Audiology Workbook

Third Edition

Audiology Workbook

Third Edition

Steven Kramer, PhD
Larry H. Small, PhD

PLURAL
PUBLISHING
INC.

5521 Ruffin Road
San Diego, CA 92123

e-mail: info@pluralpublishing.com
website: http://www.pluralpublishing.com

Typeset in 11/13 Garamond book by Flanagan's Publishing Services, Inc.
Printed in the United States of America by McNaughton & Gunn

Library of Congress Cataloging-in-Publication Data:
ISBN-13: 978-1-59756-969-9
ISBN-10: 1-59756-969-0

Contents

Preface

This third edition of *Audiology Workbook* is composed of an abundance of questions and activities designed as a means for undergraduate and beginning graduate students to reinforce their knowledge of concepts and procedures traditionally covered in introductory hearing science and clinical audiology courses. Our intent was to develop a workbook that required focused work and thought in areas that are typically difficult to understand without a lot of practice, in areas that include acoustics, anatomy, physiology, interpreting and describing audiograms, masking, immittance, screening for hearing loss, otoacoustic emissions, and auditory brainstem testing. In addition, there are exercises designed to reinforce knowledge of auditory disorders, and a chapter entirely devoted to case studies in order to help students learn how to integrate basic diagnostic test results and relate them to a variety of hearing disorders. New to this edition is a separate chapter on vestibular anatomy, physiology, disorders, and assessments for those who wish to learn more about this area of audiology.

The activities and questions are comprehensive and challenging and are designed so they may be answered with relatively short answers; the questions may also be appropriate as items for group discussion. As with the previous editions, there is a complete set of answers at the back of the workbook to guide the student in the learning process. This workbook serves as a useful companion to any introductory textbook in audiology, along with some additional literature and input from the instructor. We hope that students who use this workbook will learn to apply and think about what they have covered in class or read in their textbook and will end up with a solid foundation and appreciation of audiology.

Features and Additions to This Edition

This third edition of *Audiology Workbook* has been extensively revised from the previous edition. This edition represents a collaboration with a new co-author, Larry Small, whose longtime teaching experience and expertise in audiology and hearing science provided an opportunity to make the workbook even more useful to students new to audiology. In addition, users of past editions of the workbook were surveyed and their feedback was important in helping us revise this edition. The workbook is an appropriate supplement to any introductory audiology textbook and/or class lectures and focuses on exercises and questions that are appropriate for any traditional audiology undergraduate or beginning Au.D. course in hearing science and audiology principles and procedures. This edition updates, expands, and reorganizes material from previous editions but retains the features that worked well, including detailed answers for all of the exercises. We have added more exercises in traditionally difficult areas such as properties of sound, anatomy/physiology, audiogram interpretation/description, and masking. In addition, there are now separate chapters on immittance, OAEs and ABRs, as well as a chapter on the vestibular system and its assessment. The popular case studies have been revised into a more consistent format with answers written similar to how they might be done in a clinical audiology report. We are excited about all the improvements in this edition that will help beginning students gain a better understanding, through crafted exercises and probing questions, about audiology concepts.

Acknowledgment

We wish to acknowledge and thank
Dr. Lesli Guthrie
for her contributions to earlier editions of this workbook.

To all current and future students who take the challenge to work through this workbook—for you will come to know and appreciate audiology.

To my wife Paula, and to all of my colleagues for their continued support during the revision of this workbook.

—Steven Kramer

To dB.

—Larry H. Small

1 Properties of Sound and Speech Acoustics

1.1 What is the speed of sound in air, in meters/second (m/s), and how does it compare to the speed of light? Is the speed of sound in air faster or slower than the speed of sound in water, and why?

1.2 Given the following frequencies, calculate the period in seconds (s) and in milliseconds (ms).

    A. 20 Hz

    B. 60 Hz

    C. 250 Hz

    D. 500 Hz

    E. 1000 Hz

F. 2000 Hz

G. 2500 Hz

H. 4000 Hz

I. 8000 Hz

J. 20,000 Hz

1.3 Given the following periods in seconds (s), calculate the frequency (Hz).

A. 0.0000625 s

B. 0.0001 s

C. 0.000125 s

D. 0.00025 s

E. 0.0005 s

F. 0.001 s

G. 0.002 s

H. 0.004 s

I. 0.008 s

J. 0.04 s

1.4 Given the following periods in milliseconds (ms), convert the period to seconds (s) and calculate the frequency (Hz).

A. 0.125 ms

B. 0.250 ms

C. 0.400 ms

   D. 0.500 ms

   E. 1.000 ms

   F. 2.000 ms

   G. 4.000 ms

   H. 25.000 ms

   I. 500.000 ms

   J. 1000.000 ms

1.5 Calculate the log (base 10) for each of the following:

   A. $\log 10^5$

   B. $\log 10^{14}$

C. $\log 10^7$

D. $\log 10^{10}$

E. $\log 10^4$

F. $\log 10$

G. $\log 1$

H. $\log 2$

I. $\log 4$

J. $\log 100$

K. $\log 10,000$

L. $\log 1,000,000$

1.6 How are sound pressure and sound intensity related to each other?

1.7 As *sound intensity* increases by a factor of 4, *sound pressure* increases by what factor?

1.8 Write the general formulas for decibels of intensity and decibels of pressure.

1.9 Write the formula for dB intensity level (dB IL).

1.10 Write the formula for dB sound pressure level (dB SPL).

1.11 Calculate the dB intensity level (dB IL) for the following sounds.

A. 10^{-7} w/m^2

B. 10^{-4} w/m^2

C. 0.000001 w/m^2

D. 10^{-3} w/m^2

E. 10^{-9} w/m^2

F. 0.000000000001 w/m^2

1.12 Given the following descriptions, calculate how the dB IL of tone 1 compares with tone 2.

A. Tone 1 is twice the intensity of tone 2.

B. Tone 1 is one-half the intensity of tone 2.

C. Tone 1 is three times more intense than tone 2.

D. Tone 1 is four times more intense than tone 2.

E. Tone 1 is 10^2 times more intense than tone 2.

F. Tone 1 is 1,000,000 times more intense than tone 2.

1.13 Calculate the dB sound pressure level (dB SPL) for the following measured sounds.

A. 20,000 μPa

B. 200 μPa

C. 10^3 μPa

D. 400,000 μPa

E. 8000 μPa

F. 2×10^8 μPa

1.14 Given the following descriptions, calculate how the dB SPL of tone 1 compares with tone 2.

A. Tone 1 has twice the pressure of tone 2.

B. Tone 1 has three times the pressure of tone 2.

C. Tone 1 has one-third the pressure of tone 2.

D. Tone 1 has 10^2 times more pressure than tone 2.

E. Tone 1 has 10^3 times more pressure than tone 2.

F. Tone 1 has 10,000 times more pressure than tone 2.

1.15 Given the following descriptions, calculate either dB IL or dB SPL as appropriate.

A. Your cousin was enrolled in voice therapy for a problem with breathy voice. Following voice therapy, her average sound pressure for speech increased from 2.5×10^2 µPa to 4.5×10^3 µPa. What was the increase in your cousin's vocal output in dB?

B. In English, the phoneme with the greatest intensity, /ɔ/, is 680 times greater in intensity than the least intense phoneme, the consonant /θ/. What is the difference in dB between these two phonemes?

C. Your grandfather purchased a new hearing aid. Unamplified, your grandmother's voice is, on average, approximately 10^0 dyne/cm². With the hearing aid, your grandfather hears her voice at an average level of 10^{-2} dyne/cm². In dB, how much does his new hearing aid amplify your grandmother's voice?

D. You purchased a new pair of noise-canceling headphones to wear on your plane ride to Hawaii last month. The intensity of the background noise on the plane (prior to wearing the headphones) was 4×10^{-2} watt/m². While wearing the headphones, the intensity of the noise was reduced to 2×10^{-3} watt/m². How much noise reduction (in dB) did the headphones provide?

1.16 You have three radios playing—each of them has an output of 68 dB SPL.

A. What is the combined dB SPL of all three radios?

B. You turn off one of the radios. What is the combined dB SPL of the remaining two radios?

1.17 You have two electric fans blowing—one has an output of 70 dB SPL and the other has an output of 75 dB SPL.

A. What is the combined dB SPL of the two fans?

B. Now you turn on a third fan with an output of 90 dB SPL. What is the combined dB SPL of all three fans?

1.18 Give three common methods used to describe the overall amplitude of a pure tone.

1.19 Solve for the root-mean-square (rms) sound pressure for each of the following values of peak sound pressure OR voltage:

A. 10^2 dynes/cm^2

B. 12 volts

C. 10.414 Pa

D. 6.5 N/m^2

1.20 A pure tone has a peak amplitude of 400 μPa. Calculate the following:

A. peak-to-peak amplitude in μPa

B. rms amplitude in μPa

C. peak amplitude in dB SPL

1.21 A pure tone has an rms amplitude of 7.07 dyne/cm². Calculate the following:

A. peak amplitude in dyne/cm²

B. peak-to-peak amplitude in dyne/cm²

C. peak amplitude in dB SPL

1.22 What is the inverse square law? How is it expressed mathematically for both sound intensity and sound pressure?

1.23 If the measured sound pressure level of a radio is 65 dB SPL at a distance of 25 m from the sound source, what is the SPL at a distance of 200 m from the sound source? (Assume nothing is in the way.)

1.24 If the measured sound pressure level of a firecracker is 100 dB SPL at a distance of 250 m from the sound source, what is the SPL at a distance 4000 m from the sound source? (Assume nothing is in the way.)

1.25 Calculate the frequency (Hz) for each of the following four time-domain waveforms.

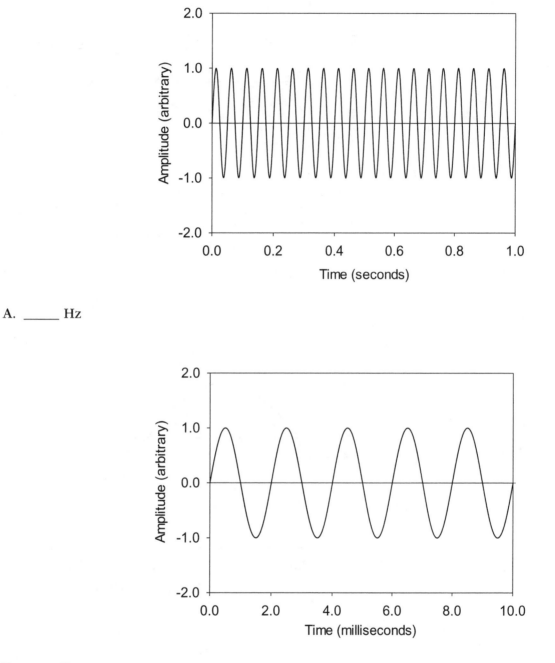

A. _____ Hz

B. _____ Hz

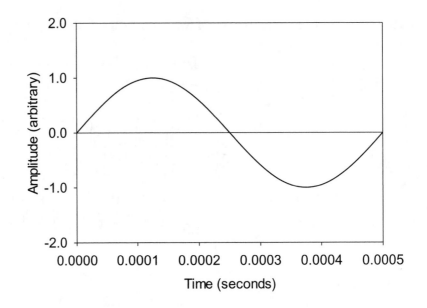

C. _____ Hz

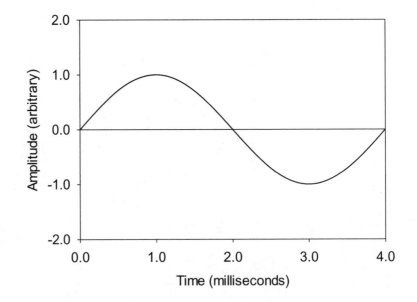

D. _____ Hz

1.26 Graph one cycle of a 1000 Hz pure tone in seconds with a peak-to-peak amplitude of 6.0 and a starting phase of 90°. Be sure to label both axes appropriately.

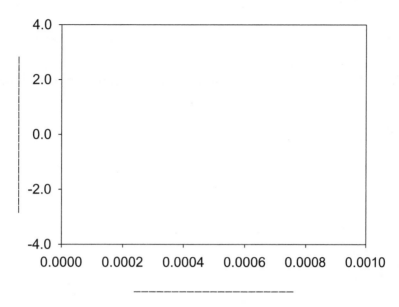

1.27 Graph one cycle of a 50 Hz pure tone in milliseconds with a peak amplitude of 1.0 and a starting phase of 180°. Be sure to label both axes appropriately.

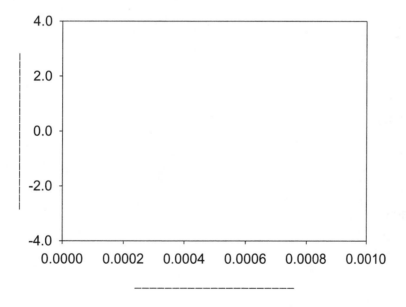

1.28 If two pure tones of the same frequency and intensity, and 180° out of phase with each other, are presented at the same time, how would the resulting waveform appear?

1.29 Given the following frequencies, calculate wavelength in meters (speed of sound in air = 343 m/s).

A. 20 Hz

B. 60 Hz

C. 440 Hz

D. 1000 Hz

E. 8000 Hz

F. 12,500 Hz

1.30 Given the following wavelengths (in meters), calculate the frequency in Hz (speed of sound = 343 m/s).

A. 0.01715 m

B. 0.0214375 m

C. 0.08575 m

D. 0.11433 m

E. 1.372 m

F. 3.4300 m

1.31 Refer to the given figure showing three sine waves at different phases and fill in the answers to the following:

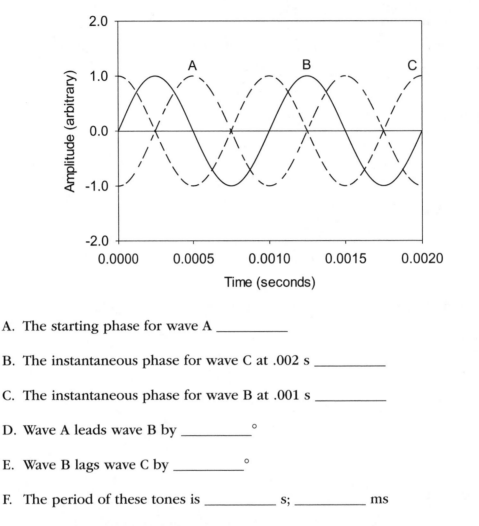

A. The starting phase for wave A _____

B. The instantaneous phase for wave C at .002 s _____

C. The instantaneous phase for wave B at .001 s _____

D. Wave A leads wave B by _____°

E. Wave B lags wave C by _____°

F. The period of these tones is _____ s; _____ ms

G. The frequency of these tones is _____ Hz

H. The wavelength of these tones is _____ m (speed of sound = 343 m/s)

1.32 What is the frequency range of normal human hearing? Draw a rough figure illustrating the threshold of audibility for humans.

1.33 What are the two main classifications of speech sounds? List at least three differences between them.

1.34 Match the following descriptions to the appropriate term.

A. _____ speech sound produced with a buildup of air pressure within the oral cavity, followed by a sudden release

B. _____ speech sound produced by a transition of a stop into a fricative

C. _____ speech sound produced by forcing the airstream through a narrow constriction formed by the articulators

D. _____ speech sound produced with the velum lowered and the oral cavity obstructed to allow the breath stream to flow through the nasal cavity

E. _____ speech sound produced by changing tongue height, tongue advancement, and lip rounding, creating no obstruction in the vocal tract

Terms:
a. vowel
b. fricative
c. affricate
d. stop
e. nasal

1.35 Calculate the first resonant frequency for the following tubes, all open at one end (quarter-wave resonators). Note: speed of sound = 343 m/s. Do not forget to convert to meters.

A. Tube length = 7 cm

B. Tube length = 10 cm

C. Tube length =14 cm

D. Tube length =17 cm

1.36 Recalculate the first resonant frequency for the four tubes from the previous exercise, assuming that each tube is now open at both ends (half-wave resonators).

A. Tube length = 7 cm

B. Tube length = 10 cm

C. Tube length =14 cm

D. Tube length =17 cm

1.37 What effect does doubling the length of a tube have on F_0?

1.38 Draw a figure to illustrate each of the following filters:

A. 2 kHz high-pass filter

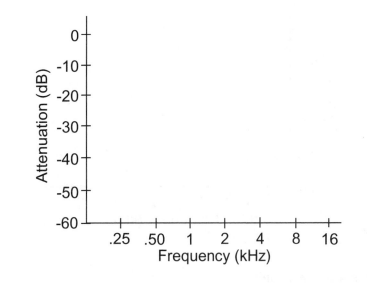

B. 2 kHz low-pass filter

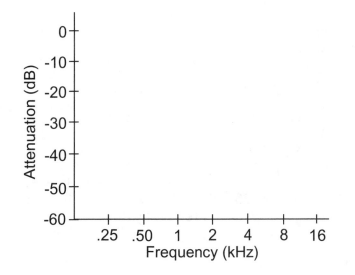

C. 1−4 kHz band-pass filter

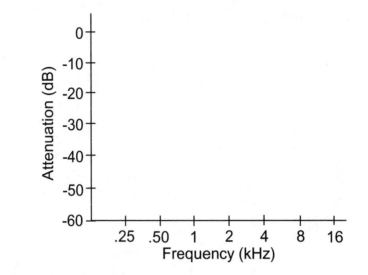

D. 1−4 kHz band-reject filter

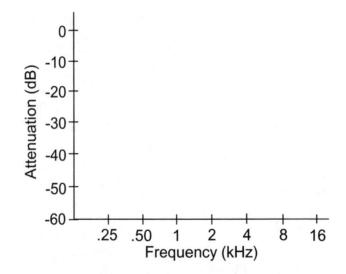

1.39 Briefly describe temporal integration.

1.40 What mechanisms do humans rely on to determine the direction from which a sound is coming (sound localization)? How might a unilateral hearing loss impact a person's ability to localize sound?

1.41 What are *equal loudness contours (phon lines)*, and how do they relate to loudness perception? What effect does intensity (dB SPL) have on the general shape of equal loudness contours?

1.42 What is a *sone*? What is the relationship between *sones* and *phons* in terms of loudness perception?

1.43 What is the *mel scale*? How does it relate to pitch perception?

2 Anatomy of the Auditory System

2.1 Identify the appropriate anatomical planes of reference for the given figures.

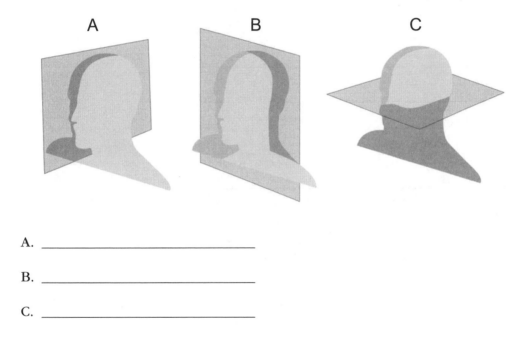

A

B

C

A. _____

B. _____

C. _____

2.2 Match each of the three planes of reference with its related results (a–c) and directions in humans (d–f), i.e., choose the two appropriate letters for each of the planes.

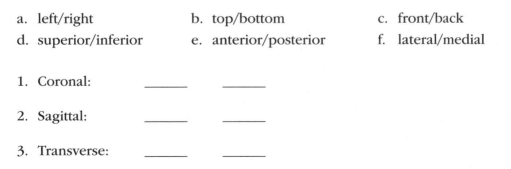

a. left/right   b. top/bottom   c. front/back

d. superior/inferior   e. anterior/posterior   f. lateral/medial

1. Coronal: _____   _____

2. Sagittal: _____   _____

3. Transverse: _____   _____

2.3 List four main divisions and two processes of the temporal bone.

1. _____   4. _____

2. _____   5. _____

3. _____   6. _____

2.4 The inner ear is found in which part of the temporal bone?

2.5 List five general divisions of the auditory system, in order, from peripheral (1) to central (5), and include the main parts of each division.

1. _____

    a. _____

    b. _____

2. _____

    a. _____

    b. _____

    c. _____

3. _____

    a. _____

    b. _____

    c. _____

4. _____

    a. _____

    b. _____

    c. _____

5. _____

    a. _____

    b. _____

2.6 Describe and/or draw the relative orientations of the cochlea and vestibular organs in the temporal bone as viewed in the skull in a transverse section.

2.7 Define/describe the pars tensa and pars flaccida of the tympanic membrane.

2.8 Name the two muscles in the middle ear along with their associated cranial nerve.

Muscle	Nerve
1.	
2.	

2.9 Name the two fluids found in the cochlea, and describe their chemical compositions.

Fluid	Composition
1.	
2.	

2.10 Name the three cochlear scalae and the type of fluid(s) found in each.

Scala	Fluid
1.	
2.	
3.	

2.11 Describe at least three differences between the inner hair cells (IHCs) and the outer hair cells (OHCs).

2.12 What is the reticular lamina and what is its significance?

2.13 List the five primary auditory nuclei within the brainstem in ascending order.

1. _____

2. _____

3. _____

4. _____

5. _____

2.14 Where are the primary auditory reception areas in the cortex located? What is the name for these areas?

2.15 Identify the labeled structures on the following coronal cross-section of the ear. From *Mosby's Guide to Physical Examination* (p. 314), by H. M. Seidel, J. W. Ball, J. E. Dains, and G. W. Benedict, 2003, St. Louis, MO: Mosby, Inc. Copyright 2003 by Mosby, Inc. Adapted with permission.

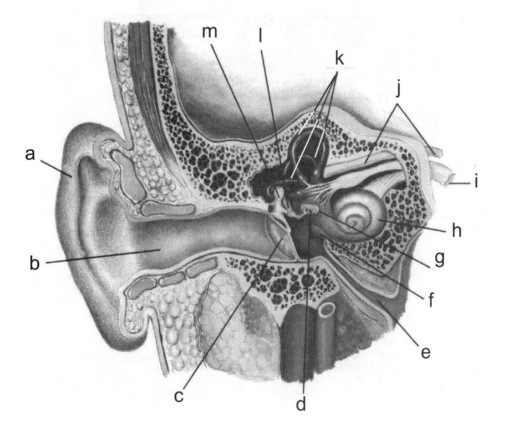

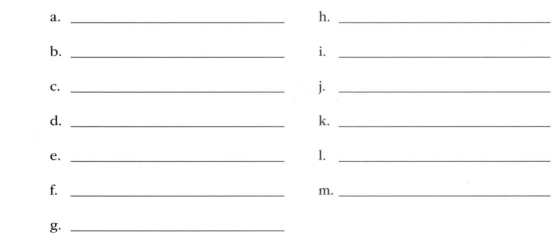

a. _____   h. _____

b. _____   i. _____

c. _____   j. _____

d. _____   k. _____

e. _____   l. _____

f. _____   m. _____

g. _____

2.16 Identify the labeled items on the following figure of the auricle.

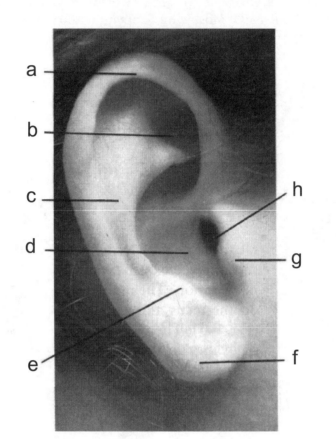

a. _____   e. _____

b. _____   f. _____

c. _____   g. _____

d. _____   h. _____

2.17 Identify the labeled items on the following figure of the ossicular chain. From *Hearing: Anatomy, Physiology, and Disorders of the Auditory System* (p. 9), by A. R. Møller, 2013, San Diego, CA: Plural Publishing, Inc. Copyright 2013 by Plural Publishing, Inc. Adapted with permission.

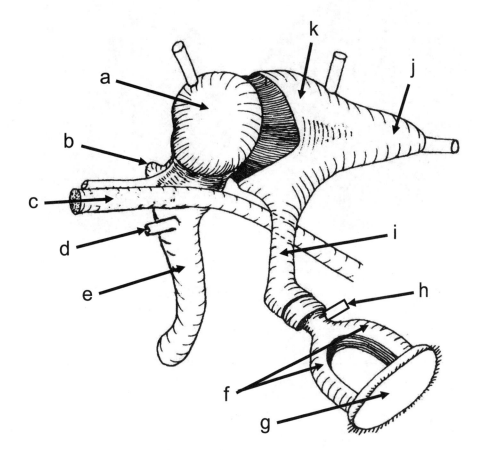

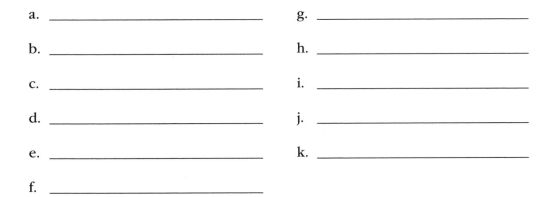

a. _____   g. _____

b. _____   h. _____

c. _____   i. _____

d. _____   j. _____

e. _____   k. _____

f. _____

2.18 Identify the labeled items on the following two otoscopic views of tympanic membranes.

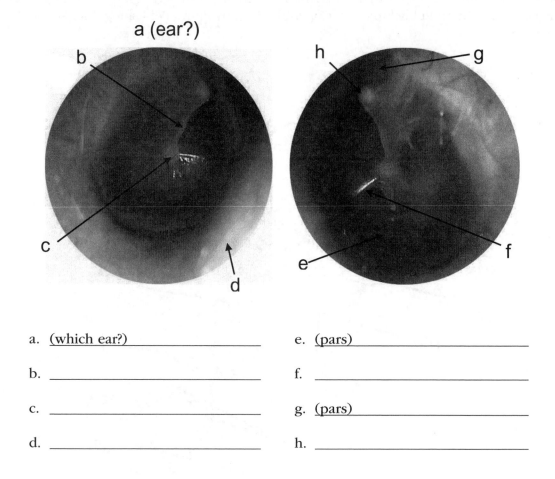

a. (which ear?) _____

b. _____

c. _____

d. _____

e. (pars) _____

f. _____

g. (pars) _____

h. _____

2.19 Identify the labeled items on the following figure of the inner ear with mid-modiolar section. From *Clinical Neurophysiology of the Vestibular System* (p. 11), by R. W. Baloh and V. H. Honrubia, 2001, New York, NY: Oxford University Press. Copyright 2001 by Oxford University Press. Adapted with permission.

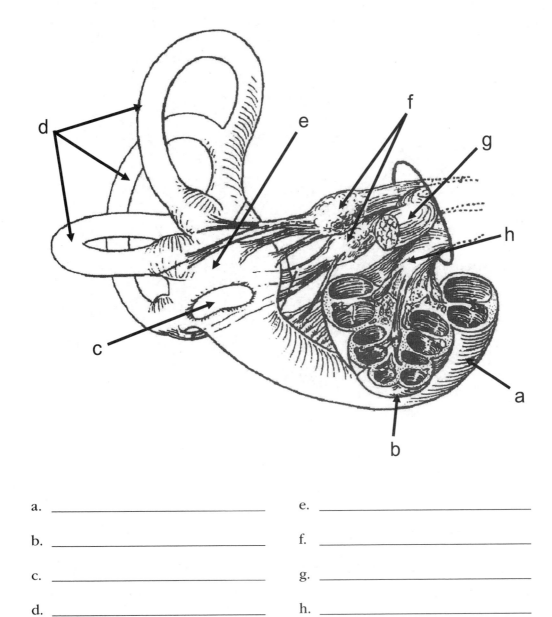

a. _____   e. _____

b. _____   f. _____

c. _____   g. _____

d. _____   h. _____

2.20 Identify the labeled items on the following figure of the inner ear labyrinths. From *Clinical Neurophysiology of the Vestibular System* (p. 29), by R. W. Baloh and V. H. Honrubia, 2001, New York, NY: Oxford University Press. Copyright 2001 by Oxford University Press. Adapted with permission.

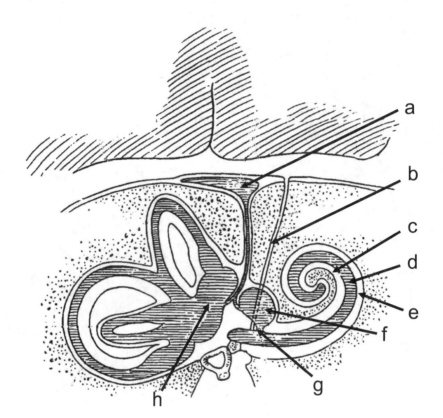

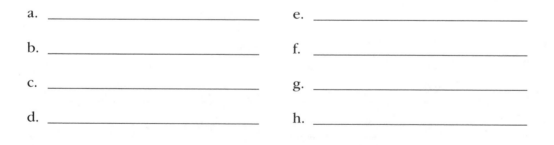

a. _____   e. _____

b. _____   f. _____

c. _____   g. _____

d. _____   h. _____

2.21 Identify the labeled items of the following figure of the cross-section of the cochlea. From *Bloom and Fawcett: A Textbook of Histology* (p. 929), by D. W. Fawcett, 1994, New York, NY: Chapman and Hall. Copyright 1994 by Chapman and Hall. Adapted with permission.

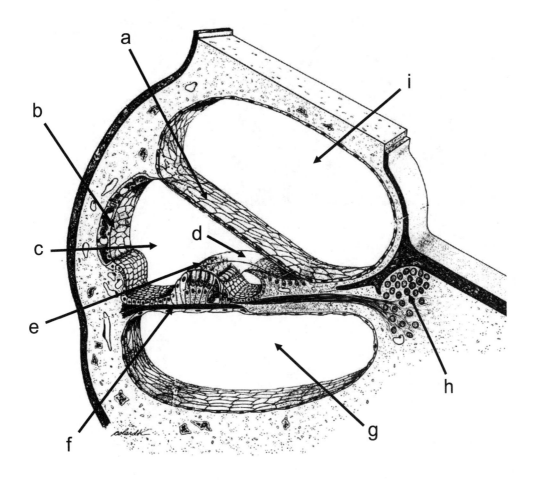

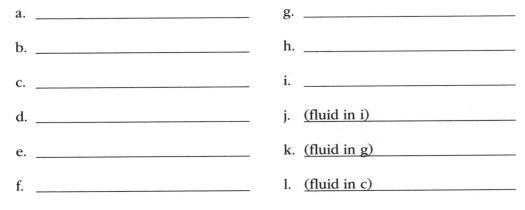

a. _____   g. _____

b. _____   h. _____

c. _____   i. _____

d. _____   j. (fluid in i) _____

e. _____   k. (fluid in g) _____

f. _____   l. (fluid in c) _____

2.22 Identify the labeled items on the following figure of the organ of Corti.

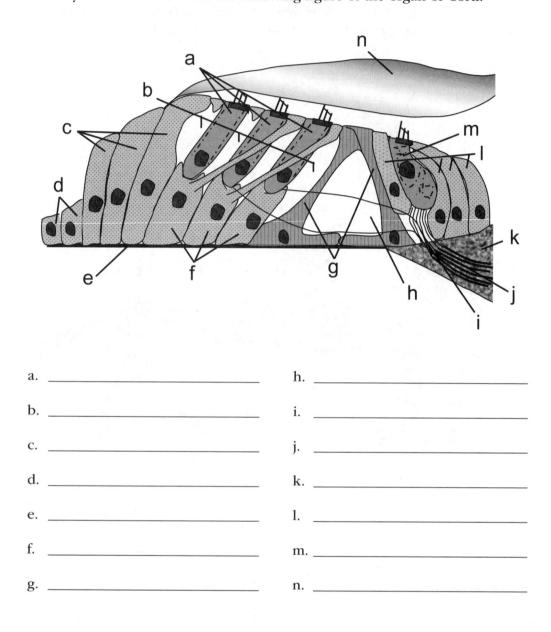

a. _____

b. _____

c. _____

d. _____

e. _____

f. _____

g. _____

h. _____

i. _____

j. _____

k. _____

l. _____

m. _____

n. _____

3 Functions of the Auditory System

3.1 Without proper function of the outer and middle ear, there would be an impedance mismatch as sound energy is transduced through the auditory system.

    A. What is meant by the term *impedance mismatch*?

    B. What is the cause of the impedance mismatch in the ear?

    C. Approximately, how much of a loss in decibels would occur due to the impedance mismatch?

3.2 In order to overcome the potential impedance mismatch described above, the outer and middle ears have important roles.

    A. What is the primary mechanism by which the outer ear amplifies incoming sound? If the average adult ear canal measures 0.025 m, what would be the average adult resonant frequency (f_{res})?

B. Describe three ways that the middle ear amplifies sound at the oval window. Calculate how much (in dB SPL) each mechanism would amplify the sound at the oval window, and how much combined amplification would occur.

3.3 What is meant by the term *transfer function*? What does the middle ear transfer function tell us about how the middle ear amplifies sound?

3.4 The tympanic membrane vibrates most efficiently when the air pressure in the middle ear space is the same as the air pressure in the outer ear canal.

A. How is this air pressure equalization maintained?

B. How does an infant eustachian tube differ from an adult eustachian tube? What are the consequences of a poorly functioning eustachian tube?

3.5 Describe the middle ear acoustic reflex pathways and its primary function? Why is the "protection from loud sounds" theory questionable?

3.6 What is meant by the term *tonotopic arrangement* in the cochlea? Describe the physical properties of the basilar membrane and how these properties relate to the processing of different frequencies in the cochlea.

3.7 Describe the mechanisms involved in the production of a traveling wave within the cochlea. Why does the traveling wave appear to move from base to apex?

3.8 Draw and label traveling wave envelopes for a 500 Hz, 2000 Hz, and 8000 Hz pure tone.

3.9 What is the meant by the endocochlear potential and how is it maintained? What is meant by the intracellular potential? Together, what is the total electrical potential between the endolymph in the scala media and the inside of the hair cells?

3.10 What is the role of the inner hair cells (IHCs) in sound transduction? Describe the shearing action of the IHC stereocilia during both the excitatory and inhibitory phases of IHC transduction.

3.11 It is well established that the role of the outer hair cells (OHCs) is different from the role of the IHCs. Describe the function and role of the outer hair cells in transduction in the cochlea.

3.12 Describe what is meant by the passive and active processes in the cochlea. Draw and label a basilar membrane tuning curve with and without normal OHCs.

3.13 Summarize the various forms of sound transduction that occur through the auditory system from the environment to the 8th cranial nerve, including the specific anatomical locations and events that underlie transduction from one form to another.

3.14 Describe two general theories that explain how humans might process (code) the frequency of an incoming sound. What are the limitations of each theory?

3.15 Describe two general theories that explain how humans might process (code) for intensity.

4 Pure-Tone Audiometry

4.1 Define what is meant by the term pure-tone audiometry.

4.2 Give at least two reasons why pure tones are used for basic audiometric testing.

4.3 List four types of audiometers, along with a brief description of each.

4.4 What is a transducer, as it pertains to audiology?

4.5 What is the difference between an input transducer and an output transducer? Give one example of each.

4.6 Briefly describe five types of transducers that are used in audiometry. Give a common model number for each.

4.7 How are the left- and right-ear earphone transducers designated in audiometry?

4.8 Describe at least two advantages of insert earphones over supra-aural earphones when testing a patient?

4.9 What is meant by sound-field audiometric testing? What is one potential disadvantage of using sound-field audiometry?

4.10 Give three situations in which you might utilize sound-field audiometric testing.

4.11 Describe the function of each of the following audiometer components.

    A. Frequency selector

    B. Attenuator

    C. Transducer selector

D. Router

E. Interrupt (Continuous) On or Off selector

F. Patient response indicator

G. VU meter

H. Talk-over microphone

4.12 What parts of the auditory system are assessed by air conduction (AC)? By bone conduction (BC)? What is meant by the air-bone gap and why is this important?

4.13 Why might BC thresholds sometimes be poorer than AC thresholds?

4.14 What information can an audiologist derive from the pure-tone thresholds obtained as part of the evaluation of a patient?

4.15 What frequencies are recommended by American Speech-Language-Hearing Association [ASHA] (2005) for testing of AC and BC thresholds? What is the recommended presentation order for testing the frequencies?

4.16 What is the recommended duration of each tone when doing pure-tone threshold audiometry? When is it advisable to use pulsed tones to obtain pure-tone thresholds?

4.17 How would one decide which ear to test first during pure-tone AC threshold testing?

4.18 What is meant by the familiarization phase of pure-tone threshold testing, and why is it used?

4.19 Describe the recommended steps involved in establishing a pure-tone threshold according to American Speech-Language-Hearing Association [ASHA] (2005) and/or American National Standards Institute [ANSI] (2004).

4.20 Give three reasons why starting at 1000 Hz is recommended. Why is it important to reevaluate a patient's threshold at 1000 Hz when testing the first ear?

4.21 When would one want to obtain a patient's pure-tone threshold at 1500 Hz?

4.22 For the three examples shown, what would be considered the appropriate ascending threshold based on the up-5-down-10 method for each of the given series of presentations? What was the patient's percentage of responses associated with the value selected as threshold?

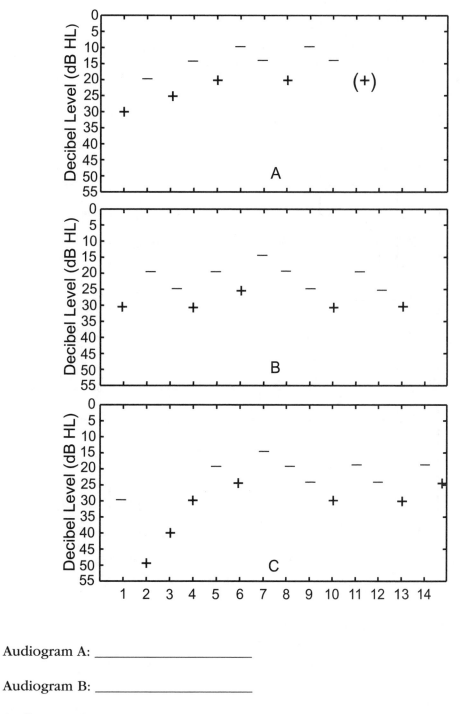

Audiogram A: _____

Audiogram B: _____

Audiogram C: _____

4.23 If a patient responded 100% of the time (2/2 presentations) at 55 dB HL and 0% (0/2 presentations) at 50 dB HL, would 55 dB HL be considered the threshold according to the ASHA (2005) guidelines? Why or why not?

4.24 Label the following audiogram where indicated.

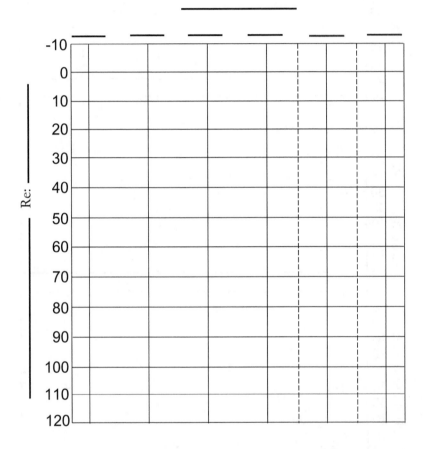

4.25 Fill in the appropriate symbols for the following Audiogram Key.

Audiogram Key	Right Ear		Left Ear	
AC unmasked				
AC masked				
BC unmasked				
BC masked				
No response				
Sound-field				

4.26 Why is it often necessary to apply masking noise to the non-test (contralateral) ear during audiometry?

4.27 For each of the audiometric transducers, when would one be concerned about the non-test ear being able to hear the signal presented to the test ear? Include the minimum interaural attenuation (IA) values.

4.28 The □ symbol on an audiogram indicates that masking noise was delivered to which ear?

4.29 What are false positive and false negative responses (as seen during pure-tone testing)? List some strategies to help control for too many false positive or false negative responses from a patient.

4.30 When might you use conditioned-play audiometry with a patient? What are the steps that an audiologist would go through to perform conditioned-play audiometry to determine audiometric thresholds?

4.31 When might you use visual reinforcement audiometry (VRA) with a patient? What are the steps involved in determining audiometric thresholds with VRA?

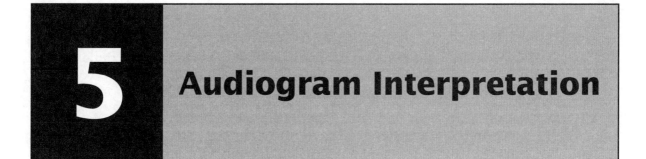

5 Audiogram Interpretation

5.1 Fill in the decibel range that corresponds to each of the following categories in reference to *degree of hearing loss*:

A. Normal adult   _____

B. Normal child   _____

C. Slight (child)   _____

D. Mild   _____

E. Moderate   _____

F. Moderately severe   _____

G. Severe   _____

H. Profound   _____

5.2 Why is degree of hearing loss based on air conduction (AC) thresholds and not bone conduction (BC) thresholds?

5.3 Match the type of hearing loss that corresponds with the appropriate description given.

    a. Conductive   b. Sensorineural   c. Mixed

    A. _____ BC thresholds are elevated (poorer than normal) and AC thresholds are elevated by the same amount (there is no air–bone gap).

    B. _____ BC thresholds are elevated and AC thresholds are elevated by a greater amount (there is an air–bone gap).

    C. _____ BC thresholds are within normal limits and AC thresholds are elevated (there is an air–bone gap)

5.4 What is meant by audiogram configuration (shape) when interpreting audiograms? Describe at least three configurations (shapes) commonly used to describe audiograms.

5.5 At which frequencies and levels might you observe the presence of tactile responses from a patient during BC testing? What might you do to verify tactile responses from a patient?

5.6 How do you determine the standard 3-frequency *pure-tone average (PTA)*? What are the primary reasons for determining PTAs with each patient?

5.7 What is the *Fletcher (2-frequency) average*? In what circumstances might you use the Fletcher average instead of the standard 3-frequency PTA?

5.8 How might you determine that a patient of yours is presenting with collapsed ear canals? What are two ways in which you might be able to minimize this problem?

5.9 How do you indicate on an audiogram that you tested at the limits of the audiometer but that the patient still did not respond? Illustrate this condition with one symbol for air conduction and one for bone conduction.

5.10 For the following questions, refer to Table 5–1.

Table 5–1. Air Conduction and Bone Conduction Reference Equivalent Values Corresponding to 0 dB HL, Based on ANSI (2010)

Transducer	Model	Frequency (Hz)							
		250	**500**	**1000**	**2000**	**3000**	**4000**	**6000**	**8000**
Supra-aural[1]	TDH-50P	26.5	13.5	7.5	11.0	9.5	10.5	13.5	13.0
Insert[2]	ER-3A	17.5	9.5	5.5	11.5	13.0	15.0	16.0	15.5
Bone[3]	B-72	67.0	58.0	42.5	31.0	30.0	35.5		

Note. Air conduction values are in dB SPL re: 20 µPa. Bone conduction values are in dB force re: 1 µN.
[1]Calibrated with 6-cc coupler.
[2]Calibrated with an occluded ear simulator. Values slightly different for HA-1 or HA-2 couplers.
[3]Calibrated with artificial mastoid for mastoid bone placement with 40 dB effective masking in non-test ear. Bone conduction calibration values are available for 6000 and 8000 Hz; however, testing at these frequencies is not in common practice and not included here.

A. What is the reference value for 0 dB HL at 1000 Hz using TDH-50P earphones?

B. Given the reference value of 15.0 dB SPL at 4000 Hz, what is the transducer?

C. What is the reference value for 0 dB HL at 8000 Hz using the bone vibrator?

D. Given the reference value of 67.0 dB SPL at 250 Hz, what is the transducer?

E. What is the reference value for 0 dB HL at 2000 Hz using the ER-3A earphones?

F. Given the reference value of 16.0 dB SPL at 6000 Hz, what is the transducer?

G. What is the reference value for 0 dB HL at 500 Hz using the TDH-50P earphones?

H. Given the reference value of 7.5 dB SPL at 1000 Hz, what is the transducer?

I. What is the reference value for 0 dB HL at 250 Hz using the bone vibrator?

J. Given the reference value of 11.0 dB SPL at 2000 Hz, what is the transducer?

5.11 Refer to the following two audiograms and answer the given set of questions. Refer to Table 5–1 shown in the previous question as needed.

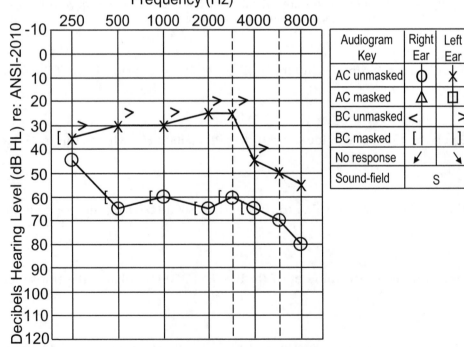

Audiogram Key	Right Ear	Left Ear
AC unmasked	Ο	Χ
AC masked	Δ	⊡
BC unmasked	<	>
BC masked	[	]
No response	↙	↘
Sound-field	S	

A. What is the dB HL for 20 dB SL re: 2000 Hz AC threshold for the right ear?

B. What is the dB HL for 10 dB SL re: 500 Hz AC threshold for the left ear?

C. What is the dB HL for 0 dB SL re: 4000 Hz AC threshold for the left ear?

D. What is the dB SL for 85 dB HL re: 250 Hz AC threshold for the right ear?

E. What is the dB SL for 60 dB HL re: 8000 Hz AC threshold for the left ear?

F. What is the dB SL for 80 dB HL re: 1000 Hz AC threshold for the left ear?

G. What is the dB SPL of a 50 dB SL signal re: 3000 Hz AC threshold delivered to the left ear by insert earphones?

H. What is the dB SPL of a 25 dB SL signal re: 500 Hz AC threshold delivered to the right ear by supra-aural earphones?

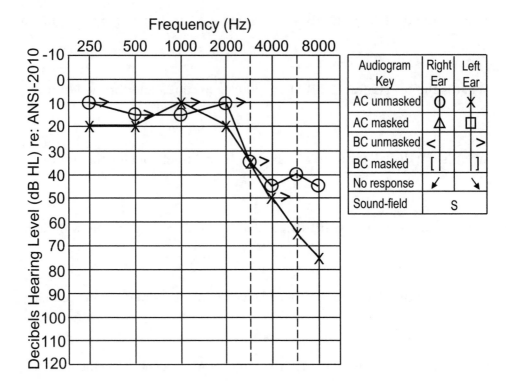

I. What is the dB HL for 20 dB SL re: 500 Hz AC threshold for the right ear?

J. What is the dB HL for 15 dB SL re: 8000 Hz AC threshold for the left ear?

K. What is the dB HL for 5 dB SL re: 3000 Hz AC threshold for the right ear?

L. What is the dB SL for 10 dB HL re: 250 Hz AC threshold for the right ear?

M. What is the dB SL for 75 dB HL re: 4000 Hz AC threshold for the left ear?

N. What is the dB SL for 75 dB HL re: 2000 Hz AC threshold for the left ear?

O. What is the dB SPL of a 10 dB SL signal re: 1000 Hz AC delivered to the right ear by insert earphones?

P. What is the dB SPL of a 25 dB SL signal re: 250 Hz AC delivered to the left ear by supra-aural headphones?

5.12 Audiometric thresholds can be documented in three different ways: single-panel audiograms, two-panel audiograms, and numerical charts. For the following three examples, convert the thresholds shown from one method of documentation to the other two methods. This will also give you practice with the symbols.

A.

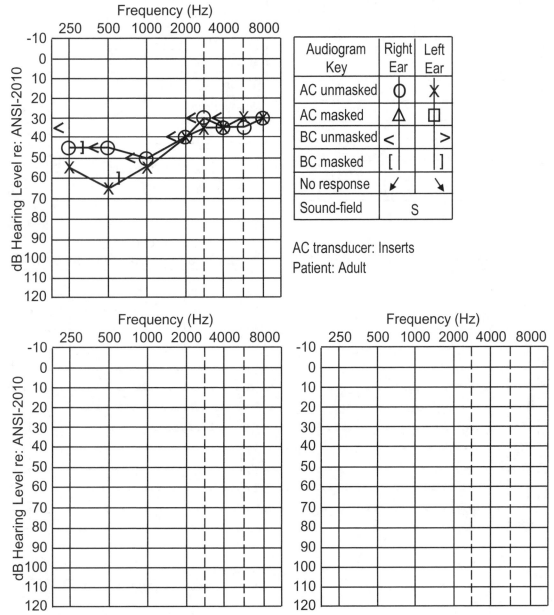

		Frequency (Hz)							
		250	500	1000	2000	3000	4000	6000	8000
Right	Air								
	Bone								
Left	Air								
	Bone								

B.

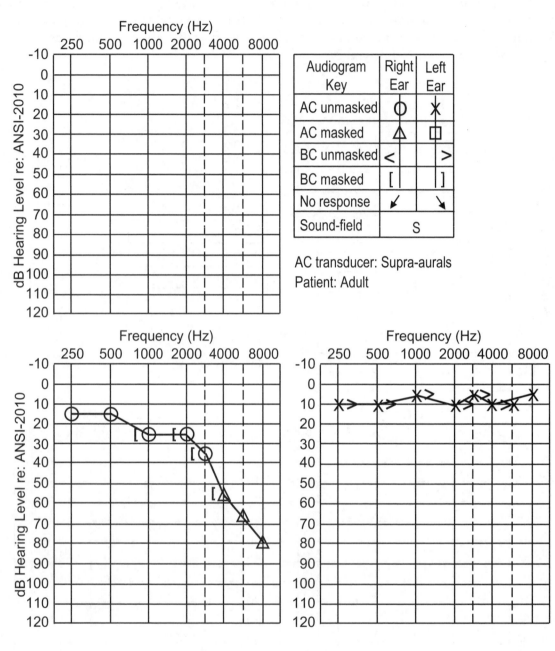

AC transducer: Supra-aurals

Patient: Adult

		Frequency (Hz)							
		250	500	1000	2000	3000	4000	6000	8000
Right	Air								
	Bone								
Left	Air								
	Bone								

C.

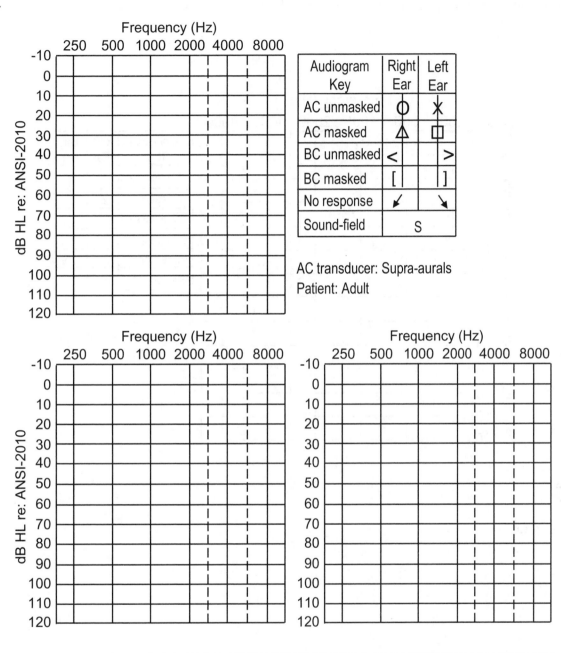

Audiogram Key	Right Ear	Left Ear
AC unmasked	O	X
AC masked	△	☐
BC unmasked	<	>
BC masked	[	]
No response	↙	↘
Sound-field		S

AC transducer: Supra-aurals

Patient: Adult

		Frequency (Hz)							
		250	500	1000	2000	3000	4000	6000	8000
Right	Air	20	30	35	45	50	50	60	70
	Bone	20	30	35	45	50	50		
Left	Air	25	35	40	50	55	55	65	70
	Bone	DNT[1]	DNT[1]	DNT[1]	DNT[1]	DNT[1]	DNT[1]		
[1]Assumed to be the same as right ear BC threshold (i.e., <15 dB air-bone gap)									

5.13 For the following audiograms, indicate the type and configuration (shape) of the hearing loss.

A.

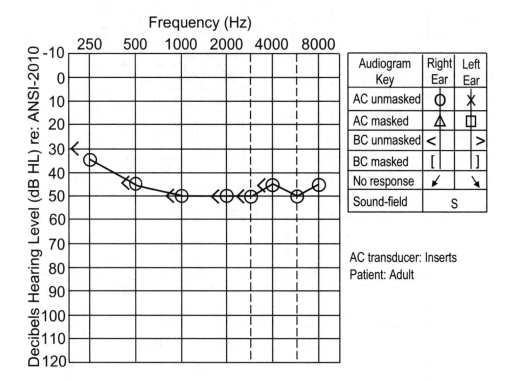

Type:

Configuration:

B.

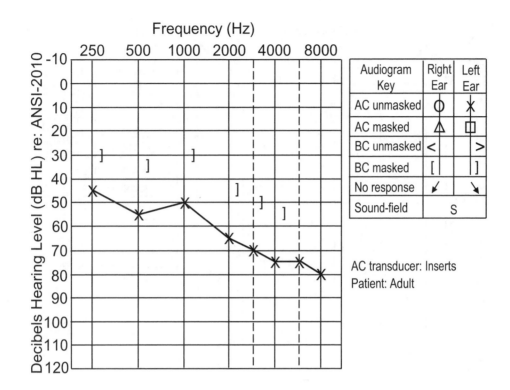

Type:

Configuration:

C.

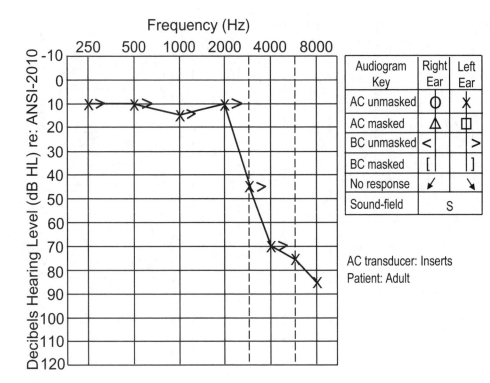

Type:

Configuration:

D.

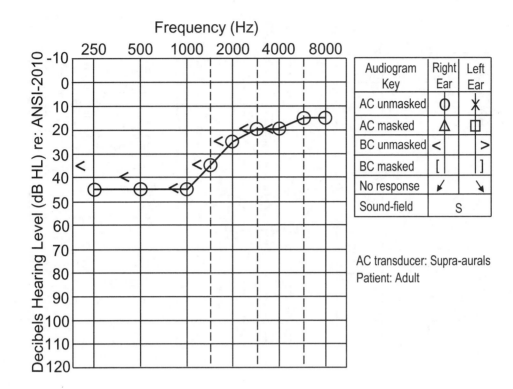

Type:

Configuration:

E.

Frequency (Hz)

Audiogram Key	Right Ear	Left Ear
AC unmasked	O	X
AC masked	△	▢
BC unmasked	<	>
BC masked	[	]
No response	↙	↘
Sound-field	S	

AC transducer: Supra-aurals
Patient: Adult

Type:

Configuration:

F.

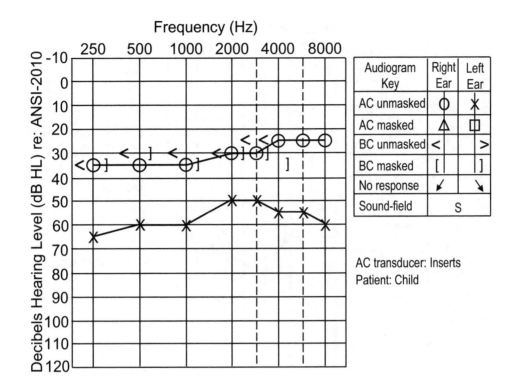

Type:

Configuration:

G.

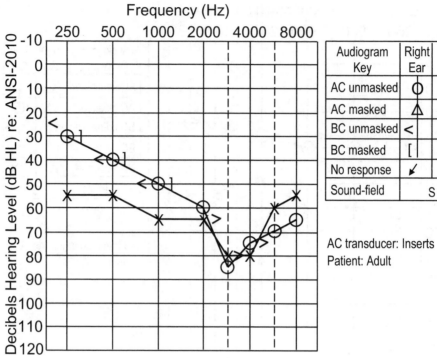

Type:

Configuration:

H.

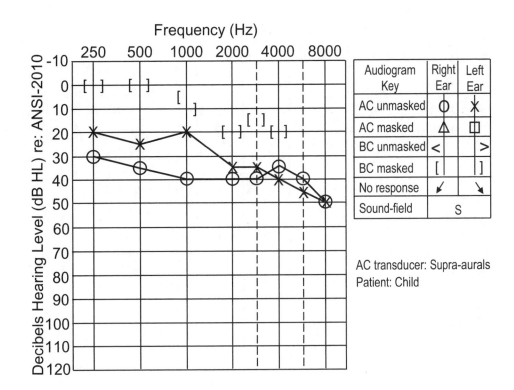

Type:

Configuration:

I.

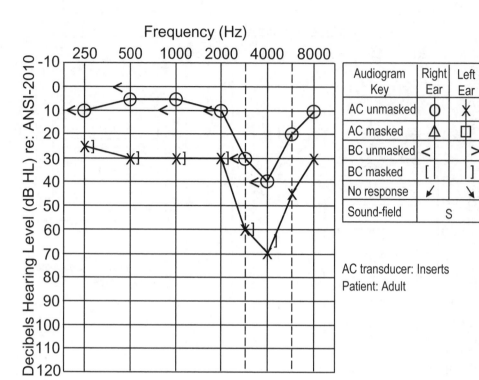

Type:

Configuration:

J.

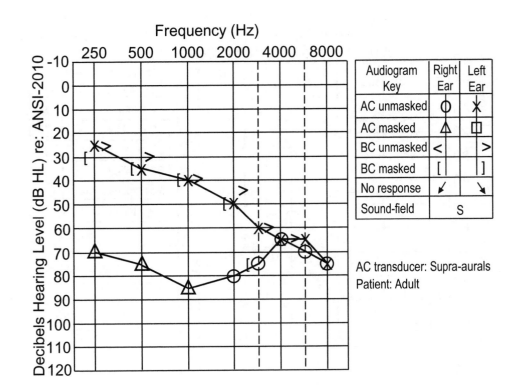

Type:

Configuration:

K.

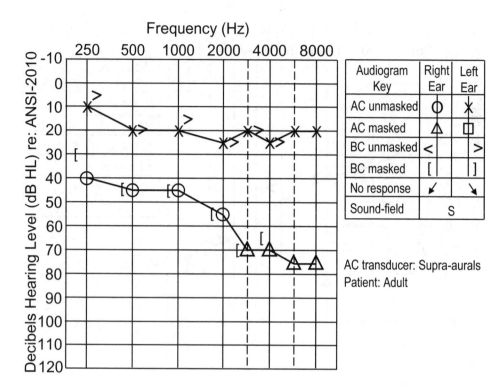

Type:

Configuration:

L.

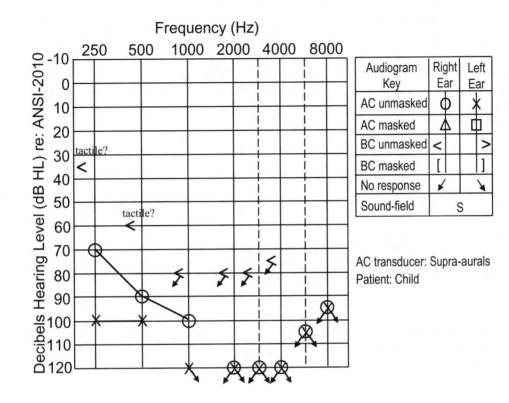

Type:

Configuration:

5.14 Given the following descriptions, plot the corresponding hearing loss on the blank single-panel audiograms. You can use unmasked symbols for this exercise. All testing for these examples was done with insert earphones. Keep in mind the given audiometer output limits for air and bone conduction (Table 5–2); however, note that output limits can vary with different audiometers. In addition, for moderately severe to profound hearing losses, bone conduction thresholds may be tactile responses at 250 Hz around 30 dB HL and at 500 Hz around 60 dB HL in cases where the loss is moderately severe to profound sensorineural, i.e., there may be a false air–bone gap in these lower frequencies (Boothroyd & Cawkwell, 1970; Nober, 1970).

Table 5–2. Output Limits of the Different Transducers for Use in the Workbook

| | **Output Limits (dB HL) by Frequency and Transducer** | | | | | | | | | |
Frequency (Hz)	**250**	**500**	**750**	**1000**	**1500**	**2000**	**3000**	**4000**	**6000**	**8000**
Supra-aural	100	115	120	120	120	120	120	120	120	105
Insert	115	120	120	120	120	120	120	120	105	95
Bone	50	70	70	80	80	80	80	75		

Note. Values may be different for other audiometers.

A. Left ear shows normal hearing sensitivity through 1000 Hz, with a gradually sloping mild to moderate sensorineural hearing loss between 2000 and 8000 Hz.

Audiogram Key	Right Ear	Left Ear
AC unmasked	O	X
AC masked	△	▢
BC unmasked	<	>
BC masked	[	]
No response	↙	↘
Sound-field	S	

B. Right ear shows a mild conductive hearing loss from 250–1000 Hz, and a sloping moderate to severe hearing loss from 2000–8000 Hz. Air–bone gaps are present from 2000–4000 Hz indicating a mixed hearing loss in that frequency range (bone conduction not tested at 6000 and 8000 Hz)

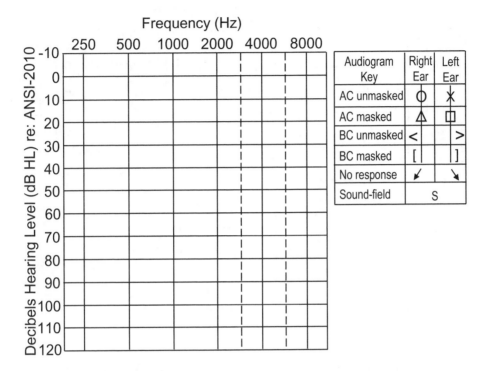

C. Right ear shows a moderate conductive hearing loss from 250–1000 Hz, rising to normal hearing at 4000 Hz.

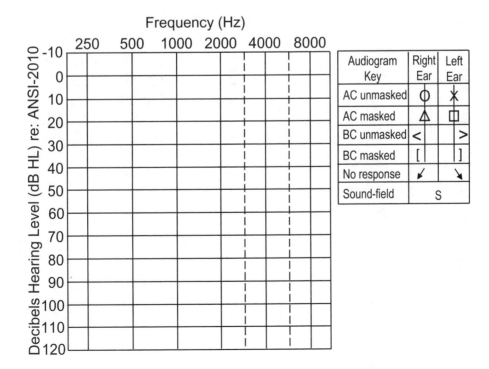

D. Left ear shows a moderate sensorineural hearing loss from 250–500 Hz, rising to normal hearing at 8000 Hz.

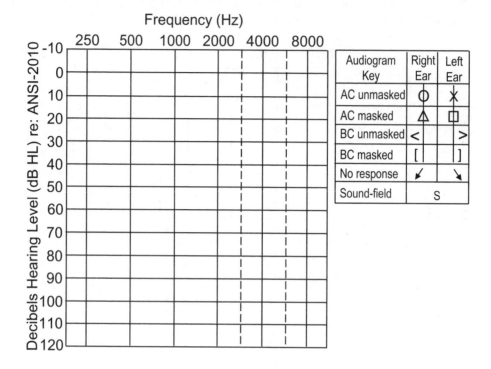

E. A bilateral, moderately severe to severe mixed sensorineural hearing loss, with 25–30 dB air–bone gaps from 250–4000 Hz.

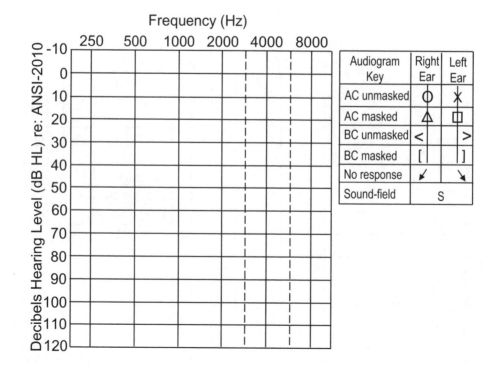

F. A bilateral, severe, relatively flat, sensorineural hearing loss from 250–4000 Hz, sloping to a profound sensorineural loss at 6000 Hz and no measurable hearing at 8000 Hz. Bone conduction tactile responses at 250 and 500 Hz.

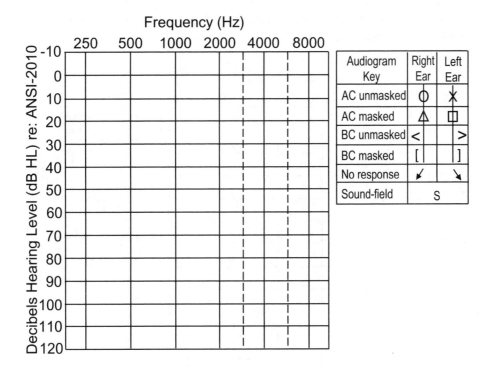

G. Normal hearing sensitivity from 250–2000 Hz, with a moderate notched sensorineural hearing loss between 3000 and 6000 Hz, bilaterally.

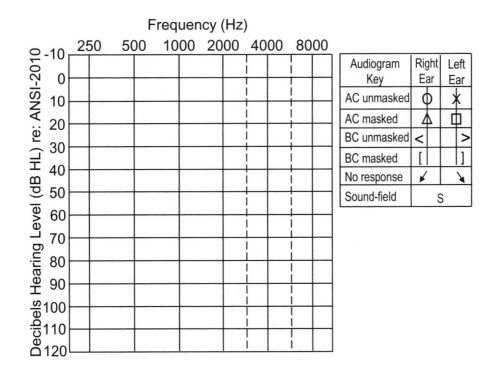

H. Right ear shows a mild, relatively flat, sensorineural hearing loss from 250–2000 Hz, sloping precipitously to a severe to profound loss from 3000–6000 Hz and no measurable hearing at 8000 Hz. Left ear shows normal hearing sensitivity from 250–3000 Hz, with 15–20 dB air–bone gaps between 250 and 1000 Hz, sloping precipitously to a severe to profound sensorineural hearing loss between 4000 and 6000 Hz and no measurable hearing at 8000 Hz.

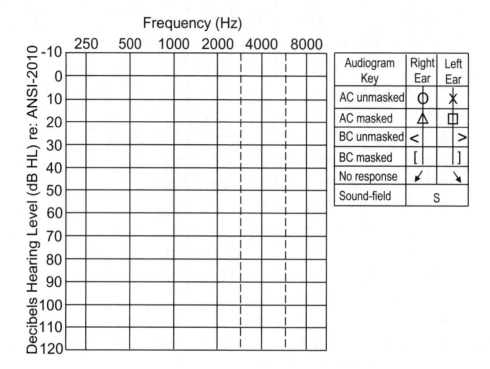

Audiogram Key	Right Ear	Left Ear
AC unmasked	O	X
AC masked	△	☐
BC unmasked	<	>
BC masked	[	]
No response	↙	↘
Sound-field	S	

I. Right ear shows borderline normal hearing sensitivity from 250–1000 Hz, sloping to a moderately severe loss between 4000 and 8000 Hz. Left ear shows a sloping moderate to severe sensorineural loss.

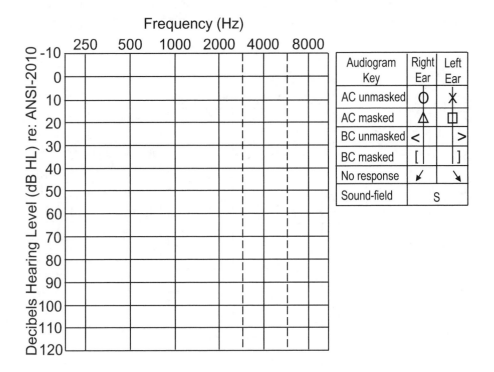

J. Right ear shows a moderate, relatively flat, conductive hearing loss. Left ear shows a mild, relatively flat, conductive hearing loss.

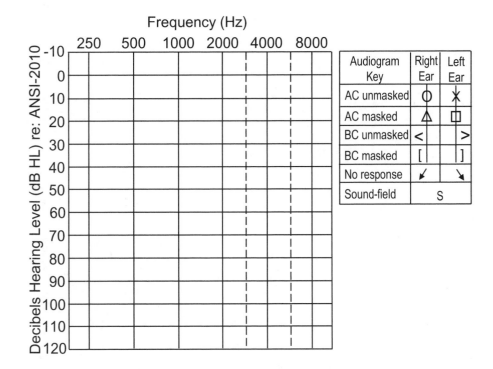

K. Right ear shows a severe to profound sensorineural hearing loss from 250–1000 Hz and no measurable responses from 2000–8000 Hz (corner audiogram). Left ear shows a moderately severe to profound sloping sensorineural hearing loss from 250–3000 Hz and no measurable responses 3000 Hz (corner audiogram). No responses to bone conducted signals observed at any frequency, except for tactile responses at 250 and 500 Hz.

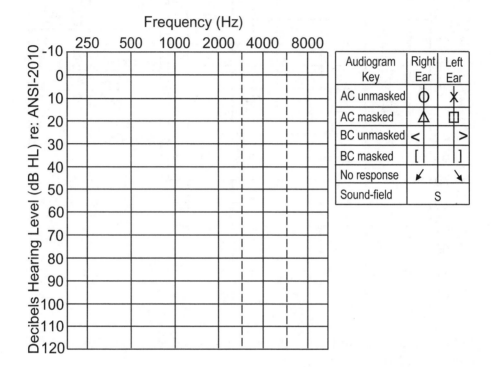

L. A bilateral, moderately severe mixed hearing loss from 250–500 Hz, with a moderate sensorineural hearing loss from 1000–2000 Hz, rising to borderline normal hearing from 4000–8000 Hz.

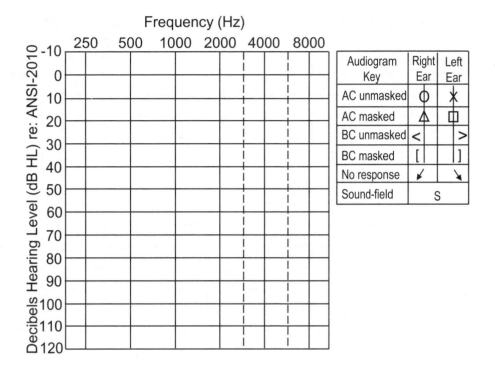

M. A bilateral, moderate to moderately severe mixed hearing loss (with 20–35 dB air–bone gaps).

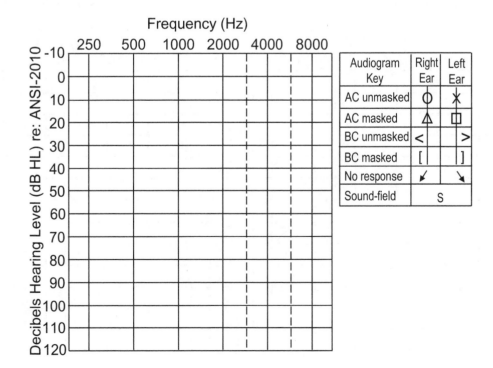

N. Right ear shows a moderate conductive hearing loss from 250–1000 Hz and a moderate mixed hearing loss above 1000 Hz (with 20 dB air–bone gaps). Left ear shows a moderate to moderately severe mixed loss (with 15–20 dB air–bone gaps).

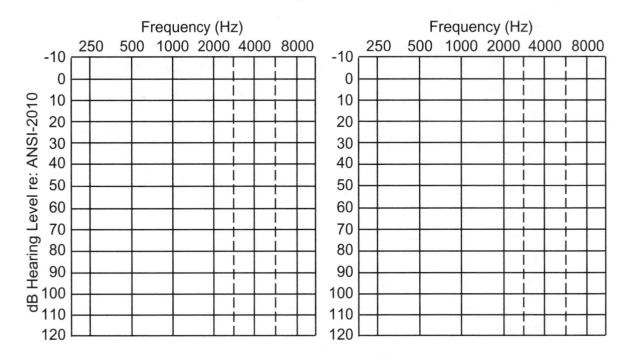

O. Right ear shows borderline normal hearing sensitivity from 250–1000 Hz, with a moderately severe to severe sensorineural notched hearing loss from 3000–6000 Hz. Left ear shows borderline normal hearing sensitivity from 250–2000 Hz, with a moderate to moderately severe notched sensorineural hearing loss from 3000–6000 Hz.

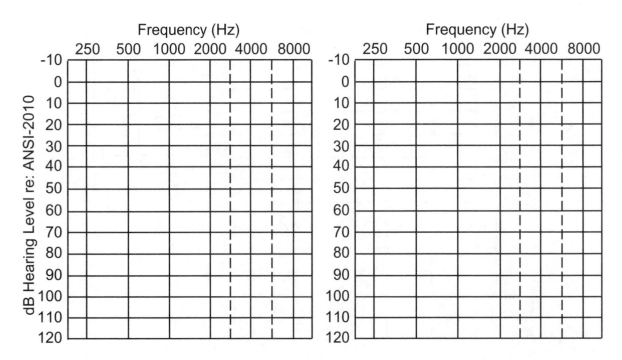

5.15 For each of the following audiograms, write a description of the hearing loss in the space provided (include degree, type, and configuration [shape] of the loss) using complete sentence format. Calculate the standard three-frequency pure-tone average (PTA) for each ear, rounded to the nearest whole number.

A.

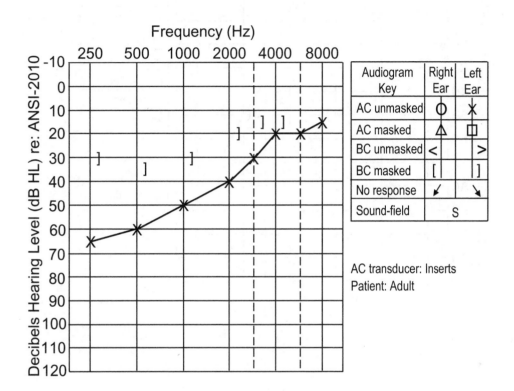

Description:

PTA:

B.

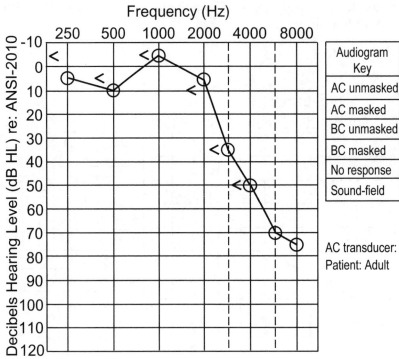

Description:

PTA:

C.

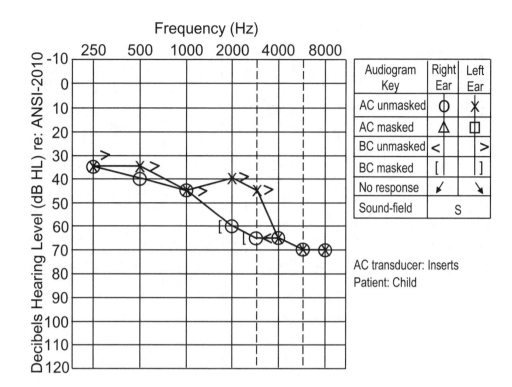

AC transducer: Inserts
Patient: Child

Description:

PTA:

D.

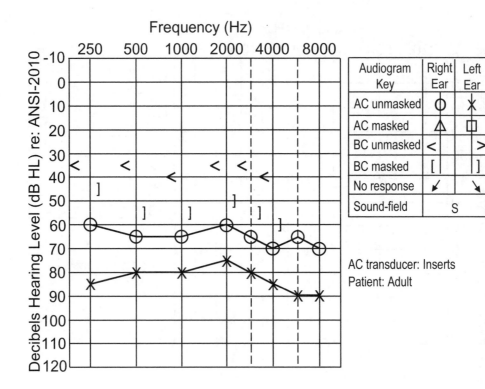

Description:

PTA:

E.

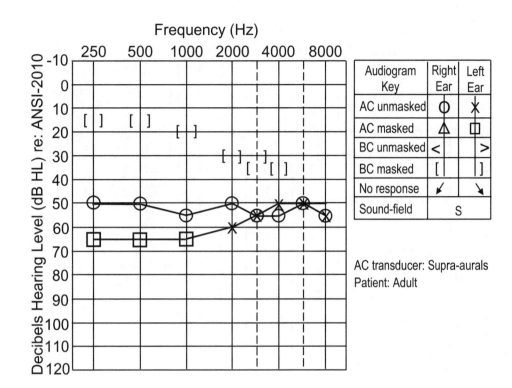

Description:

PTA:

F.

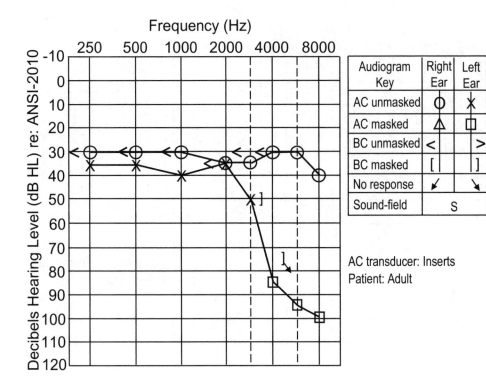

Description:

PTA:

G.

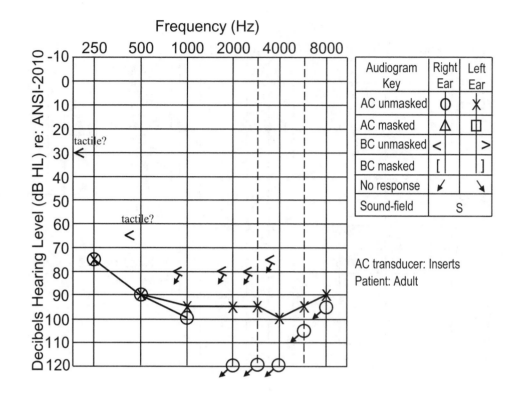

Description:

PTA:

H.

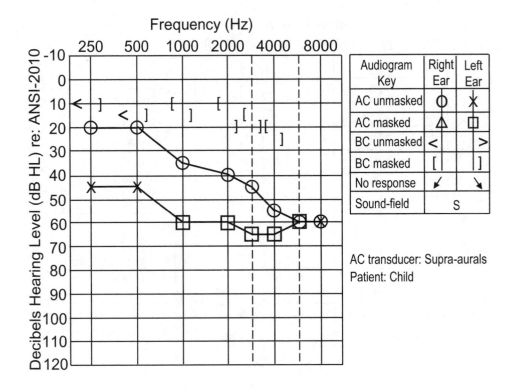

Description:

PTA:

I.

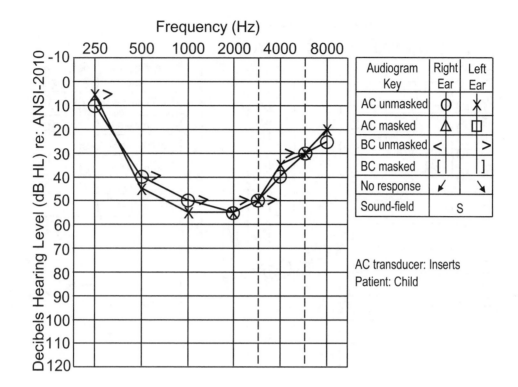

Description:

PTA:

J.

Description:

PTA:

K.

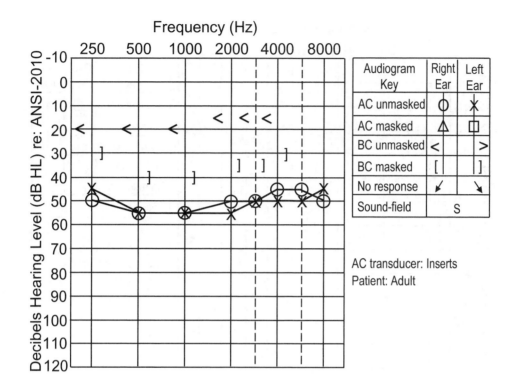

Description:

PTA:

L.

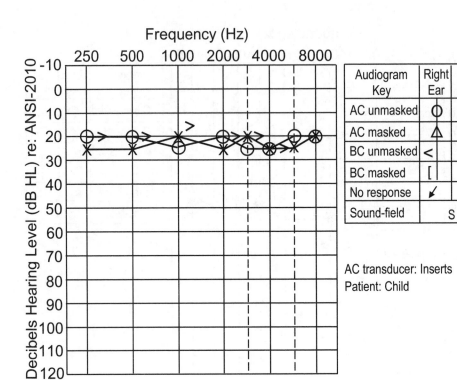

Description:

PTA:

M.

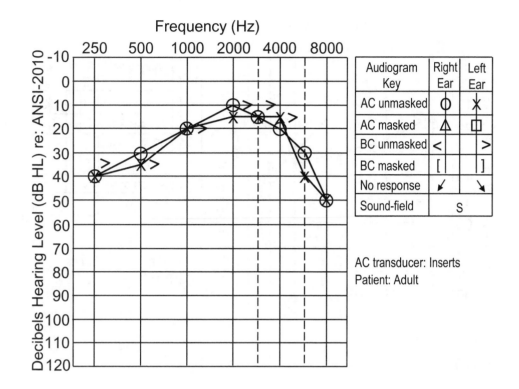

Description:

PTA:

N.

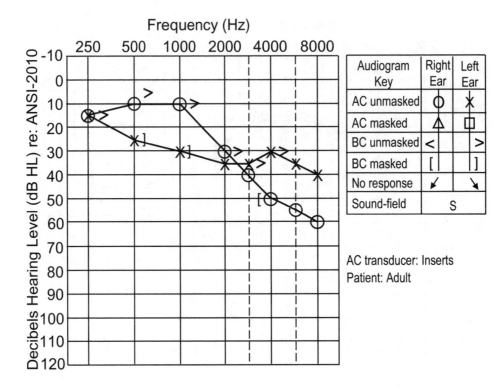

Description:

PTA:

O.

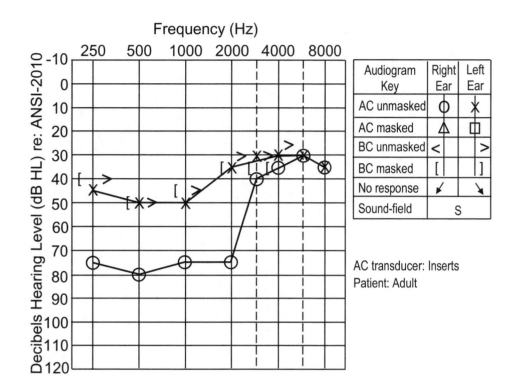

Description:

PTA:

6 Speech Audiometry

6.1 Why is speech audiometry an essential part of the basic audiometric test battery?

6.2 What is the purpose of monitoring the VU meter for speech testing?

6.3 If you are presenting words to a patient with the audiometer dial set at 40 dB HL and the VU meter is showing −5 dB, what dB HL is the audiometer actually producing? What would you do to rectify this situation?

6.4 Why is it important to always calibrate the presentation level of recorded word lists when performing speech audiometry? Describe the steps necessary for calibration of a recorded word list.

6.5 Give at least two reasons for obtaining a speech recognition threshold (SRT).

6.6 When would it be appropriate to obtain a speech detection threshold (SDT) instead of an SRT? What information does the SDT provide?

6.7 How close should the SRT be to a patient's pure-tone average (PTA) in order to be in "good" agreement? Which typically yields a better threshold, the SRT or the PTA?

6.8 If the PTA and the SRT are not in "good" agreement, what may be some possible reasons for this discrepancy? Give at least three reasons.

6.9 Why is it especially useful to use spondee pictures with children and difficult-to-test patients?

6.10 List at least five factors that need to be considered before evaluating a patient's word recognition score (WRS).

6.11 Why might it be a good idea to begin a hearing evaluation with speech audiometry instead of pure-tone testing when testing children or difficult-to-test patients?

6.12 What is considered to be the normal conversational level for speech?

6.13 When determining the WRS, why might it be problematic to use a single presentation level at:

25 dB sensation level (dB SL)?

40 dB SL?

Most comfortable loudness level (MCL)?

6.14 Why would it be advantageous to test WRS at a relatively high level, e.g., UCL-5 dB? What are the recommended presentation levels suggested by Guthrie and Mackersie (2009)?

6.15 Why would it be advantageous to determine the WRS at more than one level?

6.16 What is phonemic regression? When might you see this phenomenon clinically?

6.17 Why might two patients with similar pure-tone audiograms and SRTs have quite different word recognition scores?

6.18 If a patient has normal hearing sensitivity through 2000 Hz and a mild sensorineural hearing loss from 3000 to 8000 Hz, what parts of the speech spectrum might he/she have difficulty hearing at a normal conversational level? What kind of words might the patient confuse because of the shape of this hearing loss?

6.19 If a patient has a mild sensorineural hearing loss from 250 to 1000 Hz, rising to normal hearing sensitivity from 2000 to 8000 Hz, what parts of the speech spectrum might the patient have difficulty hearing at a normal conversational level? What kind of words might the patient confuse because of the shape of this hearing loss?

6.20 If a patient had a moderate flat sensorineural hearing loss from 250 to 8000 Hz, what parts of the speech spectrum might the patient have difficulty hearing at a normal conversational level?

6.21 What is the impact of a cochlear hearing loss on the dynamic range? What is the impact of a conductive hearing loss on the dynamic range?

6.22 If a patient's level of uncomfortable loudness (UCL) is 90 dB HL and the SRT is 35 dB HL, what is the dynamic range? If the patient's UCL is 95 dB HL and the SRT is 55 dB HL, what is the dynamic range?

6.23 What is the purpose of the speech intelligibility index (SII)?

6.24 Estimate the SII using the two "count-the-dots" methods, as proposed by Humes (1991) and by Killion and Mueller (2010) for the same given hearing loss. Note: There are 33 dots on the Humes audiogram, each dot contributing 3% to overall speech intelligibility, i.e., 33 × 3% = 99%. There are 100 dots on the Killion and Mueller audiogram, each dot contributing 1% to overall speech intelligibility, i.e., 100 × 1% = 100%.

A. Humes (1991)

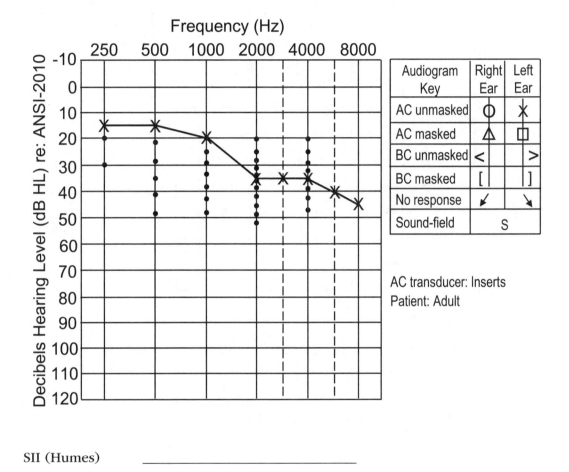

SII (Humes) _____

B. Killion and Mueller (2010)

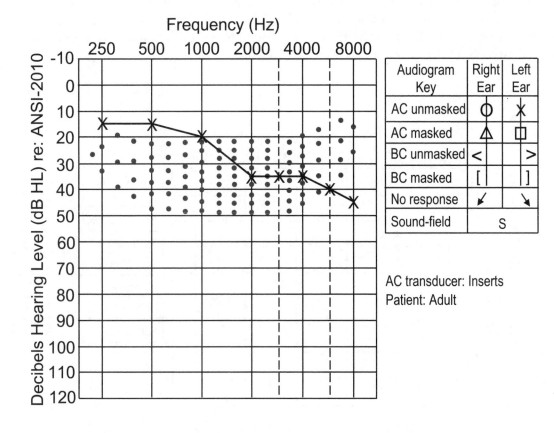

SII (Killion and Mueller) _____

C. What differences/similarities do you see when comparing the Humes (1991) and Killion and Mueller (2010) methods that might account for any observed differences in the calculated SII?

6.25 Using the same two SII methods as above, recalculate the SIIs for the hearing loss displayed in exercise 6.25, but with the patient's 8000 Hz threshold now at 20 dB HL. What changes in the SIIs do you see for these methods? What might account for any differences that you see?

A. SII (Humes) _____

B. SII (Killion and Mueller) _____

6.26 Given the following pairs of word recognition scores, determine if they are significantly different from each other based on the critical difference scores from the binomial distribution. Refer to Table 6–1 at the end of this chapter.

	Significantly different? (yes or no)
A. 96% and 68% for a 25-word list (whole word scoring)	_____
B. 52% and 72% for a 50-word list (whole word scoring)	_____
C. 72% and 56% for a 25-word list (whole word scoring)	_____
D. 68% and 88% for a 25-word list (phoneme scoring)	_____
E. 48% and 76% for a 10-word list (whole word scoring)	_____
F. 56% and 40% for a 50-word list (whole word scoring)	_____
G. 40% and 56% for a 25-word list (phoneme scoring)	_____
H. 76% and 88% for a 25-word list (whole word scoring)	_____
I. 64% and 88% for a 50-word list (whole word scoring)	_____
J. 76% and 88% for a 25-word list (phoneme scoring)	_____
K. 40% and 12% for a 25-word list (whole word scoring)	_____
L. 68% and 88% for a 50-word list (whole word scoring)	_____
M. 68% and 88% for a 25-word list (whole word scoring)	_____
N. 48% and 76% for a 25-word list (phoneme scoring)	_____

6.27 Given the following word recognition scores (%) and pure-tone averages (dB HL), determine if the word recognition score is considered to be poorer than expected for the degree of cochlear hearing loss based on the data from Dubno et al (1995). Refer to Table 6–2 at end of this chapter.

Poorer than expected?
(yes or no)

A. 96% and 40 dB   _____

B. 88% and 38.3 dB   _____

C. 52% and 41.7 dB   _____

D. 84% and 35 dB   _____

E. 60% and 36.7 dB   _____

F. 40% and 60 dB   _____

G. 24% and 65 dB   _____

H. 56% and 38.3 dB   _____

I. 96% and 48.3 dB   _____

J. 60% and 48.3 dB   _____

K. 68% and 30 dB   _____

L. 56% and 53.3 dB   _____

M. 36% and 71.7 dB   _____

N. 28% and 66.7 dB   _____

6.28 Write the formula used to calculate a rollover ratio.

6.29 Given the following PB$_{max}$ and PB$_{min}$ scores, calculate the respective rollover ratios. For each calculation, determine if the rollover ratio suggests an 8th nerve problem (use the rollover ratio cutoff value of 0.35 as significant for 8th nerve problem).

	Rollover ratio	8th nerve problem? (yes or no)
A. PB$_{max}$ = 68% and PB$_{min}$ = 52%	_____	_____
B. PB$_{max}$ = 96% and PB$_{min}$ = 68%	_____	_____
C. PB$_{max}$ = 56% and PB$_{min}$ = 28%	_____	_____
D. PB$_{max}$ = 76% and PB$_{min}$ = 72%	_____	_____
E. PB$_{max}$ = 76% and PB$_{min}$ = 48%	_____	_____
F. PB$_{max}$ = 28% and PB$_{min}$ = 16%	_____	_____
G. PB$_{max}$ = 92% and PB$_{min}$ = 72%	_____	_____
H. PB$_{max}$ = 32% and PB$_{min}$ = 20%	_____	_____
I. PB$_{max}$ = 88% and PB$_{min}$ = 68%	_____	_____
J. PB$_{max}$ = 64% and PB$_{min}$ = 56%	_____	_____
K. PB$_{max}$ = 36% and PB$_{min}$ = 20 %	_____	_____
L. PB$_{max}$ = 100% and PB$_{min}$ = 76%	_____	_____
M. PB$_{max}$ = 84% and PB$_{min}$ = 60%	_____	_____
N. PB$_{max}$ = 96% and PB$_{min}$ = 60%	_____	_____

6.30 Why is it useful to test speech understanding in noise? List two speech-in-noise tests.

6.31 What is meant by the term signal-to-noise ratio (SNR) loss?

6.32 List three special considerations when testing word recognition abilities in children.

6.33 Explain why masking is most often needed when obtaining word recognition scores.

6.34 Describe the characteristic of the masking noise used for speech audiometry.

Table 6–1. Critical Difference Values for PB Words Based on the Binomial Distribution

95% Confidence		Number of Items (phoneme scoring = 2.5 number of words)						Number of Items (phoneme scoring = 2.5 number of words)			
		10	25	50	63			10	25	50	63
The lower of the two scores being compared (in %)	0	33	15	8	6	The lower of the two scores being compared (in %)	50	91	77	70	68
	1	36	17	10	9		51	91	78	71	68
	2	38	20	12	11		52	92	79	71	69
	3	40	22	14	13		53	93	80	72	70
	4	41	23	16	14		54	93	81	73	71
	5	43	25	18	16		55	94	81	74	72
	6	45	27	19	17		56	95	82	75	73
	7	47	29	21	19		57	95	83	76	74
	8	48	30	22	20		58	96	84	77	75
	9	50	32	24	22		59	96	84	78	76
	10	51	33	25	23		60	97	85	78	77
	11	53	35	27	25		61	97	86	79	77
	12	54	36	28	26		62	98	87	80	78
	13	55	38	29	27		63	98	87	81	79
	14	57	39	31	29		64	99	88	82	80
	15	58	40	32	30		65	99	89	83	81
	16	59	42	33	31		66	100	90	83	82
	17	61	43	34	32		67	100	90	84	82
	18	62	44	36	34		68	100	91	85	83
	19	63	45	37	35		69	100	92	86	84
	20	64	47	38	36		70	100	92	87	85
	21	65	48	39	37		71	100	93	87	86
	22	66	49	41	38		72	100	93	88	86
	23	68	50	42	40		73	100	94	89	87
	24	69	51	43	41		74	100	95	89	88
	25	70	53	44	42		75	100	95	90	89
	26	71	54	45	43		76	100	96	91	89
	27	72	55	46	44		77	100	96	92	90
	28	73	56	47	45		78	100	97	92	91
	29	74	57	48	46		79	100	97	93	92
	30	75	58	50	47		80	100	98	94	92
	31	76	59	51	48		81	100	98	94	93
	32	77	60	52	50		82	100	99	95	94
	33	77	61	53	51		83	100	99	95	94
	34	78	62	54	52		84	100	100	96	95
	35	79	63	55	53		85	100	100	97	96
	36	80	64	56	54		86	100	100	97	96
	37	81	65	57	55		87	100	100	98	97
	38	82	66	58	56		88	100	100	98	97
	39	83	67	59	57		89	100	100	99	98
	40	83	68	60	58		90	100	100	99	98
	41	84	69	61	59		91	100	100	100	99
	42	85	70	62	60		92	100	100	100	99
	43	86	71	63	61		93	100	100	100	100
	44	87	72	64	62		94	100	100	100	100
	45	87	73	65	63		95	100	100	100	100
	46	88	74	66	64		96	100	100	100	100
	47	89	75	67	65		97	100	100	100	100
	48	89	75	68	66		98	100	100	100	100
	49	90	76	69	67		99	100	100	100	100

Note. Find where lower score (*row*) intersects number of items scored (*column*).

Source: Courtesy of Arthur Boothroyd and Carol Mackersie. Modified with permission.

Table 6–2. Lower 95% Confidence Limits for WRS as a Function of PTA (500, 1000, 2000 Hz) in Ears with Cochlear Hearing Loss

PTA (dB HL)	Lower 95% Confidence Limit for WRS (percent) Based on 25-Item Nu-6 Word Lists	PTA (dB HL)	Lower 95% Confidence Limit for WRS (percent) Based on 25-Item Nu-6 Word Lists
−3.3	100	36.7	68
0.0	100	38.3	64
1.7	100	40.0	64
3.3	96	41.7	60
5.0	96	43.3	56
6.7	96	45.0	56
8.3	96	46.7	52
10.0	96	48.3	52
11.7	92	50.0	48
13.3	92	51.7	48
15.0	92	53.3	44
16.7	88	55.0	44
18.3	88	56.7	40
20.0	88	58.3	40
21.7	84	60.0	36
23.3	84	61.7	36
25.0	80	63.3	32
26.7	80	65.0	32
38.3	76	66.7	32
30.0	76	68.3	28
31.7	72	70.0	28
33.3	72	71.7	24
35.0	68		

Note. Data shown are for 25-item NU-6 word lists. See Dubno et al. for results using a 50-item word list.

Source: From "Confidence-Limits for Maximum Word-Recognition Scores," by J. R. Dubno, F. S. Lee, A. J. Klein, L. J. Matthews, & C. F. Lam, 1995, *Journal of Speech, Language, and Hearing Research, 38.* Copyright 1995 by American Speech-Language-Hearing Association. Adapted with permission.

7 Clinical Masking

7.1 What is meant by interaural attenuation (IA)? What are recommended minimum IAs for supra-aural, insert, and bone conduction transducers?

7.2 Explain why a supra-aural earphone has a lower IA than an insert earphone.

7.3 What is the general rule for making decisions about the need to perform masking for air conduction thresholds?

7.4 What is the general rule for making decisions about the need to perform masking for bone conduction thresholds?

7.5 The occlusion effect (OE) is something that needs to be considered when masking for bone conduction threshold. Answer the following:

    A. What is the occlusion effect and why does this occur?

B. Why is there less of an occlusion effect when using an insert earphone for the masker, and how does the occlusion effect change with deeper insertion depth?

C. Why is the occlusion effect important to consider when obtaining masked bone conduction thresholds?

D. Which test frequencies are most impacted by the occlusion effect, and what are the typical values of the occlusion effect at those frequencies?

7.6 Describe the masking stimuli used during pure-tone testing and why these types of maskers are preferred.

7.7 Define effective masking (EM) and give an example.

7.8 Define central masking.

7.9 What is a "masking dilemma," and when is it observed clinically? When faced with the possibility of a masking dilemma, what should you do?

7.10 Given the following examples showing unmasked thresholds for the test ear (TE) and non-test ear (NTE), determine if you would have to mask when obtaining pure-tone air conduction (AC) or bone conduction (BC) thresholds for the TE.

A. AC with TDH-50 and BC with B-71

	TE	NTE	Masking Needed?
AC	55	10	
BC	10	10	

B. AC with TDH-50 and BC with B-71

	TE	NTE	Masking Needed?
AC	35	10	
BC	5	5	

C. AC with TDH-50 and BC with B-71

	TE	NTE	Masking Needed?
AC	50	45	
BC	40	40	

D. AC with TDH-50 and BC with B-71

	TE	NTE	Masking Needed?
AC	75	40	
BC	30	30	

E. AC with ER-3A and BC with B-71

	TE	NTE	Masking Needed?
AC	35	5	
BC	5	5	

F. AC with ER-3A and BC with B-71

	TE	NTE	Masking Needed?
AC	20	15	
BC	15	15	

G. AC with ER-3A and BC with B-71

	TE	NTE	Masking Needed?
AC	60	10	
BC	10	10	

H. AC with ER-3A and BC with B-71

	TE	NTE	Masking Needed?
AC	75	40	
BC	30	30	

I. AC with ER-3A; BC not tested

	TE	NTE	Masking Needed?
AC	75	20	
BC	DNT	DNT	

7.11 For the next FIVE audiograms, fill in the given tables with "M" to indicate where masked thresholds would be needed for each of the transducers.

Audiogram A

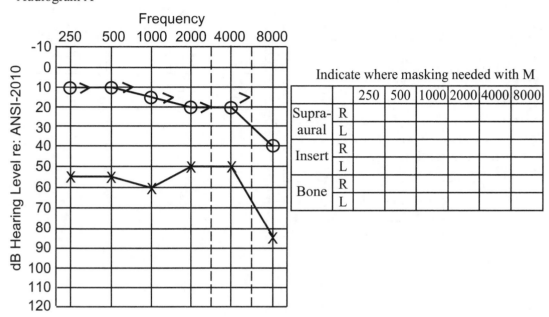

Indicate where masking needed with M

		250	500	1000	2000	4000	8000
Supra-	R						
aural	L						
Insert	R						
	L						
Bone	R						
	L						

Audiogram B

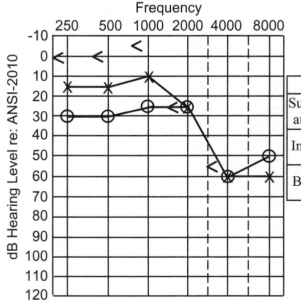

Indicate where masking needed with M

		250	500	1000	2000	4000	8000
Supra-	R						
aural	L						
Insert	R						
	L						
Bone	R						
	L						

Audiogram C

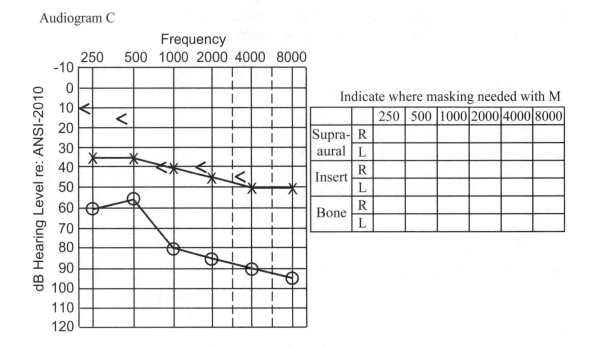

Indicate where masking needed with M

		250	500	1000	2000	4000	8000
Supra-aural	R						
	L						
Insert	R						
	L						
Bone	R						
	L						

Audiogram D (no conductive component in left ear)

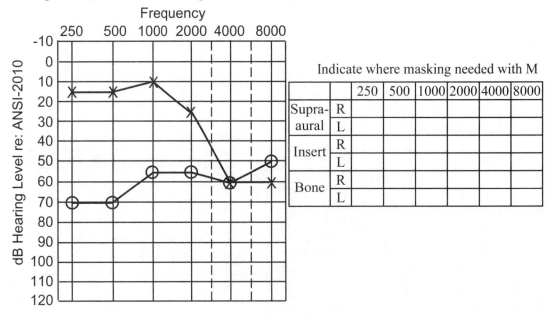

Indicate where masking needed with M

		250	500	1000	2000	4000	8000
Supra-aural	R						
	L						
Insert	R						
	L						
Bone	R						
	L						

Audiogram E

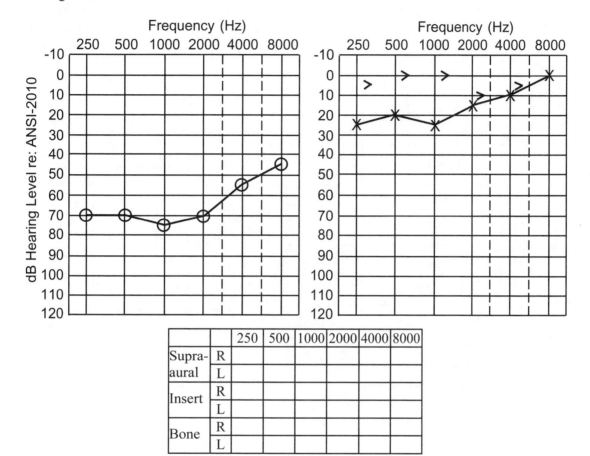

		250	500	1000	2000	4000	8000
Supra-aural	R						
	L						
Insert	R						
	L						
Bone	R						
	L						

7.12 For the audiogram shown below, fill in the table with "D" to indicate which thresholds may potentially be masking dilemmas. For the BC masked thresholds, indicate if there could be a dilemma when using supra-aural (TDH-49) or insert (ER-3) to present the masking noise to NTE.

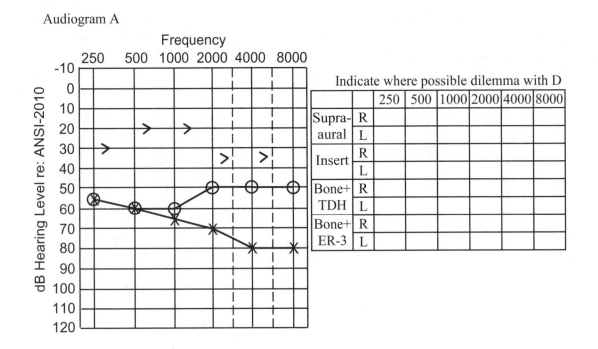

Audiogram A

Indicate where possible dilemma with D

		250	500	1000	2000	4000	8000
Supra-aural	R						
	L						
Insert	R						
	L						
Bone+ TDH	R						
	L						
Bone+ ER-3	R						
	L						

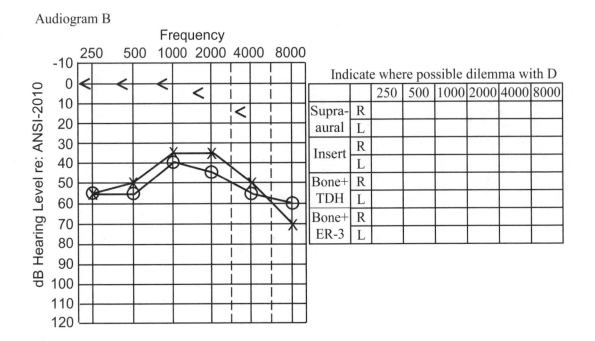

Audiogram B

Indicate where possible dilemma with D

		250	500	1000	2000	4000	8000
Supra-aural	R						
	L						
Insert	R						
	L						
Bone+ TDH	R						
	L						
Bone+ ER-3	R						
	L						

7.13 For the next two audiograms, determine, for each ear, the frequencies at which contralateral masking would be necessary to obtain thresholds for both AC and BC using either supra-aural or insert earphones, as indicated. Then for those conditions in which masking would be needed, use the following formulas to find the *minimum masking level* and *maximum masking level*. All formulas are from Yacullo (1996).

Minimum Masking Level

For AC: AC threshold in the non-test ear (AC NTE) + 10 dB

For BC: AC NTE + 10 dB + occlusion effect (OE)

Use the following values to correct for OE when using a supra-aural earphone:

250 Hz	20 dB
500 Hz	15 dB
1000 Hz	5 dB

Only use an OE of 10 dB at 250 Hz when using insert earphones (Yacullo, 1996).

Note: The OE is only applied when the patient has normal hearing or a sensorineural hearing loss in the NTE.

In the same table grid, indicate the *maximum* effective masking levels you can use to avoid potentially overmasking in the test ear. Use the following formulas to calculate the maximum masking level:

Maximum Masking Level

For both AC and BC: BC TE ear + interaural attenuation (IA) − 5 dB;

where IA = AC in the test ear (TE) − BC NTE *or* 40 dB, whichever is larger when using supra-aural headphones,

or

where IA = AC in the TE − BC NTE or 55 dB, whichever is larger when using insert earphones.

A. For this patient, supra-aural earphones were used. Correct answers for 500 Hz are filled in to get you started. Fill in the rest of the table where masking is needed. Masker levels are to be recorded for the appropriate non-test ear (NTE).

Audiogram A

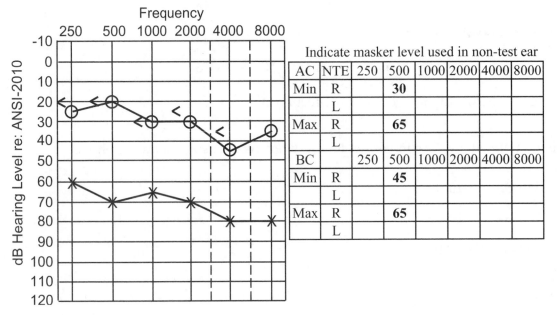

Indicate masker level used in non-test ear

AC	NTE	250	500	1000	2000	4000	8000
Min	R		30				
	L						
Max	R		65				
	L						
BC		250	500	1000	2000	4000	8000
Min	R		45				
	L						
Max	R		65				
	L						

B. For the following patient, insert earphones were used. Assume there is not any conductive loss in the right ear. Masker levels are to be recorded for the appropriate non-test ear (NTE).

Audiogram B

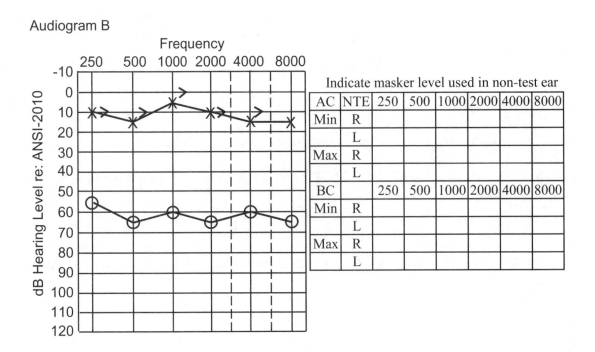

Indicate masker level used in non-test ear

AC	NTE	250	500	1000	2000	4000	8000
Min	R						
	L						
Max	R						
	L						
BC		250	500	1000	2000	4000	8000
Min	R						
	L						
Max	R						
	L						

7.14 The following five cases ask that you indicate all of the steps involved with *how to mask*, and are for the more advanced undergraduate student or beginning AuD student. For each of the cases, there is a single-panel audiogram on the top left showing the unmasked thresholds and the patient's final masked threshold. Your tasks are to:

1. Fill in the table below the audiogram to show all the steps you would need to go through to get from the given unmasked threshold to the given masked threshold. Use the plateau method of masking, with 10 dB increments of test tone and masker, to achieve a 20 dB plateau; in some cases if the 10 dB steps overshoot the given threshold, the last level will be 5 dB less than the previous level. An alternate method is to use 5 dB steps.

2. Fill in the masking profile grid (top right) to illustrate where the patient responded "Yes" as a function of masker level. You should see an undermasking stage and/or a plateau. Don't forget to include any occlusion effect when masking for bone conduction (BC) as needed. OE values are given in question 7.13. You may want to look at the answer for Case A to see if you are on the right track.

Case A. RE AC; supra-aural earphones at 500 Hz.

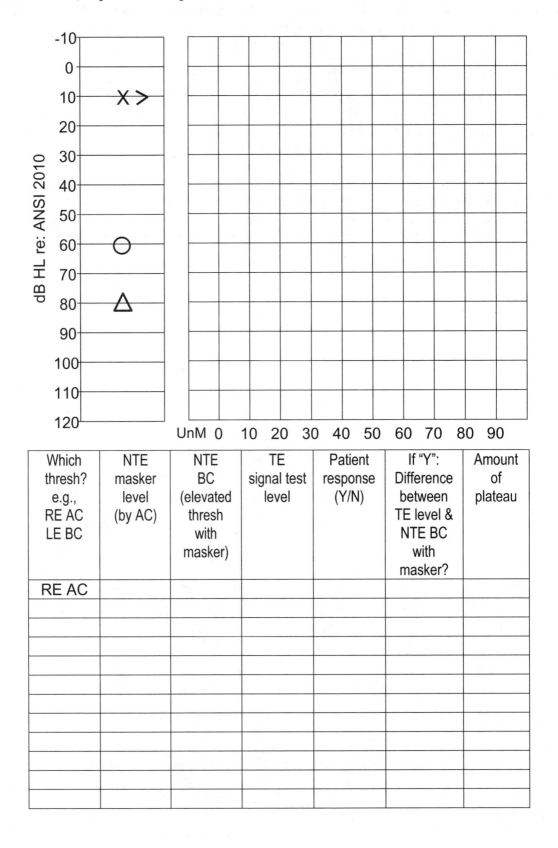

Which thresh? e.g., RE AC LE BC	NTE masker level (by AC)	NTE BC (elevated thresh with masker)	TE signal test level	Patient response (Y/N)	If "Y": Difference between TE level & NTE BC with masker?	Amount of plateau
RE AC						

Case B. LE BC; supra-aural earphones at 500 Hz.

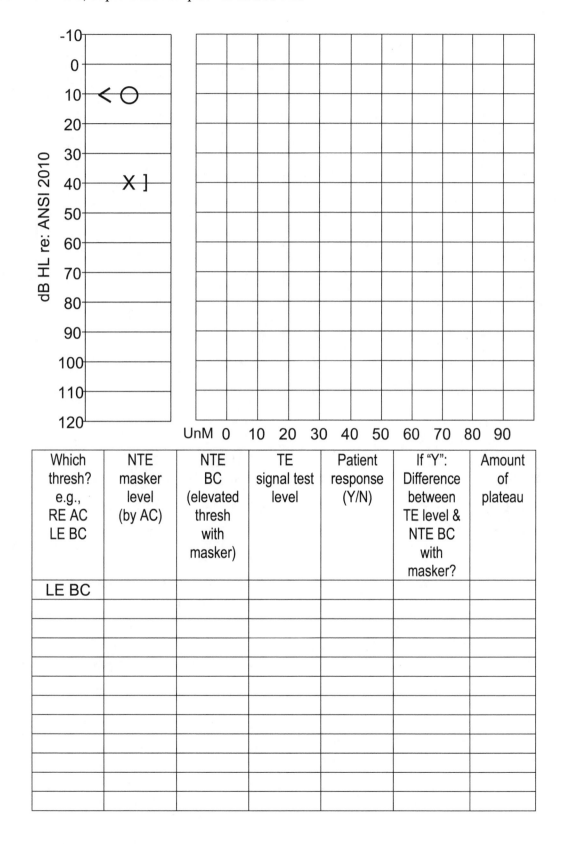

Which thresh? e.g., RE AC LE BC	NTE masker level (by AC)	NTE BC (elevated thresh with masker)	TE signal test level	Patient response (Y/N)	If "Y": Difference between TE level & NTE BC with masker?	Amount of plateau
LE BC						

Case C. LE AC; insert earphones at 1000 Hz.

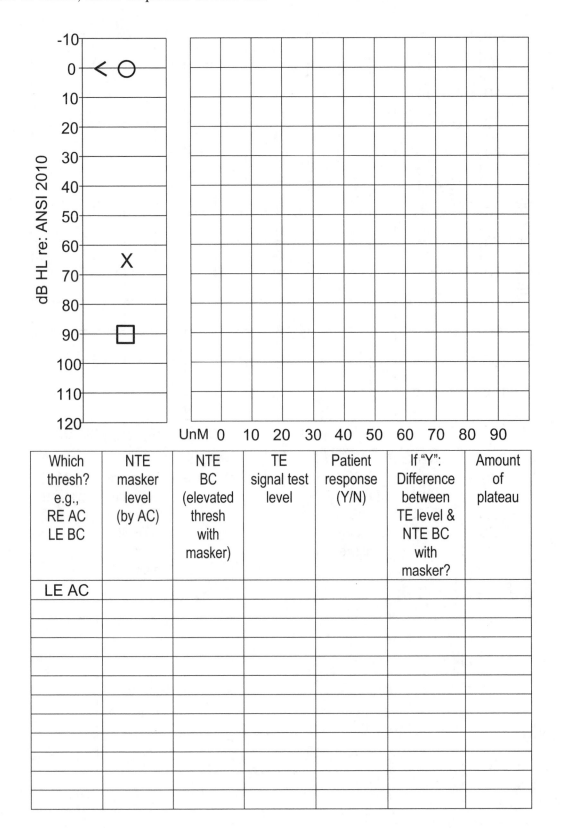

Which thresh? e.g., RE AC LE BC	NTE masker level (by AC)	NTE BC (elevated thresh with masker)	TE signal test level	Patient response (Y/N)	If "Y": Difference between TE level & NTE BC with masker?	Amount of plateau
LE AC						

Case D. LE BC; insert earphones at 1000 Hz.

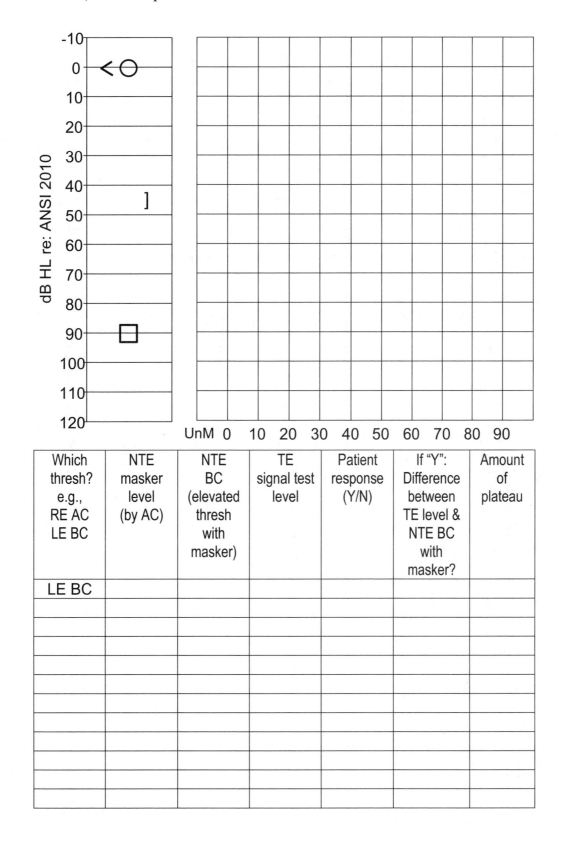

Which thresh? e.g., RE AC LE BC	NTE masker level (by AC)	NTE BC (elevated thresh with masker)	TE signal test level	Patient response (Y/N)	If "Y": Difference between TE level & NTE BC with masker?	Amount of plateau
LE BC						

Case E. Supra-aural earphones at 1000 Hz. Note: This will be a masking dilemma for AC and BC both ears.

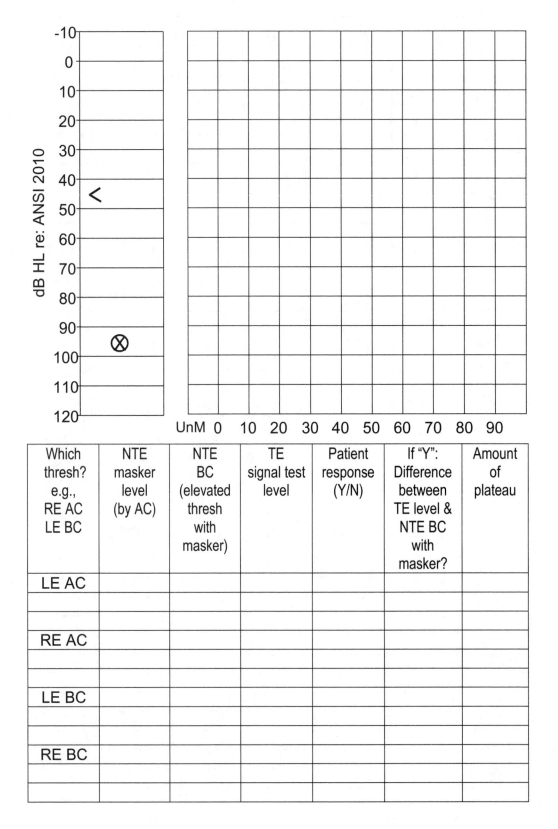

Which thresh? e.g., RE AC LE BC	NTE masker level (by AC)	NTE BC (elevated thresh with masker)	TE signal test level	Patient response (Y/N)	If "Y": Difference between TE level & NTE BC with masker?	Amount of plateau
LE AC						
RE AC						
LE BC						
RE BC						

7.15 When is it necessary to mask when determining the speech recognition threshold (SRT)?

7.16 When is it necessary to mask when determining a word recognition score (WRS)?

7.17 Describe the masking stimuli used during speech testing.

7.18 For the following three audiograms, determine the level of speech masking you would use to obtain the SRT and WRS for the poorer ear and fill in the noise levels for NTE in the open boxes (answers may vary):

Case A. Tested with TDH-50 earphones.

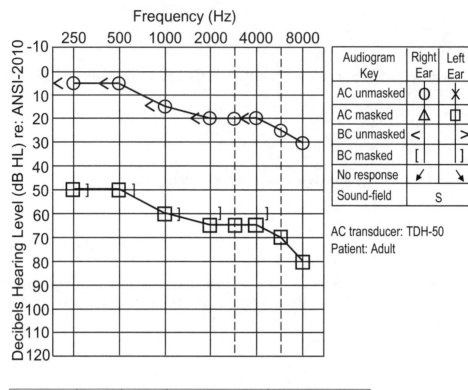

Ear	PTA	SRT	WRS (1)		WRS (2)	
			%	dB HL	%	dB HL
R	13	15	96	55	DNT	DNT
L	58	60	68	80	78	95
Noise L						
Noise R						

Case B. Tested with ER-3A earphones.

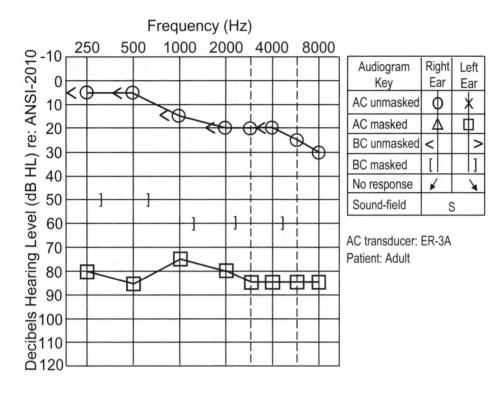

Audiogram Key	Right Ear	Left Ear
AC unmasked	O	X
AC masked	△	▢
BC unmasked	<	>
BC masked	[	]
No response	↙	↘
Sound-field	S	

AC transducer: ER-3A
Patient: Adult

Ear	PTA	SRT	WRS (1) %	WRS (1) dB HL	WRS (2) %	WRS (2) dB HL
R	13	15	100	55	DNT	DNT
L	80	80	62	95	72	105
Noise L						
Noise R						

Case C. Tested with supra-aural earphones.

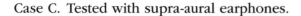

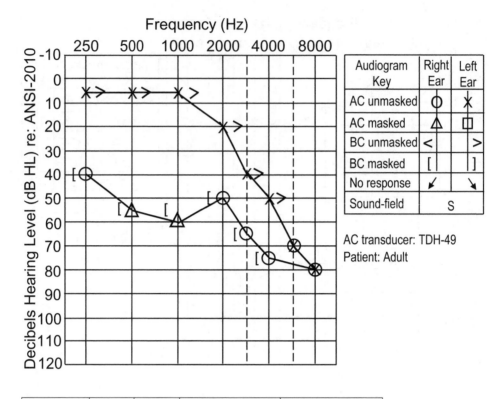

Audiogram Key	Right Ear	Left Ear
AC unmasked	O	X
AC masked	△	▢
BC unmasked	<	>
BC masked	[	]
No response	↙	↘
Sound-field	S	

AC transducer: TDH-49
Patient: Adult

Ear	PTA	SRT	WRS (1)		WRS (2)	
			%	dB HL	%	dB HL
R	55	55	82	70	86	85
L	10	10	88	50	DNT	DNT
Noise L						
Noise R						

7.19 Plot the audiograms for the descriptions given, using masked symbols where necessary. Assume these audiograms are from adult patients.

A. Mild sensorineural hearing loss in the right ear and a moderate to severe, sloping sensorineural loss in the left ear.

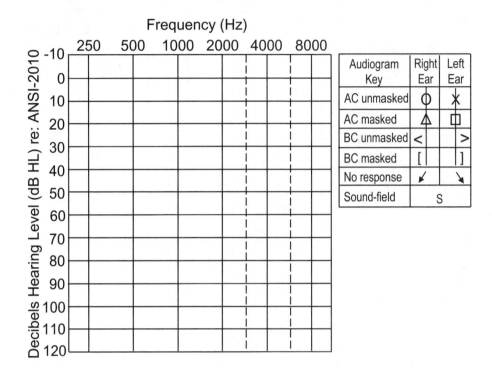

Audiogram Key	Right Ear	Left Ear
AC unmasked	⊕	X
AC masked	△	☐
BC unmasked	<	>
BC masked	[	]
No response	↙	↘
Sound-field	S	

B. Mild conductive hearing loss in the right ear and a moderate conductive hearing loss in the left ear.

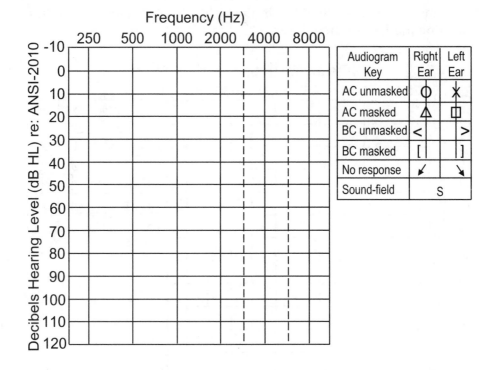

C. Borderline normal hearing sensitivity in the left ear and a profound sensorineural hearing loss in the right ear, with no measurable hearing above 4000 Hz.

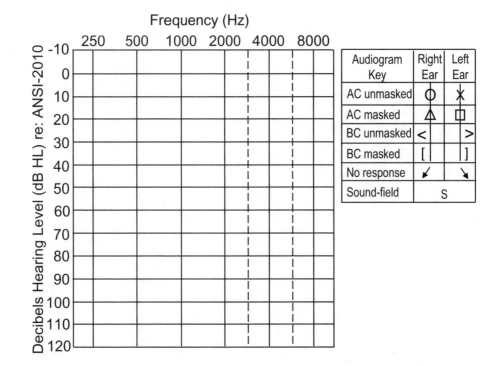

 **Immittance**

8.1 Describe the functions of the following components of an immittance instrument.

  A. probe-tone generator/speaker

  B. microphone

  C. automatic gain circuit (AGC)

  D. air-pressure pump (manometer)

  E. reflex-eliciting tone

8.2 Describe each of the following measures obtained during tympanometry, including its measurement units. What results would one expect for each measure in a normal functioning outer/middle ear for an adult? for a child 18 months to 10 years of age? Refer to Table 8–1 at the end of this chapter for normative values.

    A. Acoustic equivalent volume (V_{ea})

    B. Admittance at the tympanic membrane (Y_{tm})

    C. Tympanometric peak pressure (TPP)

    D. Tympanometric width (TW)

8.3 What is the difference between a compensated (baseline-on) and a non-compensated (baseline-off) tympanogram?

8.4 For each of the following five tympanograms, provide a brief description, the tympanogram type based on Jerger's classification scheme (e.g., A, B, C), and an associated condition/disorder of the ear.

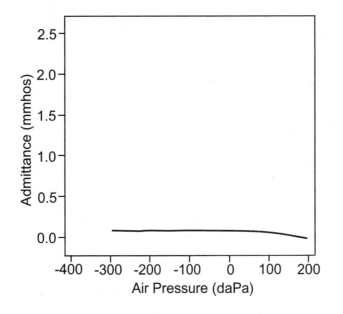

A. Description:

Type:

Possible disorder:

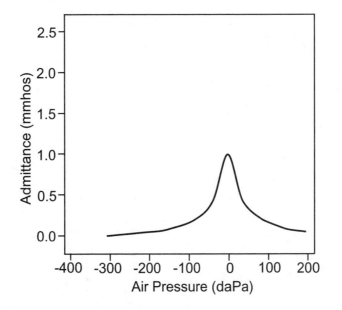

B. Description:

Type:

Possible disorder:

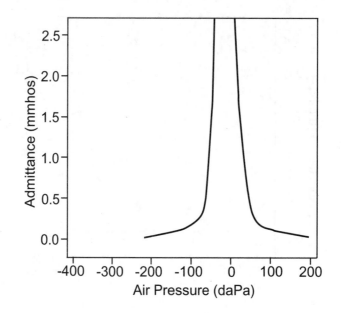

C. Description:

Type:

Possible disorder:

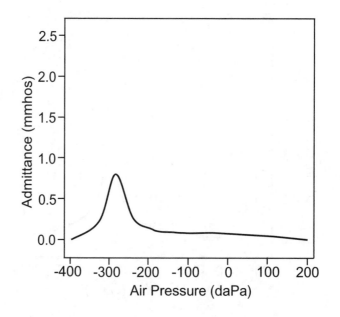

D. Description:

Type:

Possible disorder:

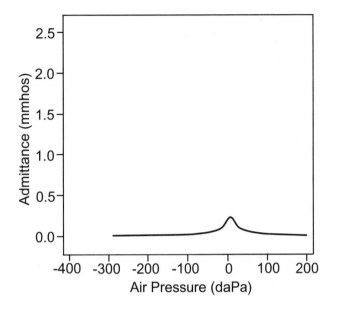

E. Description:

Type:

Possible disorder:

8.5 For the tympanogram shown below from an adult, draw lines to show how to obtain the tympanometric width (TW). Is the TW shown in this example within normal limits? Refer to Table 8–1 at the end of the chapter for assistance with this exercise.

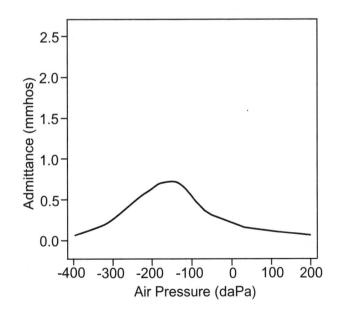

Tympanometric width: _____

8.6 Refer to the non-compensated (baseline-off) tympanograms shown below. Fill in the approximate values (try to use a straight edge to be accurate).

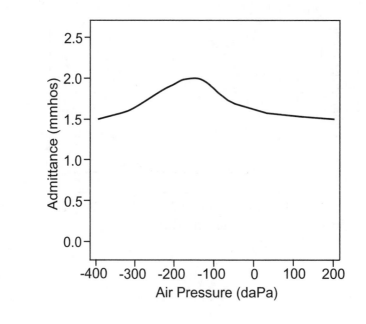

A. V_{ea} = _____

Y_{tm} = _____

TPP = _____

TW = _____

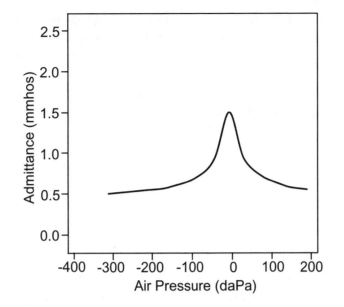

B. V_{ea} = _____

Y_{tm} = _____

TPP = _____

TW = _____

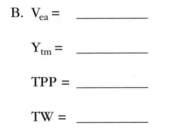

8.7 Refer to the compensated (baseline-on) tympanograms shown below. Fill in the approximate values (try to use a straight edge to be accurate). How would you obtain the V_{ea} for a non-compensated tympanogram? For the first example, assume the ear has a perforation.

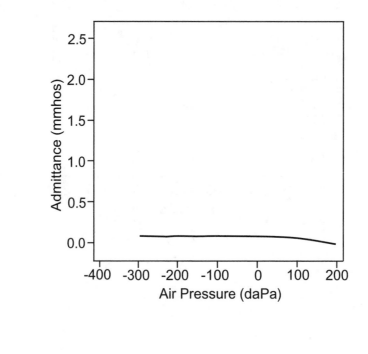

A. V_{ea} = _____

Y_{tm} = _____

TPP = _____

TW = _____

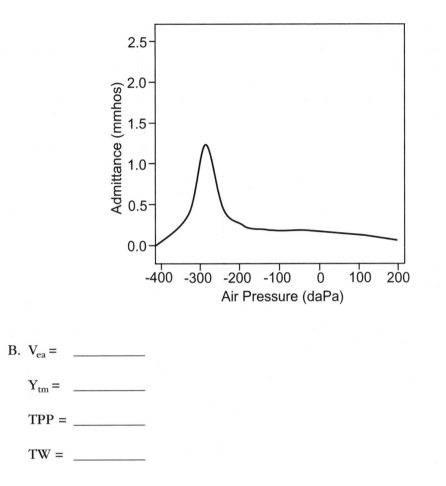

B. V_{ea} = _____

Y_{tm} = _____

TPP = _____

TW = _____

8.8 Draw and label the parts of the auditory system and pathways that represent the ipsilateral and contralateral acoustic reflex for stimulation of the left ear only (you do not need to include stimulation of the right ear).

8.9 What strategy should one use to help determine which level (dB HL) to select as the acoustic reflex threshold from a series of recordings?

8.10 Given the examples in the following table, fill in the expected acoustic reflex threshold patterns. The columns are arranged based on how one would typically have the equipment set up for testing; Ipsi first, then Contra with the probe remaining in place (in this case starting with the probe in the right ear). For cochlear losses, consider only 1000 Hz reflex eliciting tone. Refer to Table 8–2 at the end of this chapter for assistance regarding 90% criterion values for normal and cochlear losses based on Gelfand, Schwander, and Silman (1990).

		R Ipsi	Stim L Probe R	L Ipsi	Stim R Probe L
1	RE: Normal hearing and function LE: 45 dB conductive loss				
2	RE: 60 dB cochlear loss LE: 40 dB cochlear loss				
3	RE: Impacted cerumen; 15 dB air–bone gap LE: 7th N problem distal to stapedial branch				
4	RE: 70 dB cochlear loss LE: Normal hearing and function				
5	RE: 8th N tumor; mild sensorineural loss LE: Normal hearing with small perforation				
6	RE: 40 dB cochlear loss LE: 40 dB conductive loss				
7	RE: 50 dB cochlear loss LE: 70 dB mixed loss (with 40 dB ABG)				
8	RE: 7th N problem proximal to stapedial branch LE: Normal hearing and function				
9	RE: 25 dB conductive loss LE: 25 dB conductive loss				
10	RE: 35 dB cochlear loss LE: normal hearing with patent PE tube				

		R Ipsi	Stim L Probe R	L Ipsi	Stim R Probe L
11	RE: Normal hearing and function LE: 8th nerve tumor with 50 dB loss				
12	RE: 35 dB cochlear loss LE: 45 dB cochlear loss				
13	RE: 40 dB mixed loss (15 dB ABG) LE: 40 dB cochlear loss				
14	RE: 25 dB conductive loss; perforation LE: Normal hearing and function				
15	Both ears normal hearing, but with intra-axial brainstem tumor				

8.11 How is acoustic reflex decay measured? What is abnormal reflex decay, and to which disorder is abnormal reflex decay associated?

Table 8–1. Normative Tympanometric Measures of Acoustic Equivalent Volume of Ear Canal (V_{ea}), Static Acoustic Admittance of the Middle Ear (Y_{tm}), Tympanometric Peak Pressure (TPP), and Tympanometric Width (TW), with AAA Child Screening Fails

Age Group	V_{ea} (mL or cc)	Y_{tm} (mmhos)	TPP (daPa)	TW (daPa)
Adults (>10 yr.)	0.80 to 2.20	0.30 to 1.70	−105 to +5	<125
Children (>18 mo. to 10 yr.)	0.60 to 1.20	0.30 to 1.05	−75 to +25	<200
Children (6 mo. to 18 mo.)	0.50 to 1.00	0.20 to 0.70	−75 to +25	<250
Infants[1] (<6 mo.)	0.20 to 0.80	0.40 to 2.10	NA	<150
AAA child screening fails	Not used	<0.20	<−200	>250

[1]1000 Hz probe tone; +200 compensation.

Source: Data compiled from the following sources: Roush et al. (1995), American Academy of Audiology (AAA) (2011), Margolis and Hunter (2000), and Hunter (2013).

Table 8–2. 90th Percentile Values for Acoustic Reflex Thresholds (ARTs) for Contralateral Recordings Based on Data from Gelfand et al. (1990)

Hearing Threshold (dB HL)	ART at 500 Hz (dB HL)	ART at 1000 Hz (dB HL)	ART at 2000 Hz (dB HL)
0	95	95	95
5	95	95	95
10	95	95	95
15	95	95	95
20	95	95	95
25	95	95	95
30	95	95	100
35	95	95	100
40	95	95	100
45	95	95	105
50	100	100	105
55	105	105	110
60	105	110	115
65	110	110	115
70	115	115	CNT
>70	CNT	CNT	

Note. For this table, the data only go to a maximum output level of 115 dB HL; CNT= could not test due to equipment limits. See Gelfand et al. for results up to 125 dB HL.

Source: From *Essentials of Audiology* (p. 202), by S. A. Gelfand, 2016, New York, NY: Thieme Medical Publishers, Inc. Copyright 2001 by Thieme Medical Publishers, Inc. Adapted with permission.

9 Otoacoustic Emissions (OAEs) and Auditory Brainstem Responses (ABRs)

9.1 What is signal averaging and how does this help improve the detection of low-level physiological responses like OAEs and ABRs?

9.2 What is an evoked otoacoustic emission (OAE), in general, and how does it relate to events in the cochlea? Name the two main types of evoked OAEs.

9.3 What are distortion products? Define the distortion product most often used to measure DPOAEs.

A. Given that f_2 = 1000 Hz, calculate f_1 (for f_2/f_1 = 1.22). Then calculate the $2f_1$-f_2 distortion product.

B. Given that f_2 = 2000 Hz, calculate f_1 (for f_2/f_1 = 1.22). Then calculate the $2f_1$-f_2 distortion product.

C. Given that f_2 = 4000 Hz, calculate f_1 (for f_2/f_1 = 1.22). Then calculate the $2f_1$-f_2 distortion product.

9.4 What are spontaneous otoacoustic emissions (SOAEs)? Why are these not used much clinically?

9.5 Why do OAEs require relatively good middle ear function?

9.6 Describe the criteria typically used to decide when TEOAEs and DPOAEs are normal.

    A. TEOAEs

    B. DPOAEs

9.7 You have been asked to perform an OAE (TEOAE or DPOAE) evaluation on a young infant:

    A. If you find OAEs are normal (present across frequency range with appropriate SNR), what does this tell you about the patient's auditory system? What does it tell you about the patient's ability to hear?

    B. If you find OAEs are abnormal (absent across the frequency range), what does this tell you about the patient's auditory system? What does it tell you about the patient's ability to hear?

9.8 Identify the labeled areas of the following recording:

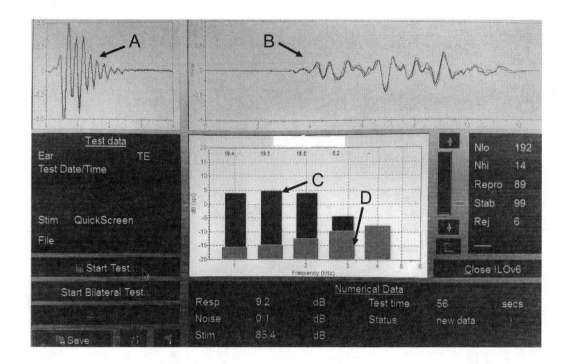

A.

B.

C.

D.

9.9 How would you interpret the results of the following two TEOAE recordings? What factors did you use to make your determinations?

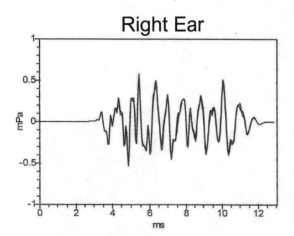

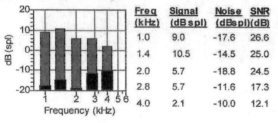

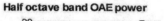

A.

Right Ear

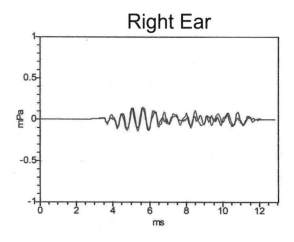

Left Ear

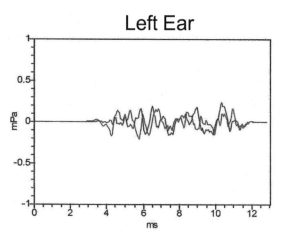

Half octave band OAE power

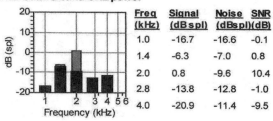

Freq (kHz)	Signal (dB spl)	Noise (dBspl)	SNR (dB)
1.0	-16.7	-16.6	-0.1
1.4	-6.3	-7.0	0.8
2.0	0.8	-9.6	10.4
2.8	-13.8	-12.8	-1.0
4.0	-20.9	-11.4	-9.5

Half octave band OAE power

Freq (kHz)	Signal (dB spl)	Noise (dBspl)	SNR (dB)
1.0	-8.2	-6.7	-1.5
1.4	-9.2	2.7	-11.8
2.0	-10.3	-7.7	-2.7
2.8	-13.3	-7.5	-5.8
4.0	-12.4	-11.0	-1.4

B.

9.10 How would you interpret the results of the following two DPOAE recordings? What factors did you use to make these determinations?

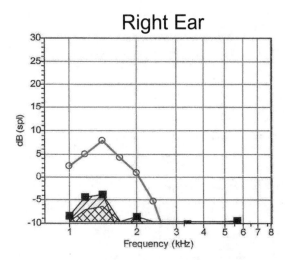

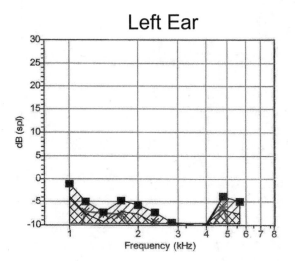

Half octave band OAE power

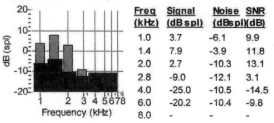

Freq (kHz)	Signal (dB spl)	Noise (dBspl)	SNR (dB)
1.0	3.7	-6.1	9.9
1.4	7.9	-3.9	11.8
2.0	2.7	-10.3	13.1
2.8	-9.0	-12.1	3.1
4.0	-25.0	-10.5	-14.5
6.0	-20.2	-10.4	-9.8
8.0	-	-	-

Half octave band OAE power

Freq (kHz)	Signal (dB spl)	Noise (dBspl)	SNR (dB)
1.0	-11.2	-2.8	-8.4
1.4	-7.4	-7.2	-0.2
2.0	-9.7	-5.2	-4.5
2.8	-12.1	-8.2	-3.8
4.0	-14.8	-10.5	-4.3
6.0	-10.1	-4.4	-5.7
8.0	-	-	-

A.

Right Ear

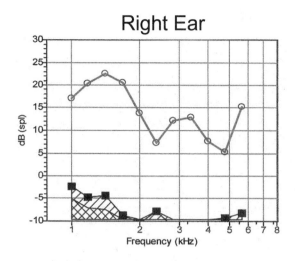

Left Ear

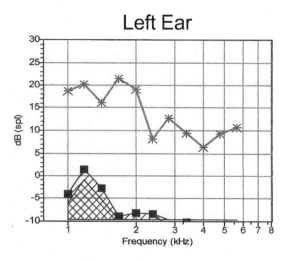

Half octave band OAE power

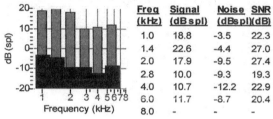

Freq (kHz)	Signal (dB spl)	Noise (dBspl)	SNR (dB)
1.0	18.8	-3.5	22.3
1.4	22.6	-4.4	27.0
2.0	17.9	-9.5	27.4
2.8	10.0	-9.3	19.3
4.0	10.7	-12.2	22.9
6.0	11.7	-8.7	20.4
8.0	-	-	-

Half octave band OAE power

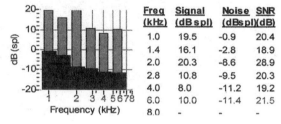

Freq (kHz)	Signal (dB spl)	Noise (dBspl)	SNR (dB)
1.0	19.5	-0.9	20.4
1.4	16.1	-2.8	18.9
2.0	20.3	-8.6	28.9
2.8	10.8	-9.5	20.3
4.0	8.0	-11.2	19.2
6.0	10.0	-11.4	21.5
8.0	-	-	-

B.

9.11 Label the seven waves (peaks) of the auditory brainstem response (ABR) in the following figure (recorded at a relatively high intensity). List the primary anatomical/neural sources that are associated with the first five waves.

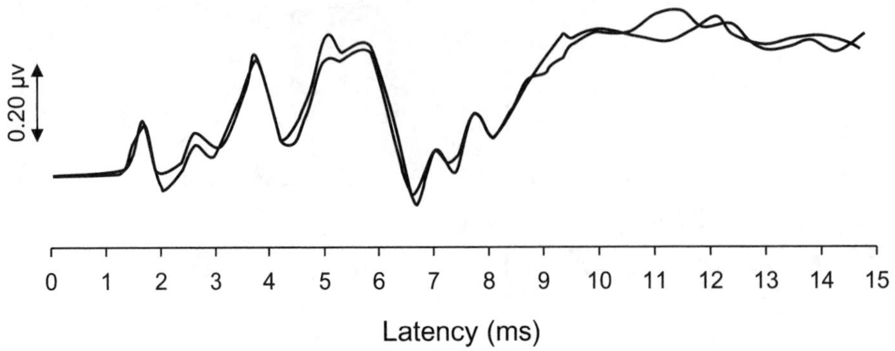

Wave I:

Wave II:

Wave III:

Wave IV:

Wave V:

9.12 Define the following terms as they pertain to ABR:

A. Absolute latency

B. Interpeak latency interval

C. Interaural latency difference

D. Amplitude

E. Amplitude ratio of V/I

9.13 Label wave V for each waveform in the following series of ABR recordings, and describe what happens to the ABR as the stimulus intensity decreases in a normal functioning auditory system.

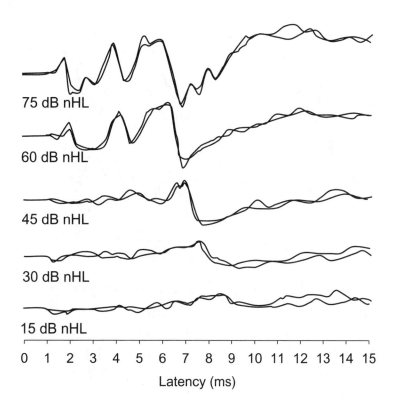

9.14 Describe the click evoked ABR outcomes you would expect if there was an acoustic neuroma (vestibular schwannoma) affecting the 8th cranial nerve of the right ear.

9.15 Label the waves on the following sets of ABR waveforms and interpret the results.

A.

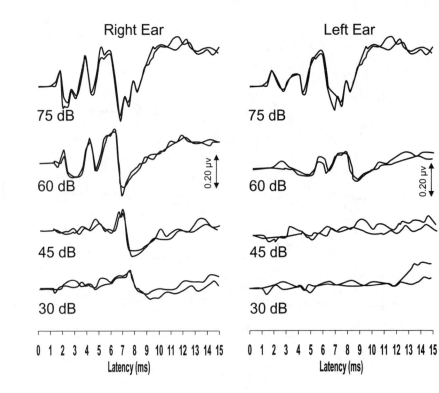

B.

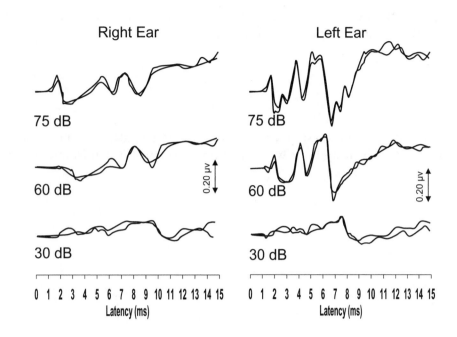

9.16 On the following latency-intensity (L-I) graph, plot how wave V (to clicks) would change across intensity for (1) mild conductive loss, (2) mild sloping high frequency sensorineural loss, (3) mild to moderately severe steeply sloping high frequency sensorineural hearing loss, and (4) moderate low frequency sensorineural loss, rising to normal at 2000 Hz.

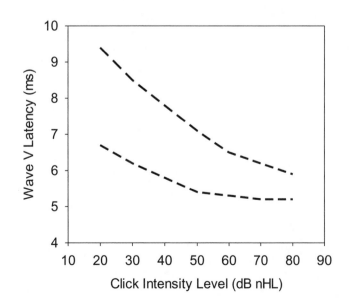

9.17 What are auditory steady state responses (ASSRs), and why might they be advantageous in defining auditory frequency-specific thresholds?

9.18 What would be your impression if you found that your patient had normal OAEs and a significant sensorineural hearing loss? What would you suspect if you found your patient had normal OAEs and absent ABRs?

10 Screening for Hearing Loss

10.1 In general, screening programs are appropriate for, and should target, disorders that are recognized as important health issues. What do you think would be the primary goal of a program for early hearing detection and intervention (EHDI)?

10.2 What are the essential elements of any effective screening test?

10.3 For a screening procedure to be effective, it must have both good validity and good reliability. Define these two terms.

10.4 Contrast the terms universal screening and targeted screening.

10.5 What are the recommended timelines for (a) an initial screening, (b) follow-up screening, (c) diagnostic testing, and (d) initiation of treatment as parts of a comprehensive universal newborn hearing screening?

10.6 What are the advantages of using automated auditory brainstem responses (AABRs) and/or otoacoustic emissions (OAEs) as a screening technique with newborns?

10.7 What are two disadvantages of screening the hearing of newborns just with OAEs?

10.8 What are the ASHA (2017) and/or AAA (2011) recommended frequencies and dB HL for pure-tone air conduction screening of school-age children? How do these differ from screening the hearing sensitivity of adults?

10.9 List three types of professionals who may perform pure-tone air conduction hearing screenings.

10.10 Based on the results from an initial preschool hearing screening, when should a child be referred for a full audiologic evaluation?

10.11 Based on the results from an initial preschool hearing screening, when should a child be referred for a medical evaluation?

10.12 Based on ASHA (2017) and AAA (2011) screening guidelines, when is it appropriate/ necessary to include 500 Hz in a screening program for children? What considerations need to be made if this frequency is included?

10.13 When performing any screening procedure (including hearing), four potential outcomes can occur: true positive, true negative, false positive, and false negative. Describe these four outcomes in relation to hearing screening.

10.14 The efficacy of a screening test is evaluated in terms of its sensitivity, specificity, positive predictive value, and negative predictive value. Define these four terms in relation to the efficacy of any particular screening test. How do you calculate each one?

10.15 You have decided to screen the hearing sensitivity of adults at your local senior center using two different levels, 10 dB HL and 50 dB HL. How would these two dB HLs affect both the sensitivity and specificity of your screening procedure? What does this tell you about the relationship between sensitivity and specificity?

10.16 The following grid displays the air conduction pure-tone data you obtained from a hearing screening you performed in your school district (463 students were screened).

Test Outcome	Hearing Loss Present	Hearing Loss Absent	TOTALS
FAIL (positive for hearing loss)	15	23	38
PASS (negative for hearing loss)	3	422	425
TOTALS	18	445	463

A. From the data given, calculate (show your work) the sensitivity, specificity, positive predictive value, and negative predictive value for the screening.

Sensitivity:

Specificity:

Positive predictive value:

Negative predictive value:

B. How would you interpret these values in terms of this test's overall effectiveness?

10.17 You have screened 180 humans for a particular disease with a recently developed screening test. The prevalence of the disease is 19% in the population.

Test Outcome	Disease Is Present	Disease Is Absent	TOTALS
FAIL (positive for the disease)	25	25	50
PASS (negative for the disease)	10	120	130
TOTALS	35	145	180

A. From the data given, calculate the sensitivity, specificity, positive predictive value, and negative predictive value for this screening test.

Humans

Sensitivity:

Specificity:

Positive predictive value:

Negative predictive value:

Test Outcome	Disease Is Present	Disease Is Absent	TOTALS
FAIL (positive for the disease)	50	19	69
PASS (negative for the disease)	20	91	111
TOTALS	70	110	180

B. You now screen 180 Martians for the same disease with the same test. The prevalence of the disease is much greater (39%) in the Martian population. From the data given, calculate the sensitivity, specificity, positive predictive value, and negative predictive value for this screening.

Martians

Sensitivity:

Specificity:

Positive predictive value:

Negative predictive value:

C. Compare the sensitivity and specificity for the two different screenings. What changes, if any, do you see? Why do you think this is so?

D. Compare the positive and negative predictive values for the two different screenings. What changes, if any, do you see? Why do you think this is so?

11 Disorders of the Auditory System

11.1 Given the following diseases or disorders, list the part of the auditory system (outer, middle, cochlea, 8th cranial nerve, central) that is primarily involved and the most probable type of hearing loss (conductive, sensorineural, none).

Disorder	Location of problem	Type of hearing loss
A. otitis externa	_____	_____
B. Meniere's disease	_____	_____
C. eustachian tube dysfunction	_____	_____
D. cholesteatoma	_____	_____
E. impacted cerumen	_____	_____
F. fistula	_____	_____
G. presbycusis	_____	_____
H. microtia	_____	_____
I. acoustic neuroma	_____	_____
J. cytomegalovirus	_____	_____
K. autoimmune inner ear disease	_____	_____
L. auricular hematoma	_____	_____
M. otitis media	_____	_____
N. meningitis	_____	_____

Disorder	Location of problem	Type of hearing loss
O. acoustic trauma	_____	_____
P. otosclerosis	_____	_____
Q. osteoma	_____	_____
R. atresia	_____	_____
S. auditory dyssynchrony	_____	_____
T. disarticulation	_____	_____
U. ototoxicity	_____	_____
V. perforation	_____	_____
W. anotia	_____	_____
X. glomus tumor	_____	_____
Y. exostosis	_____	_____

11.2 Describe the differences between a genetic hearing loss, a congenital hearing loss, and an acquired hearing loss. Give an example of each.

11.3 What is the difference between an acute disorder and a chronic disorder?

11.4 Briefly describe the primary cause and pathophysiology (i.e., what is the main change that occurs in the auditory system) for the following disorders:

    A. otitis externa

B. exostosis

C. atresia

D. otitis media

E. cholesteatoma

F. disarticulation

G. otosclerosis

H. glomus tumor

I. Meniere's disease

J. presbycusis

K. autoimmune inner ear disease

L. acoustic trauma/noise-induced hearing loss

M. ototoxicity

N. acoustic neuroma

O. auditory dyssynchrony/neuropathy

11.5 For each of the given disorders, list the common symptoms and at least one treatment option.

A. otitis externa

B. exostosis

C. atresia

D. otitis media

E. cholesteatoma

F. disarticulation

G. otosclerosis

H. glomus tumor

I. Meniere's disease

J. presbycusis

K. autoimmune inner ear disease

L. acoustic trauma/noise-induced hearing loss

M. ototoxicity

N. acoustic neuroma

O. auditory dyssynchrony/neuropathy

11.6 List four different classifications of ototoxic agents. Which of these types of ototoxic agents is often associated with a reversible hearing loss when treatment ends?

11.7 Describe two types of temporal bone fractures and the type of hearing loss generally associated with each.

11.8 What are some of the reasons that a patient might feign a hearing loss?

11.9 What is the Stenger phenomenon? Describe how the Stenger test is administered to a patient suspected of feigning a hearing loss in the right ear and how the results would suggest either a true hearing loss or a functional hearing loss.

12 Case Studies

The following case studies are designed to test your ability to describe and integrate information from a short case history and different audiometric tests for a variety of common auditory disorders. For each case, fill in the requested missing test data that would be consistent with the history and any given test data, then provide the following:

1. <u>Summary of results</u> to include: (1) description of audiogram (there will be some variability in actual values; however, air conduction thresholds should match the PTA, and the type of loss should be consistent with immittance and history); (2) description/type of tympanograms, including V_{ea} if relevant to the diagnosis; (3) summary of speech results, including consistency between PTA and SRT, and, if differences in WRS between ears, indicate if they are or are not statistically significant based on critical differences from the binomial distribution (see Table 6–1 in Chapter 6); and (4) interpretation of any additional test results/comments if relevant.
2. <u>Audiologic impression and medical diagnosis.</u> The diagnoses made in this chapter are for academic purposes; only physicians make actual medical diagnoses.
3. (For the more advanced student). <u>Recommendations</u> for medical and/or audiologic follow-up, further audiologic testing, and/or the need for amplification.

Key to Abbreviations

V_{ea} = acoustic equivalent volume

Y_{tm} = admittance at the tympanic membrane

TPP = tympanometric peak pressure

NP = no peak

NR = no response

DNT = did not test

ARTs = acoustic reflex thresholds

Ipsi R = ipsilateral reflex right ear

Ipsi L = ipsilateral reflex left ear

Stim L/Probe R = contralateral reflex with stimulus in left ear, probe in right ear

Stim R/Probe L = contralateral reflex with stimulus in right ear, probe in left ear

PTA = pure-tone average

SRT = speech recognition threshold

SDT = speech detection threshold

WRS = word recognition score

IPL = interpeak latency interval

RE = right ear

LE = left ear

Case Study 1

Susan Stapes, a 7-year-old girl, was seen for audiologic testing due to recent parent and teacher concerns regarding her difficulty hearing from the right ear. Her history is significant for frequent colds, otitis media, and excessive cerumen buildup.

Given the following results, fill in the audiogram and ARTs for both ears.

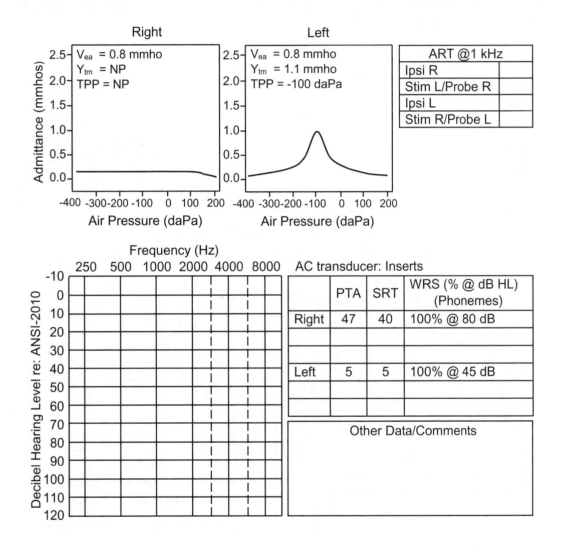

Results:

Impression/Diagnosis:

Recommendations:

Case Study 2

Steven Saccule, a 29-year-old male, was seen for audiologic testing following complaints of difficult hearing from the right ear. He reported that the onset was gradual but seemed to have worsened during the past month. He also reported that hearing loss "tended to run in the family."

Given the following results, fill in the V_{ea}, Y_{tm}, TPP, and ARTs, PTA, SRT, and WRS for one selected presentation level, for both ears.

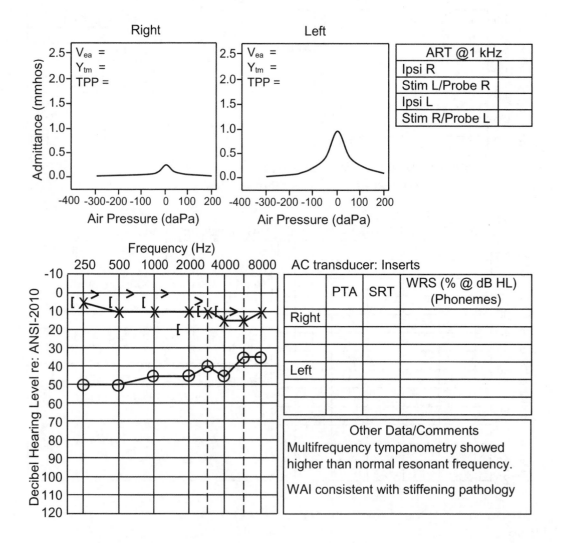

Results:

Impression/Diagnosis:

Recommendations:

Case Study 3

Vanessa Vestibule, a 71-year-old female, was seen for audiologic testing after her husband convinced her that she has difficulty hearing conversations and the television and talking with her right ear on the phone. She reported that she has gradually noticed increased difficulty, especially in noisy situations. She reported having bilateral ringing in her ears, but denied any dizziness, noise exposure, or family history of hearing loss.

Given the following results, fill in the tympanograms (compensated), ARTs, PTA, and SRT for both ears.

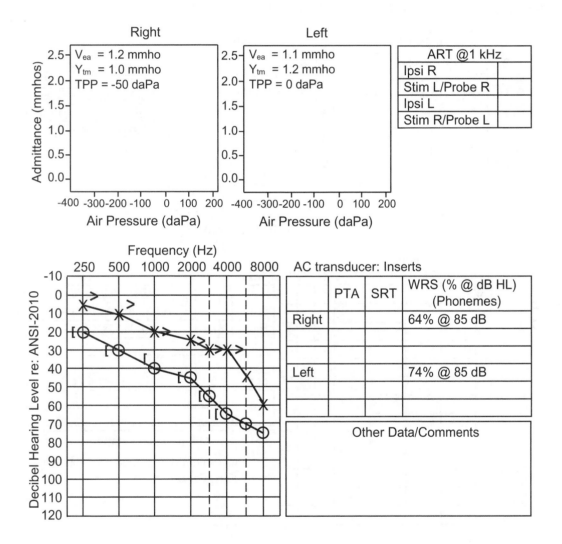

Right

V_{ea} = 1.2 mmho
Y_{tm} = 1.0 mmho
TPP = -50 daPa

Left

V_{ea} = 1.1 mmho
Y_{tm} = 1.2 mmho
TPP = 0 daPa

ART @1 kHz	
Ipsi R	
Stim L/Probe R	
Ipsi L	
Stim R/Probe L	

AC transducer: Inserts

	PTA	SRT	WRS (% @ dB HL) (Phonemes)
Right			64% @ 85 dB
Left			74% @ 85 dB

Other Data/Comments

Results:

Impression/Diagnosis:

Recommendations:

Case Study 4

Pam Perilymph, a 55-year-old female, was referred for audiologic testing as part of her physical exam upon retirement as a police officer. She reported frequent use of firearms at the firing range and that she always wore her dispatch radio on her right shoulder during her patrol shifts. She reported using ear protection when on the firing range, but rarely during her patrol shifts so she could hear her radio. She also reported frequent use of recreational vehicles (ATVs). She complained of bilateral tinnitus that was quite bothersome. She reported that she could hear pretty well, but had some difficulty in noisy situations. She denied any vertigo or aural fullness.

Given the following results, fill in the audiogram and SRTs for both ears.

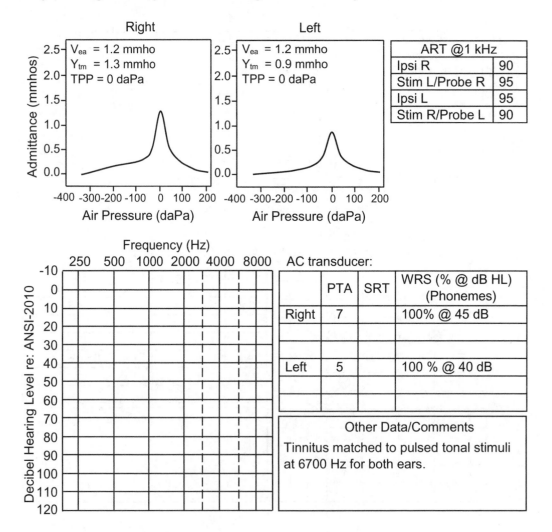

ART @1 kHz	
Ipsi R	90
Stim L/Probe R	95
Ipsi L	95
Stim R/Probe L	90

AC transducer:

	PTA	SRT	WRS (% @ dB HL) (Phonemes)
Right	7		100% @ 45 dB
Left	5		100 % @ 40 dB

Other Data/Comments

Tinnitus matched to pulsed tonal stimuli at 6700 Hz for both ears.

Results:

Impression/Diagnosis:

Recommendations:

Case Study 5

Chris Concha, an 8-year-old boy, was brought in for an audiologic evaluation by his mother due to increased concerns about Chris's hearing. His mother reported that Chris has a history of bilateral, mild to moderate, sloping sensorineural hearing loss since birth; he has been doing quite well with his binaural hearing aids and is a good student. Chris said that he thinks his hearing has worsened recently and his hearing aids were not helping him as much. He recently experienced a bad cold and currently feels his ears are "plugged." No other problems were reported.

Given the following results, fill in the audiogram and ARTs for both ears.

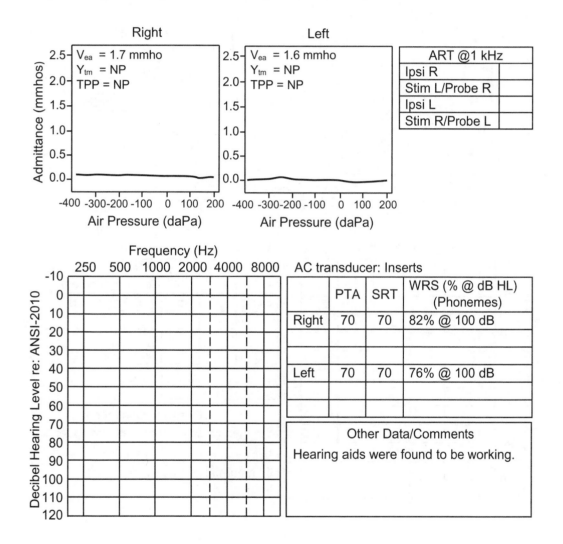

Results:

Impression/Diagnosis:

Recommendations:

Case Study 6

Liz Latency, a 22-year-old female, was seen for an audiologic evaluation due to noticing difficulty hearing in her left ear after getting hit by a ball during a softball game. She stated that she was in the process of consulting with a lawyer about the accident. She denied any ear pain, drainage, tinnitus, or aural fullness. She also reported that over the past two years she frequently goes out to bars/clubs where there is very loud music.

Given the following results, fill in the audiogram, PTA, V_{ea}, Y_{tm}, TPP, and ARTs for both ears.

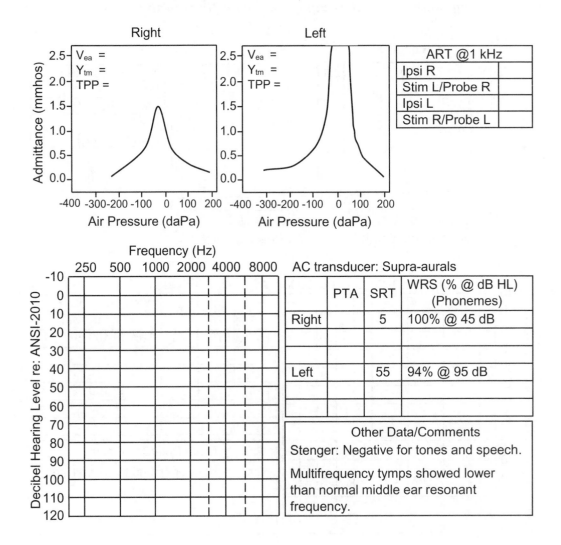

	PTA	SRT	WRS (% @ dB HL) (Phonemes)
Right		5	100% @ 45 dB
Left		55	94% @ 95 dB

ART @1 kHz	
Ipsi R	
Stim L/Probe R	
Ipsi L	
Stim R/Probe L	

AC transducer: Supra-aurals

Other Data/Comments

Stenger: Negative for tones and speech.

Multifrequency tymps showed lower than normal middle ear resonant frequency.

Results:

Impression/Diagnosis:

Recommendations:

Case Study 7

Lenny Labyrinth, a 45-year-old male, was seen for audiologic testing after falling off a scaffold and hitting the left side of his head. He reported having difficulty understanding speech, especially when using the telephone on his left ear. He also reported that he has had a high-pitched ringing in his left ear that he noticed prior to his accident. He was not sure what caused his fall, but since the fall he has noticed some slight unsteadiness.

Given the following results, fill in the ARTs and rollover ratio for both ears.

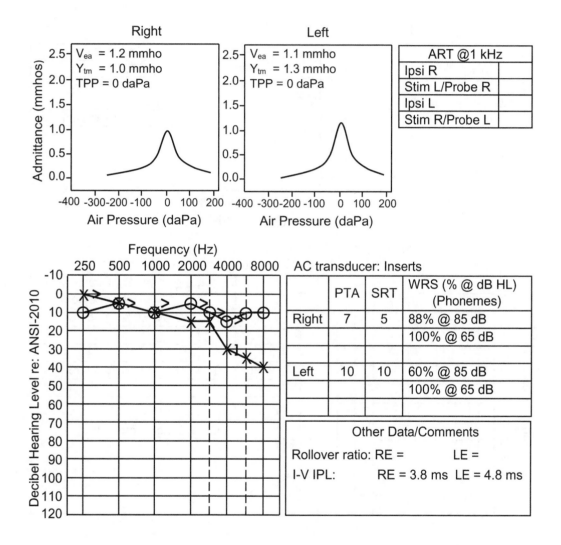

ART @1 kHz	
Ipsi R	
Stim L/Probe R	
Ipsi L	
Stim R/Probe L	

AC transducer: Inserts

	PTA	SRT	WRS (% @ dB HL) (Phonemes)
Right	7	5	88% @ 85 dB
			100% @ 65 dB
Left	10	10	60% @ 85 dB
			100% @ 65 dB

Other Data/Comments

Rollover ratio: RE =   LE =

I-V IPL: RE = 3.8 ms LE = 4.8 ms

Results:

Impression/Diagnosis:

Recommendations:

Case Study 8

Sabina Stereocilia, a 21-year-old female, was seen for an audiologic evaluation following an incident 4 days ago in which she was cleaning her ears with a cotton swab and her boyfriend bumped into her, causing her great pain in her right ear. She reported that the pain has subsided, but she notices that her hearing "has been a bit off" since the incident. She denied any dizziness or ringing in her ears.

Given the following results, fill in the audiogram, tympanograms, and ARTs for both ears.

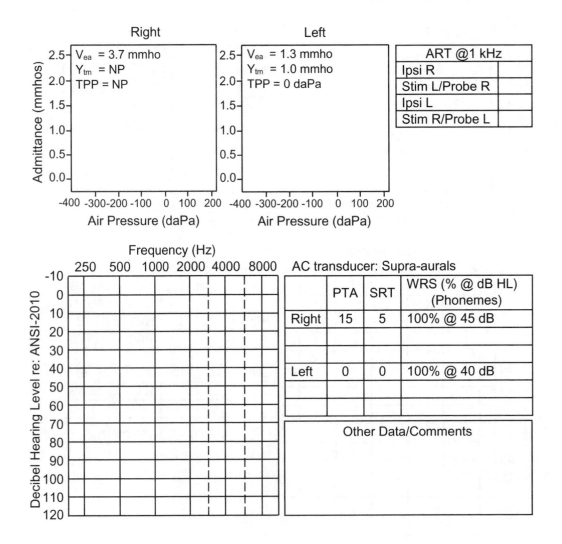

Results:

Impression/Diagnosis:

Recommendations:

Case Study 9

Sergei Spondee, a 26-year-old male, was seen for an audiologic evaluation after noticing severe ringing in his ears over the past two weeks. He reported that his hearing seems fine, although he occasionally confuses some words, and has a more difficult time in noise environments. He reported that he had recently been treated for a severe urinary tract infection but could not recall the name of the medication.

Given the following results, fill in the high frequency PTA for both ears.

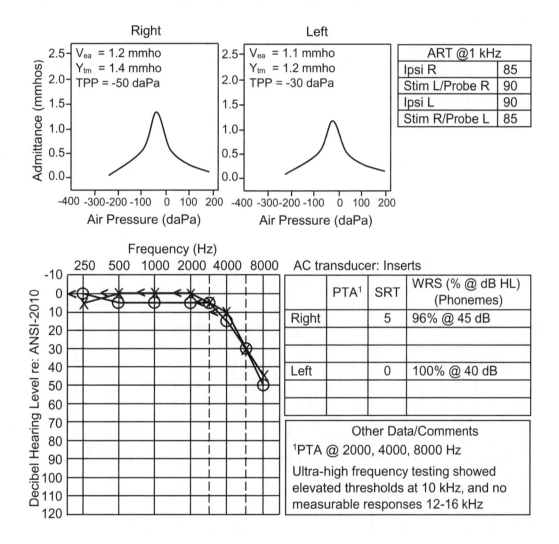

Results:

Impression/Diagnosis:

Recommendations:

Case Study 10

Dion Decibel, a 44-year-old male, was referred by his ENT physician for an audiologic evaluation due to reported episodes of vertigo occurring over the past three months, as well as a perforation noted in his right ear. Mr. Decibel reported some hearing difficulties, especially in his left ear, accompanied by a "buzzy" sound in his ear and a feeling of aural fullness. He denied any ear pain, known family history of hearing loss, or excessive noise exposure on a regular basis.

Given the following results, fill in the tympanograms, V_{ea}, Y_{tm}, TPP, ARTs, and PTAs for both ears.

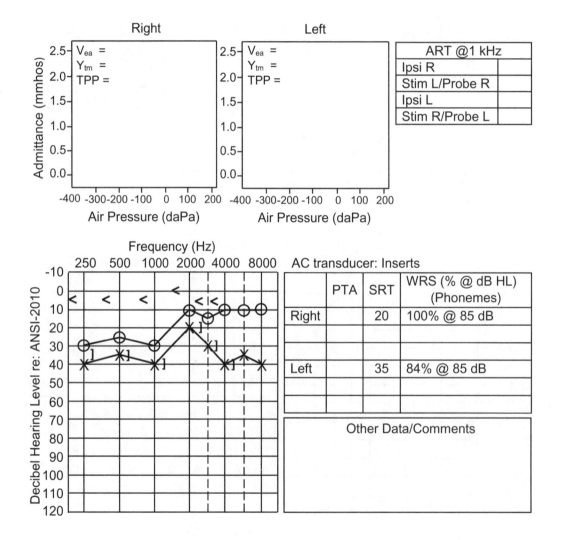

Results:

Impression/Diagnosis:

Recommendations:

Case Study 11

Madeline Malleus, a 15-year-old female, was referred by her ENT physician for an audiologic evaluation due to a recently noticed hearing problem. She reported a history of frequent ear infections in both ears when younger, but also recently had an ear infection in her left ear after an airplane flight. At today's visit, she complained of some hearing loss and feeling of fullness in both ears. She denied any dizziness or history of excessive exposure to noise.

Given the following results, fill in the audiogram and tympanogram for both ears.

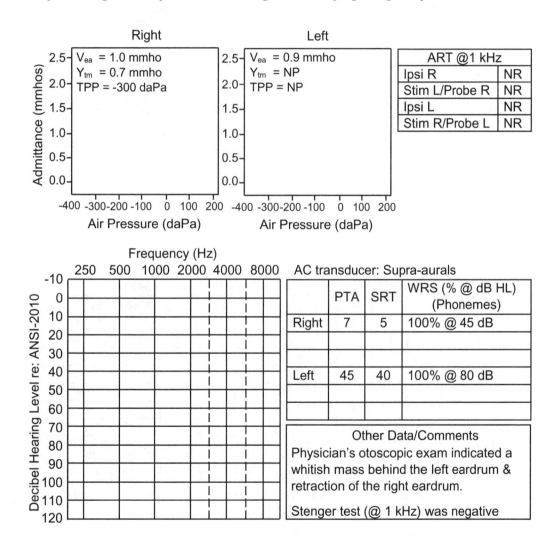

Results:

Impression/Diagnosis:

Recommendations:

Case Study 12

Reilly Rinne, a 4-year-old boy, was seen today for an audiologic evaluation as a follow-up to insertion of bilateral pressure equalization (PE) tubes about 2 months ago. His preoperative audiogram had shown a bilateral moderate conductive loss, and thresholds improved to near normal following the insertion of the tubes. At today's visit, Reilly's mother reported noticing occasional drainage from his right ear, and recently has noticed that his attention/hearing seemed to fluctuate. Reilly's speech and language seem to be age appropriate.

Given the following results, fill in the audiogram and ARTs for both ears.

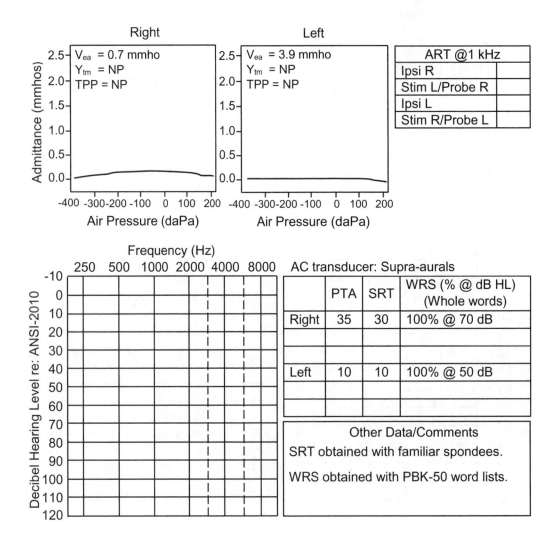

ART @1 kHz	
Ipsi R	
Stim L/Probe R	
Ipsi L	
Stim R/Probe L	

AC transducer: Supra-aurals

	PTA	SRT	WRS (% @ dB HL) (Whole words)
Right	35	30	100% @ 70 dB
Left	10	10	100% @ 50 dB

Other Data/Comments

SRT obtained with familiar spondees.

WRS obtained with PBK-50 word lists.

Results:

Impression/Diagnosis:

Recommendations:

Case Study 13

Steven Stapes, a 45-year-old male, was referred for an ENT consult and audiologic evaluation by the Urgent Care attending physician who saw him two days ago. Steven drove himself to the Urgent Care after he woke up in the morning noticing that he could not hear in his right ear and that he noticed some ringing and a feeling of fullness in that ear. He denied having any noticeable dizziness.

Given the following results, fill in the audiogram, V_{ea}, Y_{tm}, TPP, and ARTs for both ears.

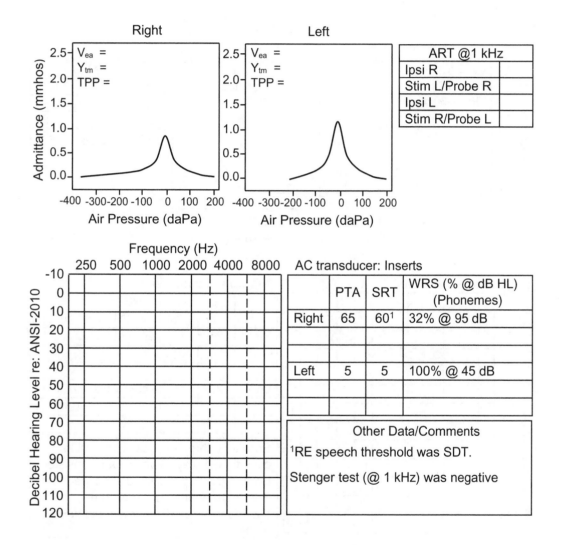

	PTA	SRT	WRS (% @ dB HL) (Phonemes)
Right	65	60[1]	32% @ 95 dB
Left	5	5	100% @ 45 dB

ART @1 kHz	
Ipsi R	
Stim L/Probe R	
Ipsi L	
Stim R/Probe L	

Other Data/Comments

[1]RE speech threshold was SDT.

Stenger test (@ 1 kHz) was negative

Results:

Impression/Diagnosis:

Recommendations:

Case Study 14

Carrie Cochlea is a 3-year-old female, whose family recently immigrated to the United States. Although specific developmental history was sketchy, her mother reported that Carrie was born very premature with a low birthweight and spent a long time in the Newborn Intensive Care Unit (NICU). Carrie's mother vaguely recalls that some type of hearing testing was done in the NICU, but she thinks it showed normal results. Mother is concerned because Carrie's speech and language development seems delayed and she acts as if she has trouble hearing/understanding.

All of the data are provided.

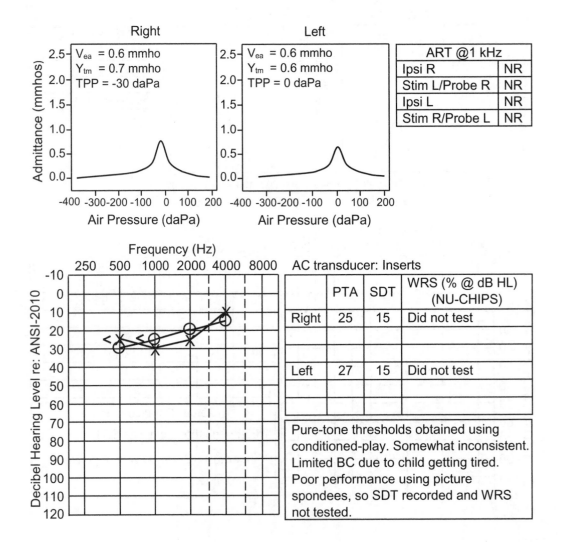

Results:

Impression/Diagnosis:

Recommendations:

Case Study 15

Ricky Resonance, a 32-year-old male, was referred by his employer for an audiologic evaluation following exposure to an explosion to the left of his factory workstation. He reported that he "couldn't hear anything out of his left ear". He also reported "unbearable ringing in his ears" since the explosion. He denied any history of exposure to other incidents of noise exposure. During the case history, the patient was observed to be straining to hear the questions and often asked for repetitions.

All of the data are provided.

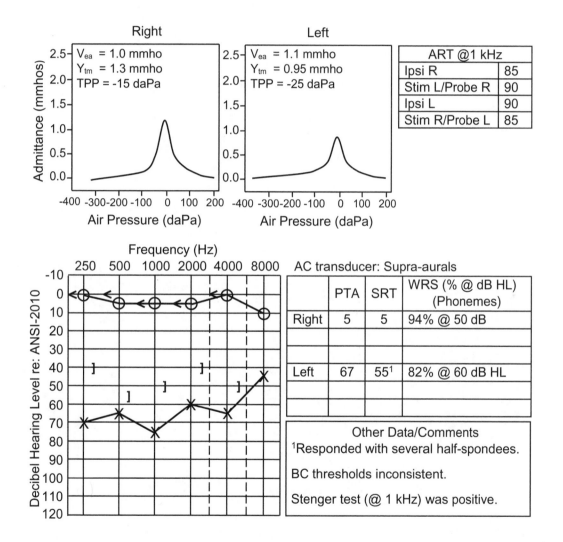

ART @1 kHz	
Ipsi R	85
Stim L/Probe R	90
Ipsi L	90
Stim R/Probe L	85

AC transducer: Supra-aurals

	PTA	SRT	WRS (% @ dB HL) (Phonemes)
Right	5	5	94% @ 50 dB
Left	67	55[1]	82% @ 60 dB HL

Other Data/Comments
[1]Responded with several half-spondees.
BC thresholds inconsistent.
Stenger test (@ 1 kHz) was positive.

Results:

Impression/Diagnosis:

Recommendations:

13 Vestibular Anatomy, Physiology, Disorders, and Assessment

13.1 What are three primary purposes of the vestibular system?

13.2 Name the five parts of the peripheral vestibular system and their associated sensory organ, as well as the type of acceleration/deceleration (angular or linear) to which each is most responsive. Give an example of how the head would move for each acceleration/deceleration.

Peripheral Vestibular Component	Sensory Organ	Acceleration/Deceleration

13.3 Label the indicated items on the following figure of the inner ear labyrinths. From *Clinical Neurophysiology of the Vestibular System* (p. 11), by R. W. Baloh and V. H. Honrubia, 2001, New York, NY: Oxford University Press. Copyright 2001 by Oxford University Press. Adapted with permission.

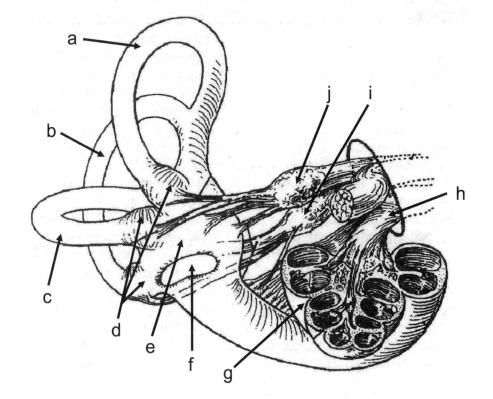

a. _____   f. _____

b. _____   g. _____

c. _____   h. _____

d. _____   i. _____

e. _____   j. _____

13.4 Label the indicated items on the following figure of the inner ear labyrinths. From *Clinical Neurophysiology of the Vestibular System* (p. 29), by R. W. Baloh and V. H. Honrubia, 2001, New York, NY: Oxford University Press. Copyright 2001 by Oxford University Press. Adapted with permission.

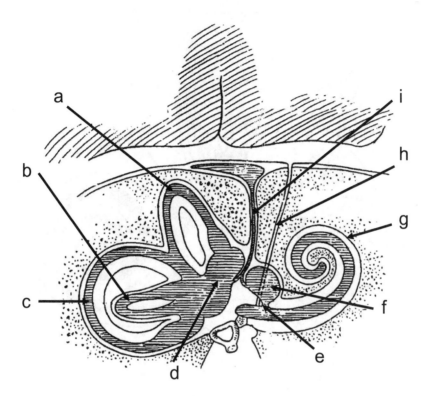

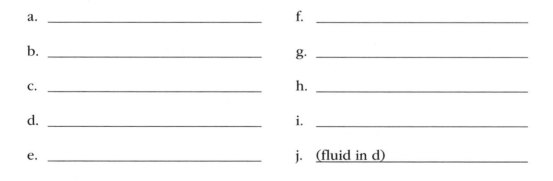

a. _____   f. _____

b. _____   g. _____

c. _____   h. _____

d. _____   i. _____

e. _____   j. (fluid in d) _____

13.5 Label the indicated items on the following figure of the inner ear labyrinths. From *A Textbook of Histology*, by W. Bloom and D. W. Fawcett, 1962, Philadelphia, PA: W.B. Saunders. Copyright 1962 by W.B. Saunders. Adapted with permission.

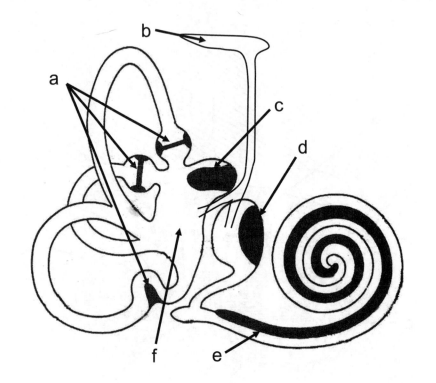

a. _____   d. _____

b. _____   e. _____

c. _____   f. (fluid) _____

13.6 Label the indicated items on the following figures of the vestibular organs. (A) From *Manual of Electronystagmography* (p. 22), by H. O. Barber and C. W. Stockwell, 1976, St. Louis, MO: Mosby, Inc. Copyright 1976 by Mosby, Inc. Adapted with permission. (B) From *Balance Disorders: A Case-Study Approach* (p. 6), by J. M. Furman and S. P. Cass, 1996, New York, NY: Oxford University Press. Copyright 1996 by Oxford University Press. Adapted with permission.

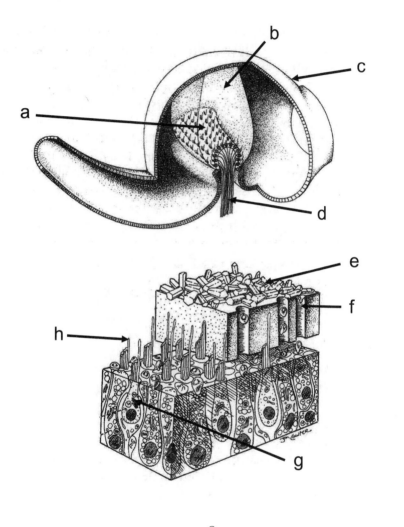

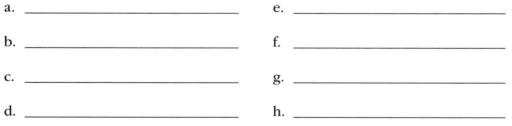

a. _____   e. _____

b. _____   f. _____

c. _____   g. _____

d. _____   h. _____

13.7 Describe the connections of the inferior and vestibular branches of the 8th cranial nerve to their corresponding parts of the peripheral vestibular organs.

13.8 In a normal vestibular system, the semicircular canals from each side of the head work together to signal rotation in the different planes. List the three functional pairings of the semicircular canals that are integrated in the vestibular nuclei.

13.9 Describe how the cristae of the semicircular canals are stimulated by head rotation (acceleration/deceleration).

13.10 Describe the neural discharge patterns of the functional pair of horizontal semicircular canals for:

    A. A normal system, for head turn to the left.

    B. A damaged vestibular organ on the right side.

13.11 Describe how the utricles from each side of the head work together with normal vestibular organs during forward and backward head accelerations.

13.12 What other sensory systems does the vestibular system interact with in order to maintain good balance function?

13.13 Describe the pathway for the vestibulo-ocular reflex (VOR), including its direct and indirect connections.

13.14 Describe the pathway for the vestibulospinal reflex (VSR), including its direct and indirect connections.

13.15 Define corneoretinal potential (CRP) and electro-oculography (EOG).

13.16 Define nystagmus. What is a saccade? Draw an example of a right beating nystagmus and a left beating nystagmus; label the slow phase and the fast phase for each of the examples.

13.17 What causes the sensation of vertigo that may occur when consuming too much alcohol?

13.18 What causes the sensation of vertigo that may occur in motion sickness, such as on a windy road, heavy seas, or in space?

13.19 For each of the following vestibular disorders (listed alphabetically), briefly describe its primary cause and pathophysiology (what is going wrong physiologically).

    A. Benign paroxysmal positional vertigo (BPPV)

B. Bilateral vestibular hypofunction

C. Endolymphatic hydrops/Meniere's disease

D. Enlarged vestibular aqueduct (EVA)

E. Labyrinthitis/vestibular neuritis

F. Perilymph fistula

G. Persistent postural-perceptual dizziness

H. Superior canal dehiscence (SCD)

I. Vestibular schwannoma

J. Vestibulotoxicity

13.20 Describe the similarities and differences of ENG and VNG nystagmus-recording methods.

13.21 Provide a brief description of the following tests (listed alphabetically) that are commonly performed in assessment of the vestibular system. Include what is expected for a normal patient.

A. Bithermal caloric

B. Gaze

C. Optokinetic

D. Paroxysmal nystagmus and the Dix-Hallpike maneuver

E. Positional

F. Saccade or occular-dysmetria

G. Spontaneous nystagmus (eyes open vs. eyes closed)

13.22 Given the following values of slow phase velocities from a bithermal, bilateral, caloric evaluation, calculate the following:

RE warm = 10 deg/s   RE cool = 13 deg/s   LE cool = 34 deg/s   LE warm = 30 deg/s

    A. Unilateral weakness

    B. Directional preponderance

13.23 Describe the basic stimuli and recording principles for the following types of vestibular evoked myogenic potentials (VEMP), as well as the main sensory organ assessed with each of the following types of VEMP recordings:

    A. Cervical VEMP (cVEMP)

        Sensory organ _____

    B. Ocular VEMP (oVEMP).

        Sensory organ _____

1 Answers for Properties of Sound and Speech Acoustics

1.1

The speed of sound in air is 343 m/s, which is much slower than the speed of light at 186,282 miles/s. The speed of sound in air is slower than it is in water because water is a denser medium with greater elasticity.

1.2

period (in seconds) = 1/frequency (in Hz)
milliseconds (ms) = seconds (s) × 1000

     A. 1/20 = 0.05 s
        0.05 × 1000 = 50 ms

     B. 1/60 = 0.0166 s
        0.0166 × 1000 = 16.6 ms

     C. 1/250 = 0.004 s
        0.004 × 1000 = 4 ms

     D. 1/500 = 0.002 s
        0.002 × 1000 = 2 ms

     E. 1/1000 = 0.001 s
        0.001 × 1000 = 1 ms

     F. 1/2000 = 0.0005 s
        0.0005 × 1000 = 0.5 ms

     G. 1/2500 = 0.0004 s
        0.0004 × 1000 = 0.4 ms

     H. 1/4000 = 0.00025 s
        0.00025 × 1000 = 0.25 ms

I. $1/8000 = 0.000125$ s
    $0.000125 \times 1000 = .125$ ms

J. $1/20{,}000 = 0.00005$ s
    $0.00005 \times 1000 = 0.05$ ms

1.3

Note: frequency (Hz) = 1/period (s)

A. $1/0.0000625 = 16{,}000$ Hz

B. $1/0.0001 = 10{,}000$ Hz

C. $1/0.000125 = 8000$ Hz

D. $1/0.00025 = 4000$ Hz

E. $1/0.0005 = 2000$ Hz

F. $1/0.001 = 1000$ Hz

G. $1/0.002 = 500$ Hz

H. $1/0.004 = 250$ Hz

I. $1/0.008 = 125$ Hz

J. $1/0.04 = 25$ Hz

1.4

Note: seconds = milliseconds/1000, frequency = 1/period

A. $0.125/1000 = 0.000125$ s
    $1/0.000125 = 8000$ Hz

B. $0.250/1000 = 0.00025$ s
    $1/0.00025 = 4000$ Hz

C. $0.400/1000 = 0.0004$ s
    $1/0.0004 = 2500$ Hz

D. $0.500/1000 = .0005$ s
    $1/0.0005 = 2000$ Hz

E. $1.000/1000 = 0.01$ s
    $1/0.01 = 1000$ Hz

F. 2.000/1000 = 0.002 s
1/0.002 = 500 Hz

G. 4.000/1000 = 0.004 s
1/0.0004 = 250 Hz

H. 25.000/1000 = 0.025 s
1/0.025 = 40 Hz

I. 500.000/1000 = 0.5 s
1/0.5 = 2 Hz

J. 1000.000/1000 = 1 s
1/1 = 1 Hz

1.5

A. 5

B. 14

C. 7

D. 10

E. 4

F. 1

G. 0

H. 0.3

I. 0.6

J. 2

K. 4

L. 6

1.6

Sound pressure and sound intensity are related to each other by the following equations:

$I = p^2$

$p = \sqrt{I}$

1.7

$I = p^2$, so as *sound intensity* increases by a factor of 4, *sound pressure* increases by $\sqrt{4}$ or 2.

1.8

dB intensity = 10 log (I_{meas}/I_{ref}), where I_{meas} = measured intensity and I_{ref} = reference intensity.

dB pressure = 20 log (P_{meas}/P_{ref}), where P_{meas} = measured pressure and P_{ref} = reference pressure.

1.9

dB IL = 10 log (I_{meas} w/m^2 / 10^{-12} w/m^2) or 10 log (I_{meas} w/cm^2 / 10^{-16} w/cm^2).

1.10

dB SPL = 20 log (P_{meas} µPa / 20 µPa) or 20 log (P_{meas} dyne/cm^2 / 2×10^{-4} dyne/cm^2).

1.11

A. dB IL = 10 log (10^{-7} w/m^2 / 10^{-12} w/m^2)
    = 10 log 10^5
    = 10 (5), where log of 10^5 = 5
    = 50 dB IL

B. dB IL = 10 log (10^{-4} w/m^2 / 10^{-12} w/m^2)
    = 10 log 10^8
    = 10 (8), where log of 10^8 = 8
    = 80 dB IL

C. dB IL = 10 log (0.000001 w/m^2 / 10^{-12} w/m^2)
    = 10 log (10^{-6} w/m^2 / 10^{-12} w/m^2)
    = 10 log 10^6
    = 10 (6), where log of 10^6 = 6
    = 60 dB IL

D. dB IL = 10 log (10^{-3} w/m^2 / 10^{-12} w/m^2)
    = 10 log 10^9
    = 10 (9), where log of 10^9 = 9
    = 90 dB IL

E. dB IL = 10 log (10^{-9} w/m^2 / 10^{-12} w/m^2)
    = 10 log 10^3
    = 10 (3), where log of 10^3 = 3
    = 30 dB IL

F. dB IL = 10 log (0.000000000001 w/m^2 / 10^{-12} w/m^2)
    = 10 log (10^{-12} w/m^2 / 10^{-12} w/m^2)
    = 10 log 1
    = 10 (0), where log of 1 = 0
    = 0 dB IL

1.12

Note: Find the dB value of tone 1 in comparison to tone 2

    A. $= 10 \log (2/1)$
       $= 10 \log 2$, where log of $2 = 0.3$
       $= 10 (.3)$
       $= 3$ dB more intense

    B. $= 10 \log (1/2)$
       $= 10 \log .5$, where log of $.5 = -0.3$
       $= 10 (-0.3)$
       $= 3$ dB less intense

    C. $= 10 \log (3/1)$
       $= 10 \log 3$, where log of $3 = 0.48$
       $= 10 (0.48)$
       $= 4.8$ dB more intense

    D. $= 10 \log (4/1)$
       $= 10 \log 4$, where log of $4 = 0.6$
       $= 10 (.6)$
       $= 6$ dB more intense

    E. $= 10 \log (100/1)$
       $= 10 \log 10^2$, where the log of $10^2 = 2$
       $= 10 (2)$
       $= 20$ dB more intense

    F. $= 10 \log (1,000,000/1)$
       $= 10 \log 10^6$, where log of $10^6 = 6$
       $= 10 (6)$
       $= 60$ dB more intense

1.13

    A. dB SPL $= 20 \log (20,000 \, \mu Pa/20 \, \mu Pa)$
       $= 20 \log 10^3$, where log of $10^3 = 3$
       $= 20 (3)$
       $= 60$ dB SPL

    B. dB SPL $= 20 \log (200 \, \mu Pa/20 \, \mu Pa)$
       $= 20 \log 10$, where log of $10 = 1$
       $= 20 (1)$
       $= 20$ dB SPL

    C. dB SPL $= 20 \log (10^3 \, \mu Pa/20 \, \mu Pa)$
       $= 20 \log (1000 \, \mu Pa/20 \, \mu Pa)$
       $= 20 \log 50$, where log of $50 = 1.70$
       $= 20 (1.70)$
       $= 34$ dB SPL

D. dB SPL = 20 log (400,000 μPa/20 μPa)
   = 20 log 20,000
   = 20 log 2×10^4, where log of 2 = 0.3 and log of 10^4 = 4
   = 20 (0.3 + 4)
   = 86 dB SPL

E. dB SPL = 20 log (8,000 μPa/20 μPa)
   = 20 log 400
   = 20 log 4×10^2, where log of 4 = 0.6 and log of 10^2 = 2
   = 20 (0.6 + 2)
   = 52 dB SPL

F. dB SPL = 20 log (200,000,000 μPa/20 μPa)
   = 20 log 10^7, where log of 10^7 = 7
   = 20 (7)
   = 140 dB SPL

1.14

Note: Find the dB value of tone 1 in comparison to tone 2

A. = 20 log (2/1)
   = 20 log 2, where log of 2 = 0.3
   = 20 (0.3)
   = 6 dB greater pressure

B. = 20 log (3/1)
   = 20 log 3, where log of 3 = 0.48
   = 20 (0.48)
   = 9.6 dB greater pressure

C. = 20 log (1/3)
   = 20 log .33, where log of .33 = −0.48
   = 20 (−0.48)
   = 9.6 dB less pressure

D. = 20 log (10^2), where log of 10^2 = 2
   = 20 (2)
   = 40 dB greater pressure

E. = 20 log (10^3), where log of 10^3 = 3
   = 20 (3)
   = 60 dB greater pressure

F. = 20 log (10,000/1)
   = 20 log 10^4, where log of 10^4 = 4
   = 20 (4)
   = 80 dB greater pressure

1.15

A. = 20 log (4.5×10^3 µPa/2.5×10^2 µPa) [Note: 20 log formula used because values are in units of pressure (µPa)]

   = 20 log 1.8×10^1 µPa, where log 1.8 = .255 and log 10^1 = 1

   = 20 (1.255)

   = 25.1 dB SPL

B. = 10 log (680/1) [Note: 10 log formula used because values are in units of intensity (watt/m²)]

   = 10 log 6.80×10^2 watt/m², where log 6.8 = .83 and log 10^2 = 2

   = 10 (2.83)

   = 28.3 dB IL

C. = 20 log (10^0 dyne/cm²/10^{-2} dynes/cm²) [Note: 20 log formula used because values are in units of pressure (dyne/cm²)]

   = 20 log 10^2 dyne/cm², where log 10^2 = 2

   = 20 (2)

   = 40 dB SPL

D. = 10 log (4×10^{-2} watt/m²/2×10^{-3} watt/m²) [Note: 10 log formula used because values are in units of intensity (watt/m²]

   = 10 log 2×10^1 watt/m², where log 2 = 0.3 and log 10^1 = 1

   = 10 (1.3)

   = 13 dB IL

1.16

A. = 68 dB SPL + 68 dB SPL + 68 dB SPL [Note: 10 log formula is used because sounds add as intensities, not pressures; recall that 68 dB SPL = 68 dB IL]

   = 68 + 10 log 3/1 (tripling dB SPL), where log 3 = 0.48

   = 68 + 10 (.48)

   = 72.8 dB SPL

B. = 68 dB SPL + 68 dB SPL

   = 68 + 10 log 2/1 (doubling SPL), where log 2 = 0.3

   = 68 + 10 (.3)

   = 71 dB SPL (whenever dB SPL is doubled, there is an increase of 3 dB)

1.17

A. The given dB SPL values are not the same. Therefore, first calculate the intensity level (I_{meas}) in watt/m² that corresponds to each dB value. Then add the intensities together. Keep in mind that sounds combine as intensities, not pressures, unless the phases of the sounds are known (and they generally are not known).

70 dB SPL = 10 log I_{meas} / 10^{-12} watt/m^2
7 dB SPL = log I_{meas} / 10^{-12} watt/m^2 (dividing both sides by 10)
I_{meas} = 10^7 × 10^{-12} watt/m^2
I_{meas} = 10^{-5} watt/m^2
75 dB SPL = 10 log I_{meas} / 10^{-12} watt/m^2
7.5 dB SPL = log I_{meas} / 10^{-12} watt/m^2 (dividing both sides by 10)
I_{meas} = $10^{7.5}$ × 10^{-12} watt/m^2, where $10^{7.5}$ = 3.16 × 10^7
I_{meas} = 3.16 × 10^7 × 10^{-12} watt/m^2
I_{meas} = 3.16 × 10^{-5} watt/m^2

Combining the two intensities from above:

1 × 10^{-5} watt/m^2 + 3.16 × 10^{-5} watt/m^2 = 4.16 × 10^{-5} watt/m^2

Now calculate dB SPL:

= 10 log 4.16 × 10^{-5} / 10^{-12}
= 10 log 4.16 × 10^7, where log 4.16 = 0.62 and log 10^7 = 7
= 10 (7.62)
= 76.2 dB SPL (or dB IL)

B. 90 dB SPL = 10 log I_{meas} / 10^{-12} watt/m^2
9 dB SPL = log I_{meas} / 10^{-12} watt/m^2 (dividing both sides by 10)
I_{meas} = 10^9 × 10^{-12} watt/m^2
I_{meas} = 10^{-3} watt/m^2

Now add all three intensities:

1 × 10^{-3} (for 90 dB) + 0.01 × 10^{-3} (for 70 dB) + 0.0316 × 10^{-3} (for 75 dB) [converting to common exponent of 10^{-3}]
= 1.0416 × 10^{-3}

Now calculate dB SPL:

= 10 log 1.0416 × 10^{-3} / 10^{-12}
= 10 log 1.0416 × 10^9, where log 1.0416 = 0.018 and log 10^9 = 9
= 10 (9.018)
= 90.18 dB SPL (or dB IL)

1.18

The amplitude of a pure tone can be described by measuring the peak amplitude (A_p), the peak-to-peak amplitude (A_{p-p}), or the root-mean-square amplitude (A_{rms}). The peak amplitude is derived by measuring the amplitude of the waveform from the baseline to either the positive or negative peak. The peak-to-peak amplitude is derived by measuring the absolute amplitude change that occurs between the positive peak and the negative peak of the waveform, i.e., 2 × A_p. To obtain A_{rms}, square each of the instantaneous amplitudes (over one cycle) to eliminate any negative values, average the squared values, and then take the square root of the average. A_{rms} may also be calculated by multiplying A_p × 0.707.

1.19

Note: root-mean-square (rms) = peak sound pressure (or voltage) × .707

    A. 10^2 dynes/cm^2 × .707 = 70.7 dynes/cm^2

    B. 12 volts × .707 = 8.484 volts

    C. 10.414 Pa × .707 = 7.363 Pa

    D. 6.5 N/m^2 × .707 = 4.596 N/m^2

1.20

    A. P-P = 2P (P = peak sound pressure)
        P-P = 2(400 µPa) = 800 µPa

    B. rms = 400 µPa × .707 = 282.8 µPa

    C. dB SPL = 20 log P_{meas}/P_{ref} , where P_{meas} = measured pressure and P_{ref} = reference pressure
        = 20 log (4 × 10^2 µPa/2 × 10^1 µPa)
        = 20 log 2 × 10^1 µPa, where log 2 = 0.3 and log 10^1 = 1
        = 20 (1.3)
        = 26 dB SPL

1.21

Note: peak sound pressure = rms/.707

    A. 7.07 dyne/cm^2/.707 = 10 dyne/cm^2

    B. P-P = 10 dyne/cm^2 × 2 = 20 dynes/cm^2

    C. dB SPL = 20 log P_{meas}/P_{ref}, where P_{meas} = measured pressure and P_{ref} = reference pressure
        = 20 log (10 dyne/cm^2/2 × 10^{-4} dynes/cm^2)
        = 20 log 5 × 10^4 dyne/cm^2, where log 5 = 0.7 and log 10^4 = 4
        = 20 (4.7)
        = 94 dB SPL

1.22

The inverse square law states that the intensity (I in watt/m^2) of a sound decreases by the square of the change in distance from the source. The inverse square law is expressed mathematically for intensity with the equation I = 1/D^2 or P = 1/D, where D = d_1/d_2. The inverse square law for pressure takes into account that p = $\sqrt{I}$.

1.23

65 – [20 log (200/25)]
= 65 – 20 log 8, where log of 8 = .9
= 65 – 20 (.9)
= 65 – 18
= 47 dB SPL

1.24

100 – [20 log (4000/250)]
= 100 – 20 log (16)
= 100 – 20 log 1.6×10^1, where log of 1.6 = .20 and log of 10^1 = 1
= 100 – 20 (1 + .20)
= 100 – 24
= 76 dB SPL

1.25

A. 20 cycles = 1 s
1/20 = 0.05 s (period)
1/0.05 = 20 Hz

B. 5 cycles = 10 ms
1 cycle = 2 ms = 0.002 s (period)
1/0.002 = 500 Hz

C. 1 cycle = 0.0005 s (period)
1/0.0005 = 2000 Hz

D. 1 cycle = 4 ms
4/1000 = 0.004 s (period)
1/0.004 = 250 Hz

1.26

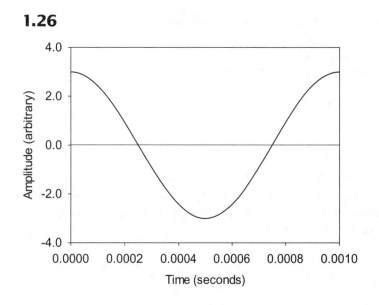

1.27

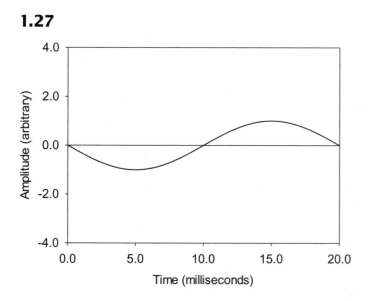

1.28

If two pure tones of the same frequency and intensity, and are 180° out of phase with each other, are played together at the same time, there would be no sound generated because each condensation point is cancelled out by an equal rarefaction point and the net displacement is zero. This would look like a flat line on the time-domain waveform.

1.29

Note: wavelength = speed of sound/frequency.

     A. 343/20 = 17.15 m

     B. 343/60 = 5.72 m

     C. 343/440 = 0.78 m

     D. 343/1000 = 0.343 m

     E. 343/8000 = 0.043 m

     F. 343/12,500 = 0.027 m

1.30

Note: frequency = speed of sound/wavelength

     A. 343/0.01715 = 20,000 Hz

     B. 343/0.0214375 = 16,000 Hz

     C. 343/0.08575 = 4000 Hz

D. 343/0.11433 = 3000 Hz

E. 343/1.372 = 250 Hz

F. 343/3.4300 = 100 Hz

1.31

A. 270°

B. 90°

C. 0° or 360°

D. 270°

E. 90°

F. .001 s or 1 ms

G. frequency = 1/period
   1/.001 s = 1000 Hz

H. wavelength = speed of sound/frequency, where speed of sound = 343 m/s
   343/1000 = .343 m

1.32

The frequency range of human hearing is 20–20,000 Hz. An illustration of the threshold of audibility across this range would be similar to the following:

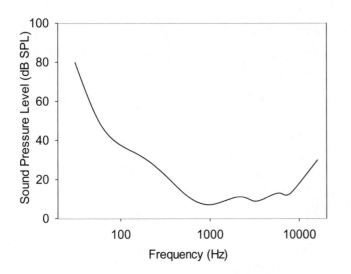

1.33

(Answers may vary)

All vowels are voiced; they all are produced with vocal fold vibration, whereas consonants can be produced with or without vocal fold vibrations, i.e., voiced or voiceless. Vowels tend to have lower frequency spectra, whereas many consonants have higher frequency spectra, especially fricatives. Vowels have greater intensity than consonants in connected speech. That is, vowels generally are perceived as being louder, and consonants generally are perceived as being softer. Consonants contribute more to word intelligibility (speech understanding) than vowels.

1.34

A. d

B. c

C. b

D. e

E. a

1.35

Note: F_0 (Hz) = c/4L, where c = speed of sound and L = length of tube (in meters).

A. 7 cm tube = 0.07 m
  $F_0 = 343/4\ (0.07)$
  $F_0 = 343/0.28$
  $F_0 = 1225$ Hz

B. 10 cm tube = 0.1 m
  $F_0 = 343/4\ (0.1)$
  $F_0 = 343/0.4$
  $F_0 = 857.5$ Hz

C. 14 cm tube = 0.14 m
  $F_0 = 343/4\ (0.14)$
  $F_0 = 343/0.56$
  $F_0 = 612.5$ Hz

D. 17 cm tube = 0.17 m
  $F_0 = 343/4\ (0.17)$
  $F_0 = 343/0.68$
  $F_0 = 504.4$ Hz

1.36

Note: F_0 (Hz) = c/2L, where c = speed of sound and L = length of tube.

A. 7 cm tube = 0.07 m
F_0 = 343/2 (0.07)
F_0 = 343/0.14
F_0 = 2450 Hz

B. 10 cm tube = 0.1 m
F_0 = 343/2 (0.1)
F_0 = 343/0.2
F_0 = 1715 Hz

C. 14 cm tube = 0.14 m
F_0 = 343/2 (0.14)
F_0 = 343/0.28
F_0 = 1225 Hz

D. 17 cm tube = 0.17 m
F_0 = 343/2 (0.17)
F_0 = 343/0.34
F_0 = 1008.8 Hz

1.37

Doubling the length of a tube would cause its resonant frequency (F_0) to be halved. This is true of both quarter-wave and half-wave resonators.

1.38

Examples of filter types:

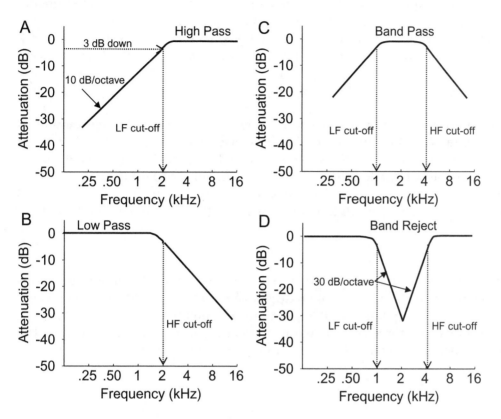

1.39

Temporal integration describes how the threshold of audibility is related to the duration of the sound. For sounds shorter than 200 ms in duration, the level must be increased in order for the sound to be audible. There is about a 10 dB increase in level needed for a tenfold decrease in duration, e.g., shortening a sound from 200 ms to 20 ms results in an increase of 10 dB.

1.40

In order to localize a sound source, humans rely on different arrival times of the sound (or interaural time differences) and/or the different intensities of sounds at the two ears (or interaural intensity differences). When a person has a unilateral hearing loss, their ability to localize is compromised, as they are unable to use these interaural timing and intensity difference cues, which rely on binaural hearing.

1.41

Equal loudness contours (also known as *phon lines*) show the amount of dB SPL across the frequencies that are perceived as equal in loudness. The phon curves are based on reference to the loudness of a 1000 Hz tone at a given dB SPL, e.g., 40 phons = loudness of 1000 Hz at 40 dB SPL; 30 phons = loudness of 1000 Hz at 30 dB SPL, etc. All points on a given equal loudness contour (phon level) are equal in loudness, but differ in dB SPL. As the human ear is not as sensitive across the frequency range (see threshold of audibility curve), it takes greater dB SPL at lower and higher frequencies to be perceived as equally loud as frequencies in the mid-range of hearing. As the level of the sounds (and phons) increases, there is less variability in perceived loudness, i.e., the phon curves flatten out considerably at the highest levels.

1.42

A sone is a unit of loudness measurement. The sone scale is a linear scale; it relates loudness to the continuum of intensity. One sone is the loudness associated with a 1000 Hz tone at 40 dB SPL. Therefore, 1 sone = 40 phons. Two sones are equal to twice the loudness of 1 sone, and 0.5 sone is equal to one-half the loudness of 1 sone. Generally, a 10 dB increase in sound pressure (10 phons) results in a doubling of loudness on the sone scale. For example, 40 dB SPL = 1 sone, 50 dB SPL = 2 sones, 60 dB SPL = 4 sones, 70 dB SPL = 8 sones, and so on.

1.43

The mel scale represents the relationship between frequency and pitch. One thousand mels is the pitch associated with 1000 Hz at a level of 40 dB above threshold. A 2000 mel tone would be judged as twice the perceived pitch of a 1000 mel tone. A doubling of pitch from 1000 mels to 2000 mels corresponds to a threefold change in frequency (from 1000 to 3000 Hz). The entire range of human hearing is compressed into a range of approximately 3500 mels.

2 Answers for Anatomy of the Auditory System

2.1

    A. sagittal

    B. coronal

    C. transverse

2.2

    1. c, e

    2. a, f

    3. b, d

2.3

(any order)

    1. tympanic

    2. mastoid

    3. petrous

    4. squamous

    5. styloid process

    6. zygomatic process

2.4

The inner ear is found in the petrous portion of the temporal bone (one on each side).

2.5

    1. outer ear

      a. auricle

      b. external auditory canal

2. middle ear
    a. tympanic membrane
    b. ossicular chain (malleus, incus, stapes)
    c. eustachian tube

3. inner ear
    a. cochlea
    b. semicircular canals (anterior/superior, posterior, horizontal/lateral)
    c. otoliths (saccule and utricle)

4. cranial (peripheral) nerves
    a. cochlear branch of 8th cranial nerve
    b. vestibular branches (superior and inferior) of 8th cranial nerve
    c. stapedial branch of 7th cranial nerve (facial nerve)

5. central auditory nervous system
    a. brainstem nuclei (cochlear nuclei, superior olivary complexes, lateral lemnisci, inferior colliculi, medial geniculate bodies)
    b. cortices (Heschl's gyrus on the superior surfaces of each temporal lobe)

2.6

The cochlea is located more anterior and medial relative to the semicircular canals. The top of the coiled cochlea "points" horizontally, in an anterior-lateral direction.

2.7

The pars tensa is the portion of the tympanic membrane that consists of three layers, the skin that lines the surface of the external ear/tympanic membrane, the mucous lining of the middle ear, and the fibrous tissue layers (concentric and radial) located between the other two layers. The majority of the tympanic membrane has the fibrous tissue layers, and is called the pars tensa. A smaller area in the superior-anterior portion of the tympanic membrane is devoid of the fibrous tissue layers and is called the pars flaccida (a.k.a. Shrapnell's membrane).

2.8

Muscle	Nerve
1. Stapedius muscle	Innervated by the stapedial branch of 7th cranial nerve (facial nerve)
2. Tensor tympani muscle	Innervated by the 5th cranial nerve (trigeminal nerve)

2.9

Fluid	Composition
1. Perilymph	Perilymph has a relatively high concentration of sodium ions (Na+) and a low concentration of potassium ions (K+).
2. Endolymph	Endolymph has a relatively high concentration of potassium ions (K+) and a low concentration of sodium ions (Na+).

2.10

Scala	Fluid
1. Scala tympani	Perilymph
2. Scala media	Endolymph above reticular lamina Perilymph in spaces below reticular lamina
3. Scala vestibuli	Perilymph

2.11
(Answers may vary)

- Stereocilia of the OHCs are arranged in a "W" shape; stereocilia of the IHCs are arranged in a "crescent" shape.
- There are three rows of OHCs and one row of IHCs.
- There are ~12,000 OHCs and ~3,500 IHCs.
- OHCs are supported by Hensen and Claudius cells and sit on top of Deiter cells; IHCs are supported by inner support/border cells.
- OHCs are surrounded by spaces of Nuel filled with perilymph; IHCs are not surrounded by fluid.
- The tops of the OHC stereocilia are in contact with the underside of the tectorial membrane; IHC stereocilia are not in contact (when at rest) with the tectorial membrane.
- The internal cell cytoplasm of the two types of hair cells are different.
- IHCs are innervated by 95% of afferent neurons; OHCs are innervated by 5% of afferents. Efferent neurons connect directly to OHCs, whereas the efferent neurons to the IHCs connect to the afferent dendrites of the IHCs rather than to the cell bodies.

2.12

The reticular lamina is a tightly arranged mosaic formed by the tops of supporting and sensory hair cells along the organ of Corti, just below the tectorial membrane. The stereocilia of the hair cells protrude above the reticular lamina. The phalangeal processes of the Deiter cells arise from the base of the cell upward to fill in the areas above the spaces of Nuel to complete the mosaic of cells that form the reticular lamina. The reticular lamina serves as a boundary within the scala media that separates endolymph (above the reticular lamina) from perilymph (below the reticular lamina).

2.13

(one on each side)

1. cochlear nucleus
2. superior olivary complex
3. lateral lemniscus
4. inferior colliculus
5. medial geniculate

2.14

The primary auditory reception areas are located on the upper surface of the temporal lobe on each side of the brain. The area on each temporal lobe is called Heschl's gyrus.

2.15

(Answers for labels: coronal-cross section.)

a. auricle
b. external auditory canal
c. tympanic membrane
d. stapes
e. eustachian tube
f. round window
g. oval window

h. cochlea
i. 8th cranial nerve (cochlear and vestibular branches)
j. 7th cranial nerve (facial nerve)
k. semicircular canals
l. incus
m. malleus

2.16

(Answers for labels: auricle landmarks.)

a. helix
b. triangular fossa
c. antihelix
d. concha

e. antitragus
f. earlobe
g. tragus
h. external auditory meatus (or canal)

2.17
(Answers for labels: ossicular chain.)

a. head of the malleus

b. lateral process of the malleus

c. chorda tympani nerve (branch of facial nerve)

d. tensor tympani muscle attachment/ ligament

e. manubrium of the malleus

f. crus (crura) of the stapes

g. footplate of the stapes

h. stapedius muscle attachment/ ligament

i. long process of the incus

j. short process of the incus

k. body of incus

2.18
(Answers for labels: photos of tympanic membranes.)

a. right ear

b. manubrium (of malleus)

c. umbo

d. ear canal wall

e. pars tensa

f. cone of light (light reflex)

g. pars flaccida (a.k.a. Shrapnell's membrane)

h. lateral process (of malleus)

2.19
(Answers for labels: inner ear with mid modiolar cross-section.)

a. basal region of cochlea

b. apex of cochlea

c. oval window

d. semicircular canals

e. vestibule (location of saccule and utricle)

f. vestibular branches of the 8th cranial nerve

g. 7th cranial nerve (facial nerve)

h. cochlear branch of 8th cranial nerve

2.20
(Answers for labels: memb labyrinths.)

a. endolymphatic sac

b. cochlear aqueduct

c. scala vestibuli

d. scala media

e. scala tympani

f. saccule

g. ductus reuniens

h. utricle

2.21
(Answers for labels: cross-section of cochlea.)

a. Reissner's membrane

b. stria vascularis

c. scala media

d. tectorial membrane

e. stereocilia (of OHCs)

f. basilar membrane

g. scala tympani

h. spiral ganglia

i. scala vestibuli

j. perilymph

k. perilymph

l. endolymph above the reticular lamina and perilymph below reticular lamina

2.22
(Answers for labels: organ of Corti.)

a. outer hair cells

b. spaces of Nuell

c. Hensen cells

d. Claudius cells

e. basilar membrane

f. Deiter cells

g. pillars of Corti

h. tunnel of Corti

i. habenula perforata

j. 8th nerve fibers

k. osseous spiral lamina

l. inner support cells

m. inner hair cell

n. tectorial membrane

3 Answers for Functions of the Auditory System

3.1

A. Impedance is opposition to the flow of energy. An impedance mismatch occurs when there is a reduction in energy transfer between two mediums that have differing physical properties, e.g., air and water. For example, water has a greater impedance than air. For the most efficient transfer of energy across two systems, or two parts of the same system, the impedance should be fairly equal. When energy is transferred from a system with low impedance to a system with higher impedance, the resulting mismatch will reduce the transfer of energy.

B. The main source of the impedance mismatch in the ear occurs because of the need to transduce sound energy from an acoustic medium (air) into a fluid medium within the inner ear. For example, if we tried to talk directly into the oval window, most of the acoustic energy would not transfer into the fluid-filled environment. This would be analogous to being underwater in a swimming pool and trying to hear someone talking from the edge of the pool.

C. There would be an approximate 99.9% loss of energy due to the impedance mismatch in the ear, i.e., only about 0.1% of the acoustic energy would be transferred into the fluid-filled inner ear. Expressing this as a ratio of the reflected (lost) energy to the transmitted (transduced) energy would be 99.9/0.1, or about 1000/1. To convert this ratio into a decibel:

dB = 10 log (1000/1)
dB = 10 (3); where log of 1000 = 3.
dB = 30

One of the roles of the outer and middle ears is to amplify the incoming vibrations in order to make up for the potential 30 dB loss that would occur due to the impedance mismatch.

3.2

A. The primary mechanism by which the outer ear amplifies sound is resonance, whereby the size and shape of the cavity results in its being more responsive to specific frequencies. The frequency that is enhanced the most is called the resonant frequency. The ear canal and auricle are irregular in shape, which can contribute to the different resonances that affect how the outer ear enhances specific frequencies. If one assumes the average size of an adult ear canal to be 0.025 m, the resonant frequency would be calculated as follows (based on a tube which is closed at one end):

f_{res} = c/4L, where c = speed of sound and L = length of tube
f_{res} = 343/(4 * 0.025)
f_{res} = 3430 Hz

B. The middle ear amplifies sound via the area ratio advantage, curved membrane advantage, and the lever advantage.

The area ratio advantage provides the largest amount of amplification. The area ratio advantage occurs due to the size difference between the tympanic membrane (e.g., 55 mm^2) and the oval window (e.g., 3.2 mm^2): Because pressure is equal to force per area (p = F/A), for a given amount of force there will be an increase in pressure on the smaller area (oval window). Using the given example, the area ratio difference would amplify the sound by about 25 dB at the oval window as calculated by:

dB = 20 log (55/3.2)
dB = 20 log (17)
dB = 25

The curved membrane advantage is related to the cone-like shape of the tympanic membrane, which tends to focus its movement in such a way that it moves the malleus with more force than if the tympanic membrane were a flat disk. The increase in pressure is about twofold, which would amplify the sound by about 6 dB at the oval window as calculated by:

dB = 20 log (2/1)
dB = 20 (.3)
dB = 6

The lever advantage occurs because of the longer length of the manubrium of the malleus relative to the length of the long process of the incus. This acts as a fulcrum where the force applied to the long arm results in more pressure being exerted at the shorter arm. The increase in pressure is about 1.3, which would amplify the sound by about 2.2 dB at the oval window as calculated by:

dB = 20 log (1.3/1)
dB = 20 (.11)
dB = 2.2

Combining all three of the middle ear advantages would result in about a 34 dB increase in pressure at the oval window [dB = 20 log (17 * 2.2 * 1.3)]. This combined effect of the middle ear amplifier effectively overcomes the predicted 30 dB loss due to the air-to-fluid impedance mismatch.

3.3

Transfer functions, in general, refer to how energy is affected by comparing measurements made at two locations in a system. The transfer function of the ear are measurements that have been made, mostly with animals, to document the changes in sound pressure and frequency that occur between the environment and end of the ear canal (outer ear transfer function), or from the tympanic membrane to the oval window (middle ear transfer function). The middle ear transfer function shows that sound is amplified about 20 dB for frequencies below about 3000 Hz. It quantifies the estimated effects of the middle ear mechanical advantages to overcome the air to fluid impedance mismatch.

3.4

A. The equalization of air pressure between the middle ear space and the external environment (air pressure in the outer ear canal) is maintained through the proper function of the eustachian tube. The eustachian tube connects the middle ear space with the nasopharynx, primarily through a cartilaginous structure that is normally closed at the nasopharynx. The eustachian tube is opened when the tensor veli palatini muscle contracts during chewing, swallowing, and/or yawning, allowing the middle ear air pressure to equalize with the environmental/atmospheric air pressure.

B. The eustachian tube of an adult is longer than that of a young child. In addition, the adult eustachian tube is oriented with about a 45° angle from the middle ear to the nasopharynx as compared with a shallower angle in the young child. These developmental differences in the eustachian tube make it more difficult for young children to maintain the normal air-filled environment in the middle ear, which in turn makes children more susceptible to middle ear infections/otitis media than adults.

3.5

The middle ear acoustic reflex in humans involves a bilateral involuntary contraction of the stapedius muscle attached to the stapes of each ear in response to relatively high levels of sound (>70 dB SPL). The reflex pathway is bilateral, e.g., stimulation from one ear results in contraction of the stapedius muscle in both ears (ipsilateral and contralateral pathway). The reflex pathway for each ear involves sensory (sound) input through the 8th cranial nerve to the ipsilateral cochlear nucleus, then to areas around the superior olivary complex on each side of the brainstem, then to the facial nucleus on each side of the brainstem, and finally to the stapedial branch of the 7th cranial nerve on each side that innervates the stapedius muscle and results in its contraction.

Contraction of the stapedius reduces the vibration of the ossicular chain by as much as 10–20 dB SPL (primarily in the lower frequencies). The primary function of the acoustic reflex is thought to reduce distortion/overload of the ossicular chain and pressure to the inner ear during relatively intense vocalizations, coughs, sneezes, or when listening to speech at high intensities. The theory that the acoustic reflex is a protective mechanism from loud impulsive noises may not be accurate, since many of these types of sounds are man-made, there is a time delay (20–100 ms) for the stapedius muscle to contract, the reflex affects only the lower frequencies, and the stapedius muscle does not stay contracted during long periods of stimulation.

3.6

The tonotopic arrangement of the cochlea refers to the fact that there is a specific relation between location along the basilar membrane and the frequency which results in its maximum displacement. The basilar membrane is narrower and stiffer at the base and becomes systematically wider and less stiff toward the apex. These physical characteristics determine how different parts of the basilar membrane respond to different frequencies. Higher frequencies are processed at the base of the cochlea and lower frequencies toward the apex of the cochlea.

3.7

The mechanisms that produce the traveling wave are determined by the width and stiffness gradients along the basilar membrane as they react to the vibrations in the fluid. Although all locations along the basilar membrane receive the same vibrational input at the same time, it is the variations in the physical characteristics of the basilar membrane that cause different areas of the basilar membrane to move up and down at different times (phases), thus creating what appears as a traveling wave. The narrower/stiffer basal end of the basilar membrane begins to move up and down sooner due to less mass/less inertia to overcome than the more apical parts of the basilar membrane that respond slightly later due to greater mass/greater inertia to overcome. Progressing apically, it takes a little longer (phase lag) for each location along the basilar membrane to overcome the inertia in order to start moving up and down to the frequency of the incoming signal. In other words, as one part of the basilar membrane is moving up and down at the incoming frequency, the adjacent area will be moving up and down at the same incoming frequency, but at a slightly different time (phase). The amplitude (height of the traveling wave) will reach a peak at the place along the basilar membrane that best matches the incoming frequency based on the tonotopic arrangement of the basilar membrane (high frequencies at the base, low frequencies at the apex).

It doesn't matter how the vibrations enter the cochlea, the reaction of the basilar membrane always appears as a traveling wave that begins at the base of the cochlea and progresses toward the apex of the cochlea membrane due to the phase lag related to the stiffness/width gradient. In fact, Bekesy demonstrated this base-to-apex basilar membrane reaction even when he delivered vibrations into the apex of the cochlea (rather than at the oval window).

3.8

The following figure shows traveling wave envelopes (arbitrary amplitude) for 500, 2000, and 8000 Hz.

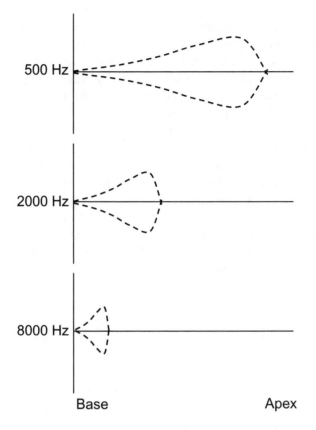

3.9

The endocochlear potential (EP) refers to the high concentration of K+ ions in the endolymph of the scala media above the reticular lamina. The EP is maintained by the stria vascularis. The EP has a +80 mV resting electrical potential. The intracellular potential refers to the electrical state within the hair cells, which is about −60 mV for IHCs and −40 mV for OHCs in a non-stimulated condition (i.e., at rest). These two electrical potentials provide a combined electrical charge (like the voltage in a battery) of 140 mV for the IHCs and 120 mV for the OHCs.

3.10

The role of the inner hair cells (IHCs) is to transduce the hydromechanical energy (up and down movement) of the traveling wave into neural impulses within the afferent cochlear branch of the 8th cranial nerve, of which 95% come from the IHCs. In response to the vibrations in the cochlear fluids, when there is sufficient displacement of the basilar membrane from the traveling wave, the IHC stereocilia come into contact with the tectorial membrane, which causes back and forth shearing of the IHC stereocilia. The back and forth shearing of the IHC stereocilia with the tectorial membrane modulates the resistance at the tops of the hair cells, thereby opening up the K+ ion channels at the tips of the stereocilia to allow an influx of K+ ions into the cell (driven by the endocochlear potential in the endolymph). When the stereocilia bend laterally toward the tallest row of stereocilia (away from the modiolus), the tip-links open up the K+ ion channels within the stereocilia, allowing for an influx of K+ ions to the hair cell (excitatory phase). When the stereocilia bend medially toward the shortest row of stereocilia (toward the modiolus), the tip-links close the K+ ion channels within the stereocilia, reducing the K+ flow to the hair cell (inhibitory phase). When the intracellular potential of the IHC is in its excitatory phase (decreased intracellular potential), there is an increase in the release of neurotransmitter substance into the synaptic cleft at the base of the IHC, which then causes the nerves to depolarize/fire and send the neural impulses along the 8th nerve fibers to the cochlear nucleus within the brainstem.

3.11

The role of the OHCs is to amplify the displacement of the basilar membrane at low to moderate intensities in order to ensure that the stereocilia of the IHCs are able to make contact (shear) with the tectorial membrane. There are about three times as many OHCs as IHCs; however, very few of the OHCs have afferent neural connections to the brainstem. Recall also that the tallest stereocilia of the OHCs are embedded in the underside of the tectorial membrane. The amplified displacement of the basilar membrane occurs through the elongation and contraction of the OHCs, which is also referred to as the motility of the OHCs. The motility of the OHCs resonates with the frequency of the basilar membrane's traveling wave displacements, thus adding energy to the system (greater displacement). The OHCs act as an electromechanical amplifier around the area of maximum displacement, and is required for the ear's good sensitivity (lower thresholds) and frequency selectivity (better tuning).

3.12

The passive process within the cochlea refers primarily to the traveling wave activity along the basilar membrane due to its physical properties (i.e., stiffness/width gradient). The passive process can be shown to occur even in cadavers. The active process within the cochlea refers to the motility (elongation/contraction) of the OHCs, which amplifies the passive traveling wave motion of the basilar membrane to allow the stereocilia of the IHCs to make contact with the tectorial membrane at low to moderate stimulus intensities, thus being responsible for the ears' good hearing sensitivity and frequency selectivity. The active process requires a physiologically intact and functioning inner ear. At moderately high to high levels of stimulation, the passive process is sufficient to allow the IHCs' stereocilia to shear with the tectorial membrane without the motility of the OHCs. The following figure illustrates basilar membrane tuning curves with and without normal functioning OHCs. With the OHCs' active process, the ear has better sensitivity and sharper frequency selectivity, whereas without the OHCs' active process, there is poorer sensitivity and broader frequency selectivity.

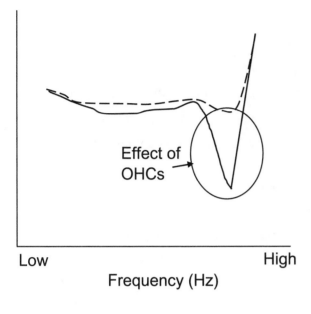

Effect of OHCs

Low   High

Frequency (Hz)

3.13

Sound begins as acoustic energy (back and forth vibrations of air molecules), which is enhanced in the auricle, concha, and ear canal through the mechanism of resonance. The acoustic energy is transduced into a mechanical form of energy at the tympanic membrane (in and out movements). The sound pressure level at the oval window is enhanced (to overcome the air-to-fluid impedance mismatch) by the area ratio of the tympanic membrane to the oval window, the curved membrane advantage of the tympanic membrane, and the lever advantage of the ossicles. Mechanical energy of the ossicles is transduced into hydromechanical energy within the fluid-filled cochlea by the movement of the stapes footplate in the oval window membrane (in and out movements of the oval window with reciprocal movements of the round window membrane). The pressure variations within the fluid-filled cochlea are received instantaneously along the basilar membrane, which produces a characteristic traveling wave that moves from the base to the area of maximum displacement depending on the incoming frequency, referred to as the passive process in the cochlea. The traveling wave reaches its peak displacement at the place that is best tuned to the incoming frequency (tonotopic arrangement). If the displacement of the traveling wave is sufficient, the IHCs' stereocilia are sheared (toward modiolus and away from the modiolus) due to contact with the tectorial membrane. The mechanical displacement of the basilar membrane around the place tuned to the incoming frequency is enhanced by the motility (elongations and contractions) of the OHCs, which, in turn, allows the IHCs' stereocilia to shear with the tectorial membrane at low to moderate intensities, referred to as the active process in the cochlea. Shearing of the IHC stereocilia (back and forth) transduces the hydromechanical energy into chemical-neural activity within the cell (decreases and increases of the intracellular potential), producing excitatory and inhibitory responses, which results in transduction to neural energy (increases and decreases in neural discharge rate). Once the neuron reaches threshold, there is an all or none neural discharge which is transmitted to neurons with the brainstem.

Alternate Answer:

Condensations and rarefactions of air molecules

In and out movements of tympanic membrane and ossicular chain

In and out movements of stapes in oval window with reciprocal movements of round window

Down and up movements of basilar membrane with resulting traveling wave

Elongations and contractions of OHCs at low/moderate intensities to enhance basilar membrane displacement

Back and forth bending (shearing) of stereocilia of IHCs

Decreases and increases of intracellular potential of IHCs

Increases and decreases of neurotransmitter substance at synaptic clefts

Increases and decreases of neural discharges

3.14

The two theories used to explain frequency coding are the place theory and the frequency theory. The place theory refers to the tonotopic arrangement of frequency by location along the basilar membrane (peak of the traveling wave occurs), as well as in the auditory nuclei and cortices. One limitation of the place theory is that it does not explain how the fundamental frequency is perceived when multiple pure tones with a harmonic relationship (e.g., 1200, 1400, and 1600 Hz) are presented, even though the fundamental frequency (200 Hz) itself is not presented (pitch of the missing fundamental).

The frequency theory refers to coding of frequency by the discharge rates or patterns of neural firings of the afferent auditory neurons. One limitation of the frequency theory is that an auditory neuron only fire at rates up to about 200 discharges/second, thus making it difficult to explain coding for tones greater than 200 Hz. The frequency theory can be expanded to include timing information in the interspike intervals (ISIs) of the neural discharges that correspond to the incoming frequency, and this can be maintained even if the neuron does not discharge on every cycle; appropriate ISIs can be seen up to about 2000 Hz. Another variation of the frequency theory is neural phase locking, whereby neurons do not have to respond to every cycle; but when they do respond, it is always at the same phase of the incoming frequency; phase locking has been shown for frequencies up to 4000–5000 Hz. It is likely that both the place and frequency theories are involved, e.g., the place theory may be used for higher frequencies and the frequency theory (with phase locking) for mid to low frequencies.

3.15

Intensity coding is not fully understood. Individual nerve fibers have been shown to only increase discharge rate over a range of 20–40 dB above their threshold. Two intensity coding theories have been posited. One explanation is that there may be a greater spread of activity from the peak of the traveling wave toward the more basal area of the basilar membrane as intensity increases, and this would then result in enough displacement to initiate the hair cell/neural responses from a wider array of neurons by stimulating the tails of the tuning curves from higher frequency neurons. Another explanation is that there may be nerve fibers that are activated at different stimulus levels, i.e., there are staggered thresholds for different neurons and these staggered thresholds, along with their 20–40 dB range of increasing discharge rate above threshold, might account for the 140 dB range of intensities to which the ear is responsive. Both of these intensity coding mechanisms have been demonstrated in animal studies.

4 Answers for Pure-Tone Audiometry

4.1

Pure-tone audiometry refers to the most basic component of the audiometric test battery whereby a patient's hearing thresholds are obtained by using pure tones over a range of frequencies from 250 to 8000 Hz. Pure-tone audiometry is performed while presenting tones via air conduction and bone conduction.

4.2

(Answers may vary.)

- Pure tones are easy to produce.
- Pure tones are easy to calibrate.
- Hearing loss does not affect all frequencies equally; therefore, patterns of pure-tone thresholds are indicative of certain pathologies, e.g., otitis media, presbycusis, noise-induced hearing loss.
- Pure-tone thresholds across the speech frequencies can provide some information relative to speech perception difficulties a patient may have.

4.3

1. Diagnostic or clinical audiometer. Found in most clinical settings. Capable of performing a wide range of audiometric tests. Two-channel devices allow for delivery of puretone or speech signals through one channel and masking noise through the other. Testing can be done over a wide range of frequencies and intensities.

2. Screening audiometer. Portable and usually smaller than a diagnostic audiometer. Can be battery operated. Typically only a single channel for air-conduction testing. Does not usually have the capability for speech testing or masking. Often limited frequency and intensity ranges.

3. Computer-based audiometer. Signal presentation and patient responses interfaced with a computer to store and manage the data. Can be entirely computer-based with appropriate software or interfaced with an instrument panel.

4. Automatic audiometer. Often referred to as a Békésy audiometer, in which the patient controls the level of the signal by depressing and releasing a button connected to the audiometer. Can also refer to an audiometer that can automatically test one or more people at the same time, as used in some industrial settings—the patient to control the presentation of pure-tone air-conducted signals.

4.4

A transducer is an electronic device that converts energy from one form to another.

4.5

An input transducer transforms acoustic energy into electrical energy. A microphone is an example of an input transducer. Output transducers transform electrical energy into acoustic energy. Earphones and loudspeakers are both examples of output transducers.

4.6

1. Supra-aural earphones are air-conduction transducers with rubber cushions that are connected by a headband and placed directly on the auricles; examples include TDH 39, TDH 49, and TDH 50.

2. Insert earphones are air-conduction transducers with disposable foam cuffs that are placed directly into the ear canals; examples include Etymotic ER-3A and ER-5A, and EarTone-3A.

3. Extended high frequency earphones are air-conduction transducers that are encased in a large cushioned cavity that completely surrounds the auricle; they are used to test frequencies above 8000 Hz. An example is the Sennheiser HDA200.

4. Sound-field speakers are air-conduction transducers that are placed in the test room and used instead of earphones in some situations. There is no one standard model; various models are available.

5. Bone conduction vibrators are electromechanical transducers that deliver sound vibrations directly to the skull. They are typically placed on the mastoid bone (one side at a time) and held in place by a metal headband; examples include the Radioear B-71, B-72, and B-81.

4.7

The transducers are color coded; red for the right ear, and blue for the left ear.

4.8

Advantages of insert earphones over supra-aural earphones include:

- Eliminates ear canal collapse during testing, which sometimes can occur with supra-aural earphones.
- Reduces occlusion effect when testing by bone conduction in conditions that require masking.
- Increases interaural attenuation values for air-conducted signals.
- Use of disposable foam cuffs eliminates the need to clean the supra-aural cushions.

4.9

Sound-field audiometric testing refers to presenting air-conducted stimuli through speakers in the sound booth. One disadvantage of sound-field testing is that it does not provide ear-specific information (response is from the better hearing ear). Also, standing waves could occur unless warble tones are used.

4.10

Three situations where one might use sound-field testing include:

1. Hearing aid evaluations
2. Evaluations of difficult-to-test patients
3. Testing children who will not tolerate the use of earphones

4.11

A. The frequency selector is used to choose the individual audiometric test frequencies.

B. The attenuator is used to increase/decrease the dB HL of the tones or speech (attenuation refers to the reduction of sound intensity, i.e., increasing attenuation makes the sound less intense).

C. The transducer selector is used to choose the method of delivery of the test stimuli, e.g., type of earphone, bone conduction vibrator, sound-field speakers.

D. The router selects the ear to which the stimulus is to be delivered.

E. The interrupter or continuous on-off selector determines if the signal is set to be always ON (stimulus turns off when presentation button "pushed") or is set to be always OFF (stimulus turns on when presentation button is "pushed") When doing speech testing or calibration, the signal should be set to be always ON.

F. The patient response indicator is a light that illuminates when the patient presses a response button, indicating that he/she heard the tone. The response indicator light is not used if patient is asked to raise his/her hand.

G. The VU (volume unit) meter allows the audiologist to monitor (and adjust) both live and recorded stimuli, ensuring proper presentation levels.

H. The talk-over microphone is used to talk to the patient during testing in order to give further instructions or to give reinforcement. The volume level of the microphone is set at a comfortable listening level for the patient. The talk-over channel is different than that used for speech testing.

4.12

During air conduction (AC) testing, the entire auditory system is evaluated, including the outer ear, middle ear, inner ear, auditory nerve, and central auditory nervous system. During bone conduction (BC) testing, the stimulus bypasses the outer and middle ears and primarily tests the sensorineural portions of the auditory system. An air–bone gap is defined as a greater than 10 dB difference between AC and BC thresholds (BC being better). An air-bone gap is indicative of a conductive component to the hearing loss. The hearing loss is considered to be conductive if BC is normal and there is the presence of an air-bone gap. The hearing loss is considered to be mixed when both AC and BC thresholds are poorer than normal and there is an air-bone gap.

4.13

(Answers may vary.)

- Patient differences in skin thickness over the mastoid process or differences in density of the mastoid air spaces
- Patient attention and fatigue
- Normal variability of the middle ear and external auditory canal
- Inherent variability within a patient
- Bone conduction standards for 0 dB HL, are based on an average for group of listeners; individuals may be above or below that average.

4.14

(Answers may vary.)

Pure-tone air conduction thresholds define the degree (amount) and shape/configuration of the hearing loss across the audiogram, illustrating how a patient's hearing thresholds vary from frequency to frequency. Bone conduction thresholds define the type of hearing loss, i.e., conductive, sensorineural, or mixed. In addition, pure-tone air conduction thresholds at 500 Hz, 1000 Hz, and 2000 Hz are often used to provide the pure-tone average (PTA), a measure that is useful for comparing pure-tone thresholds with speech recognition thresholds.

4.15

For AC, the recommended frequencies include 250, 500, 1000, 2000, 3000, 4000, 6000, and 8000 Hz (ASHA, 2005). In addition, 125 Hz may be included for patients with low frequency residual hearing (steep slope above 500 Hz) or in cases with a low frequency loss rising to normal in the higher frequencies. The order for testing is typically 1000 Hz, followed by 2000, 3000, 4000, 6000, 8000, 250, and 500 Hz (with retesting at 1000 Hz before testing 250 and 500 Hz). For BC, the recommended frequencies include 250, 500, 1000, 2000, 3000, and 4000 Hz. ASHA (2005) recommends starting at 1000 Hz with further testing at 2000, 3000, 4000, 250, and 500 Hz (with retest at 1000 Hz).

4.16

The recommended presentation duration is 1–2 s when testing pure-tone thresholds. It is advisable to use pulsed tones with young children, difficult-to-test patients, and patients who complain of tinnitus.

4.17

The patient's better ear should be tested first, if information is available. If the patient does not have a better ear, testing can begin with either ear.

4.18

The familiarization phase involves presenting a pure tone at a suprathreshold level prior to beginning the actual threshold, e.g., 30 dB SL. This is done to make sure the patient understands the directions and is able to perform the given response task (raising a hand, pushing a button, giving a verbal response, etc).

4.19

1. Provide the patient with instructions regarding the task and what you want him/her to do.

2. Place the appropriate transducer on the patient in the proper position.

3. Select the desired frequency for testing.

4. Begin testing with a familiarization phase by presenting the pure tone at a level that is relatively easy to hear (e.g., 30–40 dB above the estimated threshold of the patient). If the patient does not hear the initial tone, increase the tone by 20 dB until the patient responds. Continue with the familiarization phase by decreasing the tone in 10–20 dB steps until the patient no longer responds; this point marks the beginning of the threshold search.

5. Begin the threshold search using the "up-5-down-10" procedure. As the level is now below threshold, increase the level in 5 dB steps until the patient responds; then decrease the level of the pure tone in 10 dB steps until the patient does not respond.

6. Continue the presentations using the up-5-down-10 procedure until the threshold is established based on the following definition: Threshold of hearing is defined as the lowest dB HL at which a patient voluntarily responds to at least 50% of the series of ascending trials. The minimum number of responses needed to determine the threshold is two out of three responses at a single level. Generally, the interpretation of the procedure is that three or four presentations are required, and at least 50% of the ascending trials must be heard.

7. If procedures are modified for other populations (e.g., young children or the disabled), make sure that this is documented in the report.

4.20

Reasons for starting at 1000 Hz include:

- It is in the middle of the range of frequencies to which the human ear is most sensitive.
- It is in the middle of the speech range.
- It is a familiar pitch to most individuals.
- It is less affected by biological noise.
- It has good test-retest reliability.

4.21

Testing is performed at 1500 Hz when there is a greater than 20 dB difference between audiometric thresholds at 1000 and 2000 Hz.

4.22

Audiogram A: threshold = 20 dB HL; response percentage = 67% (2/3) or 75% (3/4)

Audiogram B: threshold = 30 dB HL; response percentage = 100% (3/3)

Audiogram C: threshold = 25 dB HL; response percentage = 50% (2/4)

4.23

In this scenario, using the ASHA procedure, 55 dB would not be considered the threshold because only two presentations were presented at the lower level of 50 dB and the criterion is that there be at least two correct responses out of a possible three or four presentations. If the patient did not respond to the next presentation at 50 dB, then 55 dB could be established as the threshold because the best the patient could do at 50 dB would be one out of four responses (25%).

4.24

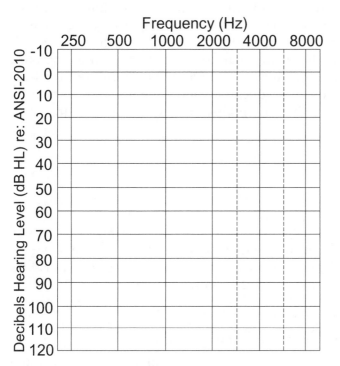

4.25

Audiogram Key	Right Ear	Left Ear
AC unmasked	O	X
AC masked	△	▯
BC unmasked	<	>
BC masked	[	]
No response	↙	↘
Sound-field	S	

4.26

It is important to apply masking to the non-test ear to ensure that tones crossing over from the contralateral test ear cannot be heard in the non-test ear.

4.27

For supra-aural earphones, the minimum interaural (IA) value is 40 dB. Therefore, one needs to be concerned about the non-test ear hearing the signal coming from the test ear when: (1) the AC threshold in the test ear is 40 dB greater than the BC threshold in the non-test ear, or (2) the AC threshold in the test ear is 40 dB greater than the AC threshold in the non-test ear. For insert earphones, the rules are the same; however, the IA values increase to at least 55 dB. The IA value for BC is 0 dB; one needs to be concerned about the non-test ear hearing the signal coming from the test ear whenever there is an air–bone gap in the test ear.

4.28

Masking noise is delivered to the right ear.

4.29

False positive responses occur when a patient responds to a tone when no tone was presented. False negative responses occur when a patient (presumably) hears a tone but does not respond. Some strategies to control for false positive responses include:

- Do not present the tones in a predictable pattern.
- Intersperse some longer and variable pauses between the presentations.
- Use a varying number of tone pulses (1, 2, or 3) instead of a continuous tone, and ask the patient to push the button the same number of times that correspond to the number of pulses heard.
- Provide more feedback to the patient.
- Reinstruct the patient to guess when tones are faint.
- Reinstruct the patient to press the button (or keep his hand raised) as long as he hears the tone, and to quit responding when the tone is no longer heard.

4.30

Conditioned-play audiometry is the technique used to test hearing in children between the ages of 2 and 4 years (or others who are difficult to test). This testing paradigm involves conditioning the child to perform a fun task (putting a toy in a bucket, putting a ring on a pole, etc.) each time she hears a sound. Once the child has demonstrated that she understands the activity, the testing phase begins. Obtain thresholds using a standard procedure (up-5-down-10), unless a modified procedure (up-10-down-20) is needed to save time and get an estimate of the thresholds. As children tend to fatigue quickly, try to obtain a couple of thresholds in each ear and then add other frequencies back and forth between ears as time permits.

4.31

Visual-reinforcement audiometry is the technique used to test hearing in children ranging in age between 6 months and 2 years (or difficult-to-test patients). This testing paradigm involves pairing an audible sound with a visual reinforcer, such as an image on a flat screen monitor and a mechanical animal or toy enclosed in a tinted plastic enclosure, and conditioning the child to turn and look at the toy whenever she hears the sound. When the child turns her head in response to the sound, a mechanical switch is used to light up the toy behind the tinted plastic and/or to set the toy in motion. The visual reinforcers are placed 45–90° away from the child's forward facing position. Once the child has demonstrated that she is consistently turning her head in response to the sound, the testing phase begins. Obtain thresholds using a standard procedure (up-5-down-10), unless a modified procedure (up-10-down-20) is needed to save time and get an estimate of the thresholds. Always attempt testing with earphones first in order to get ear-specific information, but testing can also be conducted in the sound field if the patient will not tolerate the earphones.

5 Answers for Audiogram Interpretation

5.1

A.	Normal adult	−10–25 dB HL
B.	Normal child	−10–15 dB HL
C.	Slight (child)	16–25 dB HL
D.	Mild	26–40 dB HL
E.	Moderate	41–55 dB HL
F.	Moderately severe	56–70 dB HL
G.	Severe	71–90 dB HL
H.	Profound	>90 dB HL

5.2

Humans hear sounds primarily through air conduction (however, they also hear through bone conduction when sounds are loud enough). Also, air conduction testing evaluates the entire auditory system, whereas bone conduction only evaluates the inner ear and the higher auditory structures, eliminating the participation of the outer and middle ear systems. The degree of hearing loss, therefore, should include effects from all parts of the auditory system; hence, air conduction is used to describe degree of hearing loss.

5.3

A. b

B. c

C. a

5.4

Audiogram configuration refers to the overall shape of the air conduction thresholds (between 250 and 8000 Hz) on an audiogram. Some common configurations are (1) flat, where air conduction (AC) thresholds between 250 and 8000 Hz do not vary by more than 20 dB; (2) rising, where AC thresholds in the higher frequencies are better than the AC thresholds in the lower frequencies; (3) sloping (falling), where AC thresholds in the lower frequencies are better than the AC thresholds for the higher frequencies; (4) precipitous, where AC thresholds steeply slope (e.g., >40 dB between thresholds measured at consecutive octave frequencies); (5) notched, where AC thresholds are worse in a narrow region, usually in the 3000–6000 Hz region.

5.5

Tactile (non-audible) responses to bone conducted signals may be typically observed on an audiogram from 25–40 dB at 250 Hz, and from 55–70 dB HL at 500 Hz (Boothroyd & Cawkwell, 1970; Nober, 1970). To verify the presence of tactile responses, patients can be asked to indicate if the tone being delivered through the bone conduction vibrator is perceived as being heard or only felt.

5.6

The standard 3-frequency PTA is determined by averaging the pure-tone AC thresholds obtained at 500, 1000, and 2000 Hz. The PTA for each patient provides a summary of his/her hearing sensitivity across the main speech frequencies (500 Hz–2000 Hz). In addition, the PTA is compared with the patient's speech recognition threshold (SRT) as a cross-check: The PTA and the SRT should be within 10 dB of each other.

5.7

The Fletcher (2-frequency) average is an average of the two better AC thresholds of 500, 1000, and 2000 Hz. The Fletcher average is performed in cases of precipitous or sharply rising hearing loss in order to give a more accurate estimate of the patient's hearing, whereas the 3-frequency PTA may be unduly influenced by the poorest threshold.

5.8

Patients who present with compliant ear canals (usually small children and older adults) may have their ear canals temporarily closed off (collapsed) while being tested with supra-aural earphones. Audiometric evidence of collapsed ear canals are erroneous air–bone gaps, indicating a conductive hearing loss when none is present. Some ways to minimize the problem would be to: (1) use insert earphones, (2) test the patient with his/her mouth held open, (3) hold the supra-aural headphone loosely on the auricle, and (4) utilize sound-field testing.

5.9

The appropriate air and/or bone conduction thresholds are plotted at the upper output limit for each frequency with a down-pointing arrow added to the symbol. This would indicate that testing was performed, but the patient's threshold was at least 5 dB worse than the audiometric limit. Examples include:

$\bigcirc$ right ear AC $\gtrsim$ left ear BC

Note that the arrow points to the right for left ear thresholds, and to the left for right ear thresholds. Arrows may be added to unmasked as well as masked symbols when no response is obtained at the output limit.

5.10

    A. 7.5 dB SPL

    B. insert earphones (ER-3A)

    C. NA; bone conduction is not normally tested at 8000 Hz

    D. bone vibrator (B-72)

    E. 11.5 dB SPL

    F. insert earphones (ER-3A)

    G. 13.5 dB SPL

    H. supra-aural headphones (THD-50P)

    I. 67 dB force (re: 1 μN)

    J. supra-aural headphones (TDH-50P)

5.11

Audiogram A

    A. 85 dB HL

    B. 40 dB HL

    C. 45 dB HL

    D. 40 dB SL

    E. 5 dB SL

    F. 50 dB SL

    G. 88 dB SPL

    H. 103.5 dB SPL

Audiogram B

    I. 35 dB HL

    J. 90 dB HL

    K. 40 dB HL

    L. 0 dB SL

    M. 25 dB SL

    N. 55 dB SL

    O. 30.5 dB SPL

    P. 71.5 dB SPL

5.12

A.

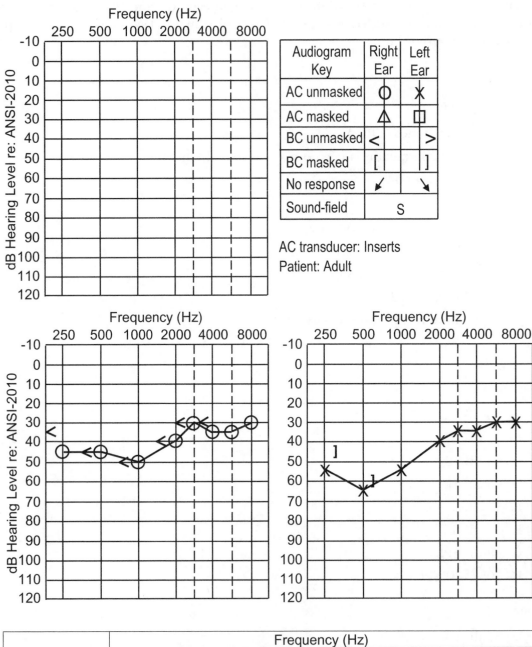

		Frequency (Hz)							
		250	500	1000	2000	3000	4000	6000	8000
Right	Air	45	45	50	40	30	35	35	30
	Bone	35	45	50	40	30	35		
Left	Air	55	65	55	40	35	35	30	30
	Bone	45	60	DNT[1]	DNT[1]	DNT[1]	DNT[1]		
[1]Assumed to be the same as right ear BC threshold (i.e., <15 dB air-bone gap)									

B.

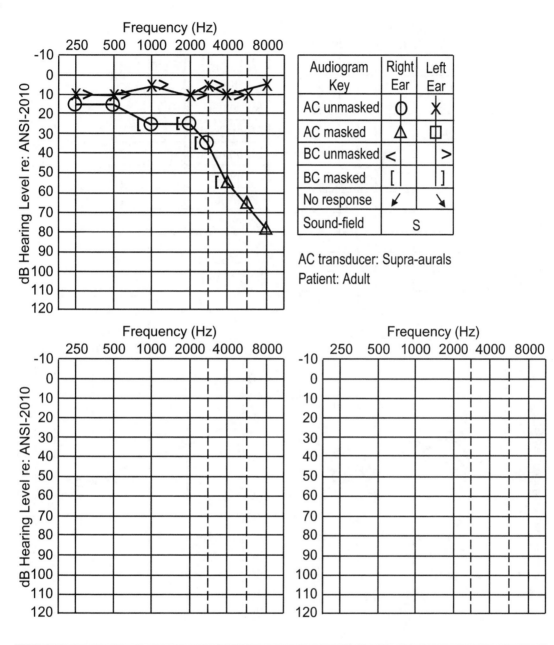

AC transducer: Supra-aurals

Patient: Adult

		Frequency (Hz)							
		250	500	1000	2000	3000	4000	6000	8000
Right	Air	15	15	25	25	35	55	65	80
	Bone	DNT[1]	DNT[1]	25	25	35	55		
Left	Air	10	10	5	10	5	10	10	5
	Bone	10	10	5	10	5	10		
[1]Assumed to be the same as left ear BC threshold (i.e., <15 dB air-bone gap)									

C.

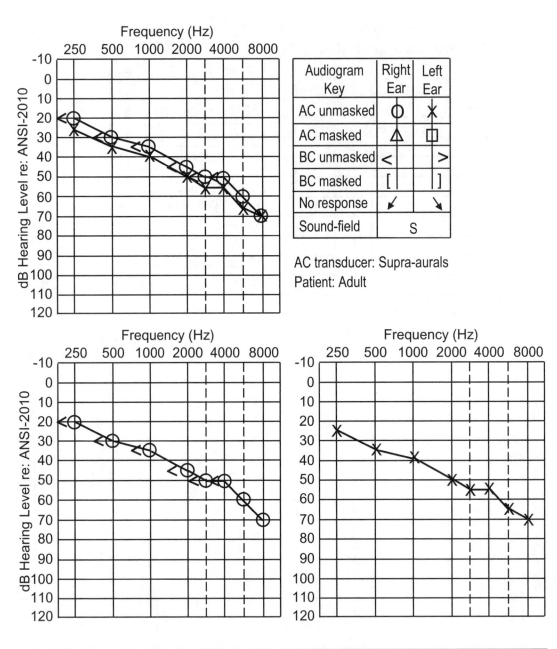

Audiogram Key	Right Ear	Left Ear
AC unmasked	O	X
AC masked	△	□
BC unmasked	<	>
BC masked	[	]
No response	↙	↘
Sound-field	S	

AC transducer: Supra-aurals
Patient: Adult

		Frequency (Hz)							
		250	500	1000	2000	3000	4000	6000	8000
Right	Air								
	Bone								
Left	Air								
	Bone								

5.13

A. Right ear: Sensorineural; relatively flat

B. Left ear: Mixed; sloping

C. Left ear: Sensorineural loss (above 2000 Hz); precipitously sloping (above 2000 Hz)

D. Right ear: Sensorineural loss (low frequencies); rising

E. Right ear: Conductive loss; sloping
   Left ear: Conductive loss; sloping

F. Right ear: Sensorineural loss; relatively flat
   Left ear: Mixed loss; relatively flat

G. Right ear: Sensorineural loss; sloping between 250 and 3000 Hz, rising above 3000 Hz
   Left ear: Mixed through 1000 Hz, sensorineural above 1000 Hz; sloping through 3000 Hz, rising above 3000 Hz

H. Right ear and left ear: conductive loss; slightly sloping (or relatively flat)

I. Right ear: Sensorineural loss 3000–6000 Hz only; notched (between 2000 and 4000 Hz)
   Left ear: Sensorineural loss; flat through 2000 Hz, notched (between 3000 and 6000 Hz)

J. Right ear: Mixed loss from 250 to 2000 Hz and sensorineural loss between 3000 and 8000 Hz; relatively flat (or slightly rising)
   Left ear: Sensorineural loss; sloping

K. Right ear: Sensorineural loss; sloping
   Left ear: Normal (or borderline normal) hearing sensitivity; flat

L. Right ear and left ear: Probable sensorineural loss; corner audiogram (low frequency residual hearing only), but could have a conductive component that cannot be determined from audiogram.

5.14

A.

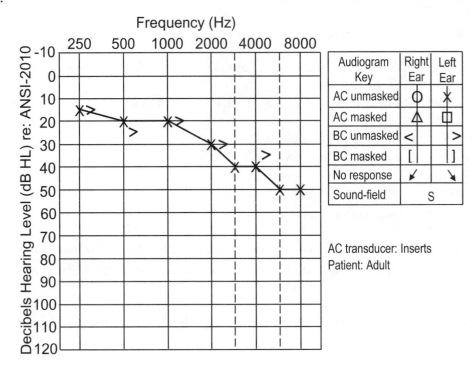

B.

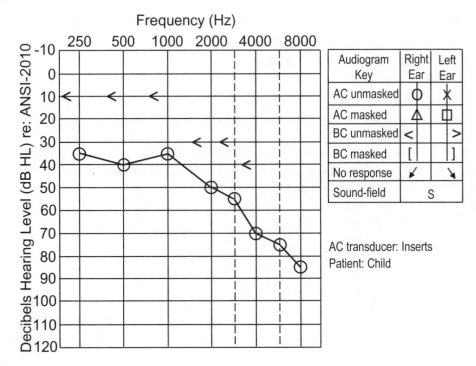

C.

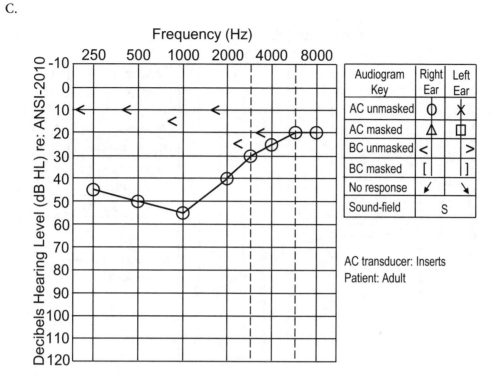

D.

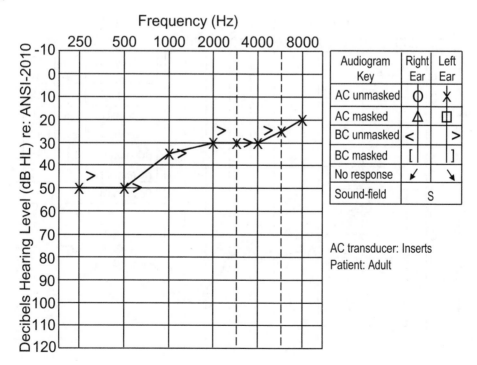

E.

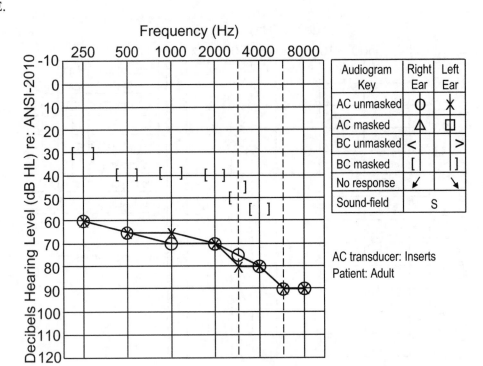

F.

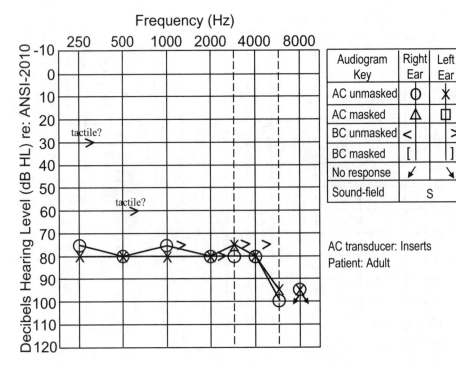

G.

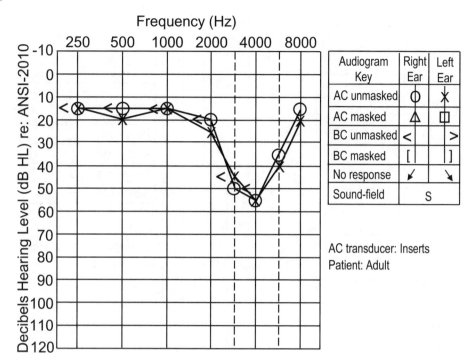

H.

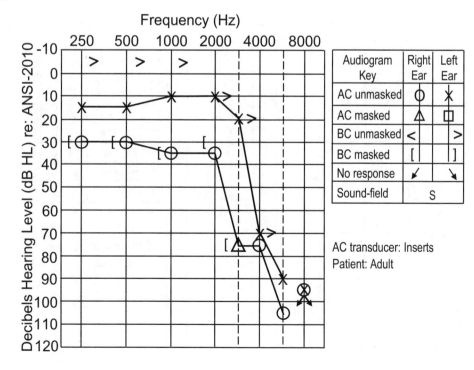

I.

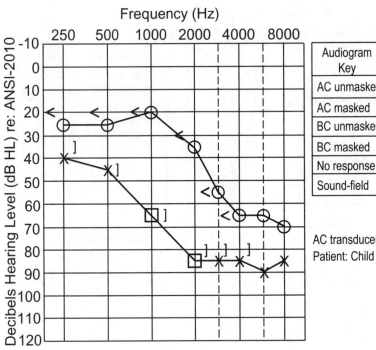

AC transducer: Supra-aurals
Patient: Child

J.

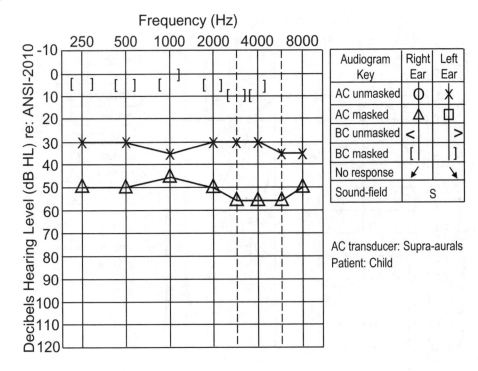

AC transducer: Supra-aurals
Patient: Child

K.

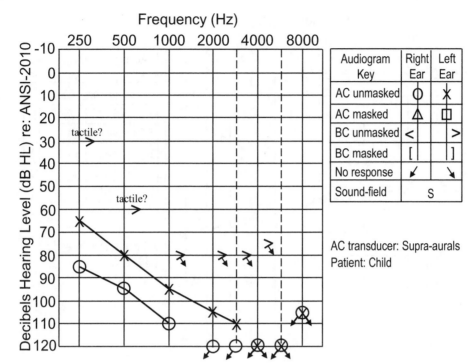

L.

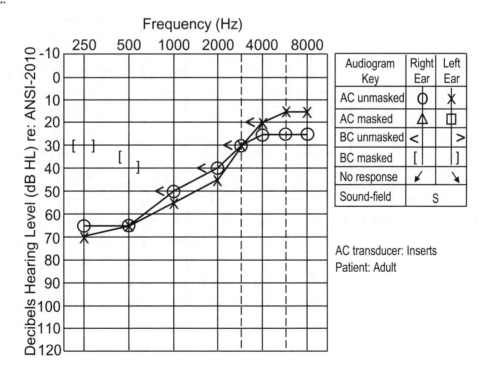

M.

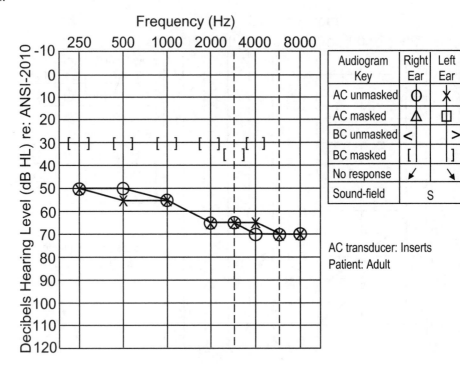

AC transducer: Inserts
Patient: Adult

N.

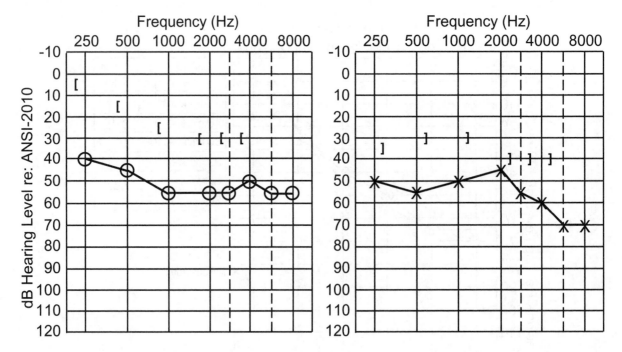

O.

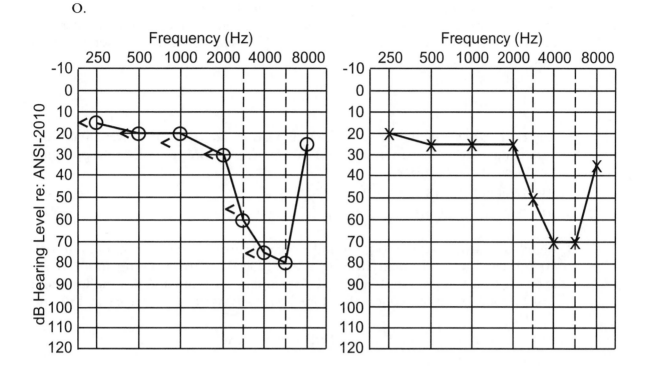

5.15

A. Left ear shows a moderately severe, low frequency, mixed hearing loss, rising to a mild mixed hearing loss at 3000 Hz and normal hearing from 4000 to 8000 Hz.

PTA left ear: 50 dB HL

B. Right ear shows normal hearing from 250 to 2000 Hz and a mild to severe sloping sensorineural loss in the higher frequencies.

PTA right ear: 3 dB HL

C. Right ear shows a mild to moderately severe sloping sensorineural hearing loss. Left ear shows a mild to moderate, flat sensorineural hearing loss from 250 to 3000 Hz, sloping to moderately severe in the higher frequencies.

PTA right ear: 48 dB HL

PTA left ear: 40 dB HL

D. Right ear shows a moderately severe, flat, mixed hearing loss (with 25–30 dB air–bone gaps). The left ear shows a severe, flat, mixed hearing loss (with 25–40 dB air–bone gaps).

PTA right ear: 63 dB HL

PTA left ear: 78 dB HL

E. Right ear shows a moderate conductive hearing loss from 250 to 1000 Hz and a moderate mixed hearing loss at 2000 Hz and higher. Left ear shows a moderately severe conductive hearing loss from 250 to 1000 Hz, rising to a moderate mixed hearing loss at 2000 Hz and higher.

PTA right ear: 55 dB HL

PTA left ear: 60 dB HL

F. Right ear shows a mild, flat, sensorineural hearing loss. Left ear shows a mild sensorineural hearing loss from 250 to 2000 Hz, sloping precipitously to a profound loss at 6000 and 8000 Hz.

PTA right era: 32 dB HL

PTA left ear: 37 dB HL

G. Right ear shows a severe to profound sloping sensorineural hearing loss through 1000 Hz and no measurable hearing above 1000 Hz (corner audiogram). Left ear shows a severe to profound, relatively flat sloping sensorineural hearing loss from 250 to 8000 Hz. Bone conduction thresholds are most likely tactile at 250 and 500 Hz.

PTA right ear: 95 dB HL (Fletcher 2-frequency average)

PTA left ear: 93 dB HL

H. Right ear shows normal hearing from 250 to 500 Hz and a mild to moderately severe, sloping conductive loss from 1000 to 8000 Hz. Left ear shows a moderate to moderately severe, sloping, conductive loss.

PTA right ear: 32 dB HL

PTA left ear: 55 dB HL

I. A bilateral, moderate, mid-frequency ("saucer-shape or "cookie-bite") sensorineural hearing loss with normal hearing at 250 and 8000 Hz.

PTA right ear: 48 dB HL

PTA left ear: 52 dB HL

J. A bilateral, mild to severe, sloping, sensorineural hearing loss.

PTA right ear: 65 dB HL

PTA left ear: 67 dB HL

K. Right ear shows a moderate, conductive hearing loss. Left ear shows a moderate mixed hearing loss.

PTA right ear: 53 dB HL

PTA left ear: 55 dB HL

L. A bilateral, slight, flat, sensorineural hearing loss.

PTA right ear: 22 dB HL

PTA left ear: 23 dB HL

M. A bilateral, mild sensorineural hearing loss from 250 to 500 Hz, rising to normal hearing from 1000 to 4000 Hz, and sloping to a moderate sensorineural hearing loss in the higher frequencies.

PTA right ear: 20 dB HL

PTA left ear: 23 dB HL

N. Right ear shows normal hearing through 1000 Hz, and sloping to a moderately severe sensorineural hearing loss in the higher frequencies. Left ear shows normal hearing from 250 to 500 Hz, and a mild sensorineural loss from 1000 to 8000 Hz.

PTA right ear: 17 dB HL

PTA left ear: 30 dB HL

O. Right ear shows a severe mixed hearing loss from 250 to 2000 Hz, rising to a mild sensorineural hearing loss in the higher frequencies. Left ear shows a moderate sensorineural loss through 1000 Hz, rising to a mild sensorineural hearing loss in the higher frequencies.

PTA right ear: 77 dB HL

PTA left ear: 45 dB HL

6 Answers for Speech Audiometry

6.1

(Answers may vary.)

Speech audiometry is an essential part of the basic audiometric test battery for several reasons: Speech is the most important signal we hear daily. The pure-tone audiogram cannot accurately predict the degree of communication deficit caused by a hearing loss; two people with the same audiogram may have quite different speech perceptual abilities. The greatest complaint from patients with hearing loss is that they have difficulty understanding speech. Also, speech audiometry is often more sensitive to the effects of hearing loss than pure-tone testing. Clinically, the speech recognition threshold (SRT) is used to check the accuracy of pure-tone thresholds. Speech audiometry can also be utilized for differential diagnosis of individuals suspected of 8th nerve disorders. For children and with many special-needs clients, speech audiometry may be the only way to assess hearing status.

6.2

By monitoring the VU meter during speech testing, the audiologist can ensure that the speech signal is properly calibrated for intensity, whether the audiologist is using live voice or recorded speech stimuli. When the VU meter is "peaked" at 0 dB (which is associated with the appropriate calibration level), the audiologist can be sure that a word presented at 10 dB HL (for example) is truly being presented at 10 dB HL and not at a greater or lesser intensity level.

6.3

If the VU meter is peaked at −5 dB, the speech signal is being presented at a level of 35 dB HL. This problem can be rectified by adjusting the level of the speech signal until the VU meter peaks at 0 dB HL (with either monitored live voice or recorded materials).

6.4

It is important to always calibrate the presentation level of recorded words to ensure that the dB level of any particular word list is accurate. For recorded materials, the VU meter is adjusted by playing the 1000 Hz calibration tone located at the beginning of the appropriate track on the CD, and then adjusting the intensity level of the VU meter to 0 dB.

6.5

The SRT serves as a cross-check for the pure-tone average. Additionally, speech stimuli are usually more familiar than pure-tone stimuli, so if the patient is not responding consistently to the pure tones, the SRT may provide the only valid information relative to the degree of hearing loss. Also, the SRT is sometimes used as a baseline for selecting the presentation level for determining a patient's word recognition score (WRS).

6.6

The SDT is determined when it is not possible to obtain an SRT with a particular patient, i.e., when the patient is not capable of repeating speech stimuli. The SDT is most often used with developmentally delayed patients, infants and young children, difficult-to-test individuals, and patients with profound hearing loss. Similar to the SRT, the SDT is a threshold measure for speech stimuli, and should coincide with the patient's best (lowest) pure-tone threshold. The SDT is approximately 5–10 dB better than the SRT.

6.7

The SRT should be within 10 dB of the PTA. The SRT is generally better (lower in dB) than the PTA.

6.8

(Answers may vary.)

- With a steeply sloping or rising audiogram, the SRT will more closely correspond to a two-frequency threshold average, using the thresholds of the better two frequencies of 500, 1000, or 2000 Hz.
- Misunderstanding of instructions (perhaps due to limited English language proficiency on the patient's part or not understanding the audiologist's dialect).
- The audiometer may not have been properly calibrated for speech stimuli.
- Pseudohypoacusis (functional hearing loss).
- Equipment malfunction.
- Developmental level of the patient.
- Tendency to have more false negatives for pure-tone testing (unwilling to guess when close to threshold).
- Patient may have a cognitive disorder or a language disorder.

6.9

Spondee pictures are important during SRT testing with many children and difficult-to-test patients because these patients may not be willing or capable of repeating spondees. Also, if a patient has a phonological disorder, the patient's verbal response may be misinterpreted by the audiologist and scored incorrectly (either correct or incorrect). Picture pointing eliminates this possibility.

6.10
(Answers may vary.)

- The specific list to be used (e.g., CID W-22 vs. NU-6)
- Number of items presented (25- vs. 50-word list)
- Scoring method (whole word vs. phoneme scoring)
- Determination of presentation level
- If more than one presentation level is used
- If testing is to be performed both in quiet and in noise
- Determination of S/N ratio when testing in noise

6.11
Starting an audiometric evaluation with speech audiometry (SRT) may save clinical time. Children and difficult-to-test patients often do not fully understand the instructions for pure-tone testing. Numerous false negative responses may be observed because these patients are not willing to guess when the pure-tone stimuli are close to true threshold. The presence of the false negative responses may not be fully realized until the SRT is performed, and there is poor correspondence between the SRT and PTA. In these populations, spondees are more interesting to listen to than pure-tone stimuli, therefore the patient responds more reliably at or near threshold for speech than for pure tones.

6.12
The normal conversational level for speech is considered to be 50 dB HL.

6.13
It would be problematic to use a single presentation level of 25 dB SL with most patients because it might be too low to achieve PB_{max}. Although presentation level of 40 dB SL might include more acoustic information, it may be uncomfortably loud with patients who exhibit signs of recruitment (typical of most cochlear hearing losses). Using the MCL may also be too low to achieve PB_{max}.

6.14
Using a presentation level of UCL-5 dB helps to maximize the possibility that the presentation level is at the patient's PB_{max} but at the same time not exceeding the patient's tolerance level to loud sound. Guthrie and Mackersie (2009) recommended UCL-5 or the following levels above the 2000 Hz threshold:

- If threshold at 2000 Hz is <50 dB HL, present at 25 dB SL
- If threshold at 2000 Hz is 50–55 dB HL, present at 20 dB SL
- If threshold at 2000 Hz is 60–65 dB HL, present at 15 dB SL
- If threshold at 2000 Hz is 70–75 dB HL, present at 10 dB SL

6.15

Testing at multiple levels will produce a PI/PB function that will better define PB_{max}. Testing at multiple levels will allow for calculation of a rollover ratio.

6.16

Phonemic regression is a disproportionate reduction in speech recognition in reference to a patient's pure-tone audiogram. Phonemic regression may occur in some patients with presby-cusis and in patients with hearing loss of retrocochlear or central origin.

6.17

Although patients with similar audiograms (and SRTs) have a similar reduction in hearing sensitivity (audibility), they may have differing abilities in terms of differential sensitivity. That is, there is most likely a difference between these patients in terms of their ability to discriminate small changes in frequency, intensity, and/or temporal information. A reduction in a patient's differential sensitivity results in reduced speech understanding. Additionally, a patient with a neural disorder will have a disproportionate reduction in speech recognition (phonemic regression) than a patient with a cochlear hearing loss, even though they have the same audiogram.

6.18

Higher harmonics of the fundamental frequency of the voice would be less audible. Audibility of noise bursts associated with stops and affricates would be reduced. In addition, perception of airstream turbulence associated with both voiced and unvoiced fricatives would be difficult. Second and third formant transitions of vowels would not be audible, leading to problems with perception of place of articulation cues of stops and fricatives. For this patient, these problems could cause difficulty distinguishing words that contain fricatives (s, f, th) or stops that differ in place of articulation. Some examples include "elf" vs. "else" or "shoe" vs. "two." Not hearing /s/ might cause problems with plurals and possessives.

6.19

An individual with a low frequency loss of this nature could have difficulty perceiving some voicing cues and the fundamental frequency (and harmonics) of women's and children's voices. In addition, perception of nasal murmur associated with the consonants /m/, /n/, and /ŋ/ could be difficult. Other problems could involve the audibility of consonant manner of production, noise bursts of stop consonants, formant transitions of glides and liquids, and the formant transitions of vowels. Some examples of words that would be difficult to distinguish with this hearing loss include "hat" vs. "hot," "pit" vs. "put," "moon" vs. "noon," "deep" vs. "leap," and "bat" vs. "rat."

6.20

With a moderately flat hearing loss from 250 to 8000 Hz, most of the speech spectrum would become inaudible when spoken at a normal conversational level without any form of amplification.

6.21

With a cochlear hearing loss, the uncomfortable loudness (UCL) usually is reduced because of recruitment, and with the elevated SRT there is a reduction in the dynamic range. With a conductive hearing loss, the UCL is typically elevated along with the SRT, so the size of the dynamic range is relatively unaffected. Depending on the degree of the conductive component, the UCL may not be measurable, as it may be beyond the limits of the audiometer.

6.22

For the first example, the dynamic range would be 55 dB. For the second example, the dynamic range would be 40 dB.

6.23

The Speech Intelligibility Index (SII) is used to estimate the percentage of the speech spectrum audible to a patient based on their particular audiogram. For example, if a patient has a hearing loss with an SII of 24%, this means that only 24% of the speech spectrum is audible. This person would have great difficulty perceiving speech, as 76% of the speech spectrum would be inaudible. Clinically, estimates of the SII may be determined by using what are known as count-the-dots audiograms (see 6.24 and 6.25).

6.24

A. Humes (1991) SII = 0.63 (21 dots above threshold × .03).

B. Killion and Mueller (2010) SII = 0.66 (66 dots above threshold × .01).

C. There is fairly good agreement between the two methods; however, the methods cannot be compared effectively because each method covers different frequency/ intensity ranges and the similarity may not hold for different thresholds. The Humes count-the-dots audiogram has only 33 dots, whereas the Killion and Mueller count-the-dots audiogram has 100 dots and is based on newer distribution of SII data. The density of the dots is greatest in the 1000 to 4000 Hz range for both methods, indicating the greater importance of these frequencies for speech intelligibility. The placement of the dots in the Humes method is strictly at the octave frequencies between 250 and 4000 Hz. The Killion and Mueller method has placement of the dots starting below 250 Hz and ranging to 8000 Hz, with the dots located continuously throughout the audiogram so as to include hearing between the octave frequencies. For instance, there are 17 dots spread out between 2000 and 4000 Hz rather than just centered at 3000 Hz. The Killion and Mueller method also takes into account thresholds above 4000 Hz. Speech perceptual cues located in the frequencies higher than 4000 Hz play an important role in speech intelligibility.

6.25

A. Humes (1991) method: SII = 0.63 (21 dots above threshold × .03).

B. Killion and Mueller (2010) method: SII = 0.71 (71 dots above threshold × .01)

When using the Killion and Mueller count-the-dots audiogram, more dots would be included above 4000 Hz, thus raising the SII approximately 5%. The Humes count-the-dots method has no dots above 4000 Hz, hence there is no change in the SII even though the patient's threshold was improved to 20 dB at 8000 Hz.

6.26

A. yes

B. yes

C. no

D. yes

E. no

F. no

G. no

H. no

I. yes

J. no

K. yes

L. yes

M. no

N. yes

6.27

A. no

B. no

C. yes

D. no

E. yes

F. no

G. yes

H. yes

I. no

J. no

K. yes

L. no

M. no

N. yes

6.28
Rollover Ratio equation:

$$RR = (PB_{max} - PB_{min}) / PB_{max}$$

6.29

A. 0.24, no

B. 0.29, no

C. 0.50, yes

D. 0.05, no

E. 0.37, yes

F. 0.43, yes

G. 0.22, no

H. 0.38, yes

I. 0.23, no

J. 0.13, no

K. 0.44, yes

L. 0.24, no

M. 0.29, no

N. 0.38, yes

6.30
Speech-in-noise measures are designed to assess how well a patient can recognize speech in the presence of different levels of background noise, thus obtaining measures of speech recognition that may be more representative of real-world listening situations. Examples of speech-in-noise tests include the Speech Perception in Noise (SPIN) test, the Synthetic Sentence Identification (SSI) test, the Quick Sentence in Noise (QuickSIN) test, and the Hearing in Noise Test (HINT).

6.31

Signal-to-noise ratio loss is defined as the decibel increase in the S/N ratio required by a hearing-impaired person to understand speech-in-noise compared to someone with normal hearing.

6.32

(Answers may vary.)

- Use age-appropriate words or words that are familiar to the child.
- Use the WIPI or NU-Chips tests for children with limited vocabularies or who are reluctant to speak.
- Use an "up-10-down-20" procedure to save time.
- Test in sound field if the child will not tolerate headphones.
- Be flexible.
- Use lots of positive reinforcement to help encourage participation.

6.33

Masking is often needed for WRS testing because the presentation level of the speech material is at a supra-threshold level and, therefore, is more likely to cross over to the non-test ear.

6.34

The masker used for speech is a noise that contains a range of frequencies that are representative of the long-term speech spectrum, making it an effective masker for the audiometric speech frequencies.

7 Answers for Clinical Masking

7.1

Interaural attenuation (IA) refers to the difference (reduction) in the level of a sound that is presented to one ear (e.g., test ear) and the amount that occurs in the other ear (e.g., non-test ear). The sound in the non-test ear occurs primarily through bone conduction (vibrations occurring in the skull). Intuitively, when the sound to the test ear is delivered by a bone oscillator, there would essentially be no difference in the sound level between the ears (IA = 0) because both ears are embedded in the skull and the levels would be the same at the two ears. Even when testing by air conduction, at a high enough level, the sound can start to be picked up through bone conduction. Although IAs vary across people and frequencies (Sklare & Denenberg, 1987), the following *minimum* IAs are used throughout this workbook:

Bone conduction = 0 dB

Supra-aural earphones = 40 dB

Insert earphones = 55 dB

7.2

The level of an air conduction sound that is needed to begin to get the skull to pick up the vibrations and potentially stimulate the non-test ear (through bone conduction) depends on the surface area of the transducer that is exposed to the listener's skull. A supra-aural earphone has a greater surface area in contact with the skull than does an insert earphone. Using the formula: Force = Pressure × Area ($F = P \times A$), it can be seen that the supra-aural earphone (larger area) would generate a greater force to the skull, thus resulting in a lower IA than an insert earphone.

7.3

Masking is needed whenever there is the possibility that the non-test ear (NTE) could hear the sound presented to the test ear (TE). For AC testing, if the difference between the TE AC threshold and the NTE BC threshold exceeds the IA, masking is needed to rule out the possibility that the AC threshold is coming from the NTE (by BC). Masking would also be needed if the difference between the TE AC threshold and the NTE AC threshold exceeds the IA value, because the NTE BC threshold would be equal to or better than the NTE AC threshold.

7.4

Masking is needed whenever there is the possibility that the non-test ear (NTE) could hear the sound presented to the test ear (TE). For BC testing, one would expect to always need to mask; however, when there are no air-bone gaps, the unmasked BC would not change with masking. Therefore, the general rule for needing masking for BC testing is when there is a difference between the unmasked BC threshold and the TE AC threshold that exceeds 10 dB (i.e., there is an air–bone gap).

7.5

A. The OE is an artificial improvement (decrease) in the BC threshold that occurs when the non-test ear is covered (occluded) by placement of a supra-aural headphone or insert earphone during masking. The source of the OE when covered with a supra-aural earphone is primarily the vibration of the cartilaginous part of the ear canal reacting to the bone-conducted vibrations. These sound waves in the ear canal cannot escape as easily to the environment when occluded, causing additional energy to be transmitted into the inner ear, resulting in an increase in the level of the test tone (i.e., better threshold).

B. The OE is less with an insert earphone because less of the cartilaginous part of the ear canal is available to vibrate and contribute to the bone-conducted sound energy. With deeper insertion depth of the insert earphone, the OE decreases due to (1) less sound energy being radiated into the canal due to a reduction in the surface area of the ear canal, (2) increased impedance at the tympanic membrane, (3) an upward shift in the resonant frequency of the remaining ear canal, and (4) damping of the ear canal wall vibrations due to the presence of the earphone (Tonndorf, 1972).

C. When masking is being performed during BC testing, the minimum masking level must be increased in the NTE due to the increase in the perceived loudness of the test tone being presented to the TE due to the OE.

D. The OE mainly occurs in the lower frequencies and is inversely related to frequency. With a supra-aural earphone, the OE values are approximately 20 dB at 250 Hz, 15 dB at 500 Hz, and 5 dB at 1000 Hz, and negligible for 2000 Hz and higher. With an insert earphone, with deep insertion, there are no OEs except 10 dB at 250 Hz.

7.6

The typical masking stimuli used during pure-tone testing are one-third-octave-wide narrow-band noises that are centered around the corresponding frequency being tested. A narrow-band noise is based on a critical band of frequencies that is needed to produce maximum masking, whereas adding frequencies wider than the critical band only adds to the intensity of the noise and does not contribute any more to the masking of the tone (Fletcher, 1940; Sanders & Rintleman, 1964).

7.7

Effective masking (EM) is the decibel level (dB HL) to which a threshold is shifted by a given level of masking noise. For example, a 40 dB EM level of a narrowband noise will elevate the threshold of a tone centered in that noise to a level of 40 dB HL. Modern audiometers are calibrated in EM levels. Therefore, if a patient's unmasked threshold in the NTE was 50 dB HL, and 70 dB EM is delivered to that ear, the threshold in the NTE would be shifted to 70 dB HL.

7.8

Central masking causes a 5–7 dB threshold shift (worsening) of the test tone in the test ear when masking noise is delivered to the contralateral (non-test) ear at a level that is not able to cross over to the test ear. This is thought to occur through some mechanism of the central nervous system (e.g., neural inhibition).

7.9

The masking dilemma is usually seen in the presence of a large bilateral conductive loss. The masking dilemma occurs when the minimum dB masking level is actually greater than the maximum dB masking level, i.e., the level at which overmasking occurs. Insert earphones have the advantage over supra-aural earphones in that a masking dilemma would require a much larger conductive loss before overmasking occurs because of their greater interaural attenuation values.

7.10

    A. AC: Yes
       BC: Yes

    B. AC: No
       BC: Yes

    C. AC: No
       BC: No

    D. AC: Yes
       BC: Yes

    E. AC: No
       BC: Yes

    F. AC: No
       BC: No

    G. AC: No
       BC: Yes

H. AC: No
   BC: Yes

I. AC: Yes
   BC: Did not test

7.11

A.

		250	500	1000	2000	4000	8000
Supra-aural	R						
	L	M	M	M			M
Insert	R						
	L						
Bone	R						
	L	M	M	M	M	M	

B.

		250	500	1000	2000	4000	8000
Supra-aural	R						
	L						
Insert	R						
	L						
Bone	R	M	M	M			
	L	M	M	M			

C.

		250	500	1000	2000	4000	8000
Supra-aural	R	M	M	M	M	M	M
	L						
Insert	R						
	L						
Bone	R	M	M	M	M	M	
	L	M	M				

D. (Assume LE BC = LE AC: No air–bone gaps in LE)

		250	500	1000	2000	4000	8000
Supra-aural	R	M	M	M			
	L						
Insert	R	M	M				
	L						
Bone	R	M	M	M	M		
	L						

E.

		250	500	1000	2000	4000	8000
Supra-aural	R	M	M	M	M	M	M
	L						
Insert	R	M	M	M	M		
	L						
Bone	R	M	M	M	M	M	
	L	M	M	M			

7.12

A.

		250	500	1000	2000	4000	8000
Supra-aural	R		D	D			
	L		D	D			
Insert	R						
	L						
Bone+ TDH	R		D	D	D	D	
	L		D	D			
Bone+ ER-3	R			D		D	
	L						

B.

		250	500	1000	2000	4000	8000
Supra-aural	R	D	D	D	D	D	D
	L	D	D				D?
Insert	R	D	D				
	L	D	D				D?
Bone+ TDH	R	D	D	D	D	D	
	L	D	D				
Bone+ ER-3	R	D	D				
	L	D	D				

7.13

A. Indicate masker level used in non-test ear.

AC	NTE	250	500	1000	2000	4000	8000
Min	R		30		40	55	45
	L						
Max	R		65		65	75	75
	L						
BC		250	500	1000	2000	4000	8000
Min	R	55	45	45	40	55	
	L						
Max	R	55	65	65	65	75	
	L						

B. Indicate masker level used in non-test ear.

AC	NTE	250	500	1000	2000	4000	8000
Min	R						
	L		25	15	20		
Max	R						
	L		60	55	60		
BC		250	500	1000	2000	4000	8000
Min	R						
	L	30	25	15	20	25	
Max	R						
	L	60	60	55	60	60	

7.14

Case A.

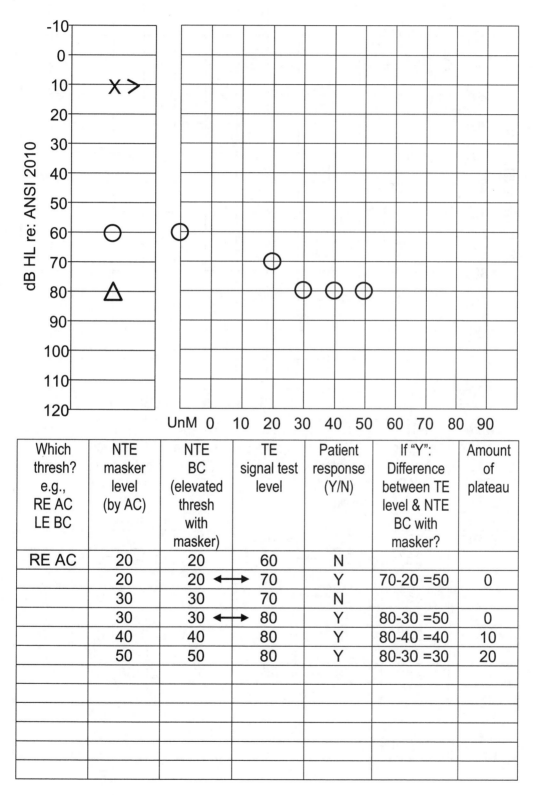

Which thresh? e.g., RE AC LE BC	NTE masker level (by AC)	NTE BC (elevated thresh with masker)	TE signal test level	Patient response (Y/N)	If "Y": Difference between TE level & NTE BC with masker?	Amount of plateau
RE AC	20	20	60	N		
	20	20 ⟷	70	Y	70-20 =50	0
	30	30	70	N		
	30	30 ⟷	80	Y	80-30 =50	0
	40	40	80	Y	80-40 =40	10
	50	50	80	Y	80-30 =30	20

Case B.

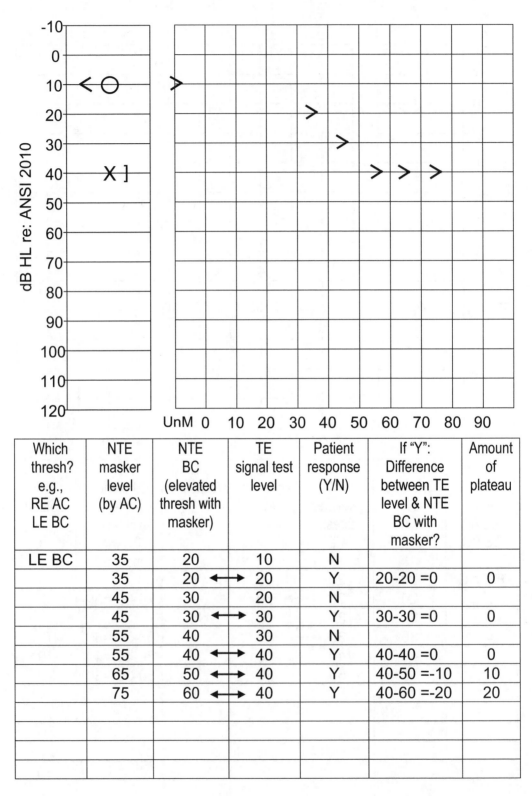

Which thresh? e.g., RE AC LE BC	NTE masker level (by AC)	NTE BC (elevated thresh with masker)	TE signal test level	Patient response (Y/N)	If "Y": Difference between TE level & NTE BC with masker?	Amount of plateau
LE BC	35	20	10	N		
	35	20 ↔ 20	20	Y	20-20 =0	0
	45	30	20	N		
	45	30 ↔ 30	30	Y	30-30 =0	0
	55	40	30	N		
	55	40 ↔ 40	40	Y	40-40 =0	0
	65	50 ↔ 40	40	Y	40-50 =-10	10
	75	60 ↔ 40	40	Y	40-60 =-20	20

Case C.

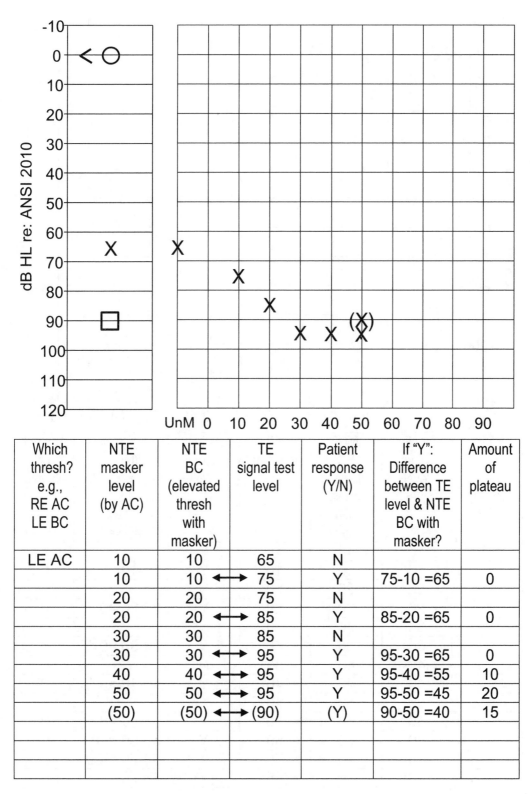

Which thresh? e.g., RE AC LE BC	NTE masker level (by AC)	NTE BC (elevated thresh with masker)	TE signal test level	Patient response (Y/N)	If "Y": Difference between TE level & NTE BC with masker?	Amount of plateau
LE AC	10	10	65	N		
	10	10 ←→	75	Y	75-10 =65	0
	20	20	75	N		
	20	20 ←→	85	Y	85-20 =65	0
	30	30	85	N		
	30	30 ←→	95	Y	95-30 =65	0
	40	40 ←→	95	Y	95-40 =55	10
	50	50 ←→	95	Y	95-50 =45	20
	(50)	(50) ←→	(90)	(Y)	90-50 =40	15

Case D.

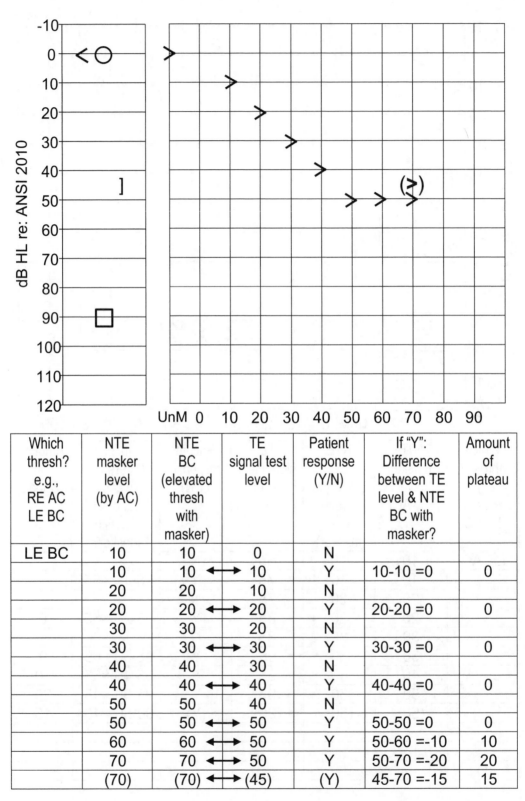

Which thresh? e.g., RE AC LE BC	NTE masker level (by AC)	NTE BC (elevated thresh with masker)	TE signal test level	Patient response (Y/N)	If "Y": Difference between TE level & NTE BC with masker?	Amount of plateau
LE BC	10	10	0	N		
	10	10 ⟷	10	Y	10-10 =0	0
	20	20	10	N		
	20	20 ⟷	20	Y	20-20 =0	0
	30	30	20	N		
	30	30 ⟷	30	Y	30-30 =0	0
	40	40	30	N		
	40	40 ⟷	40	Y	40-40 =0	0
	50	50	40	N		
	50	50 ⟷	50	Y	50-50 =0	0
	60	60 ⟷	50	Y	50-60 =-10	10
	70	70 ⟷	50	Y	50-70 =-20	20
	(70)	(70) ⟷	(45)	(Y)	45-70 =-15	15

Case E.

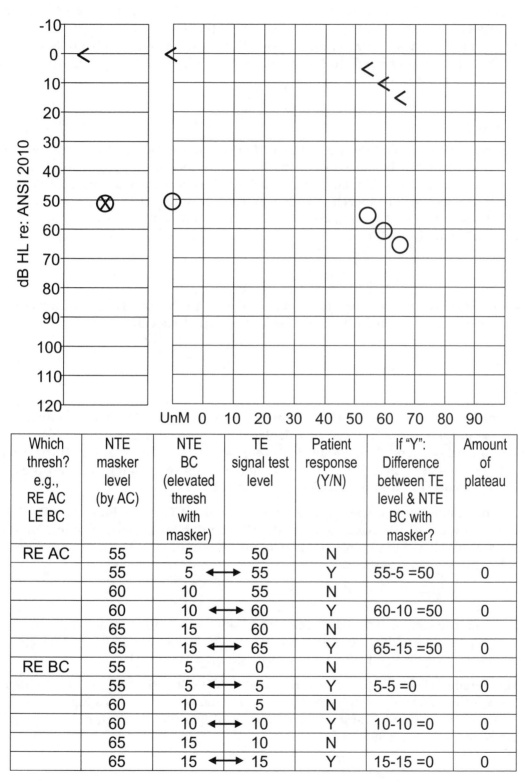

Which thresh? e.g., RE AC LE BC	NTE masker level (by AC)	NTE BC (elevated thresh with masker)	TE signal test level	Patient response (Y/N)	If "Y": Difference between TE level & NTE BC with masker?	Amount of plateau
RE AC	55	5	50	N		
	55	5 ↔	55	Y	55-5 =50	0
	60	10	55	N		
	60	10 ↔	60	Y	60-10 =50	0
	65	15	60	N		
	65	15 ↔	65	Y	65-15 =50	0
RE BC	55	5	0	N		
	55	5 ↔	5	Y	5-5 =0	0
	60	10	5	N		
	60	10 ↔	10	Y	10-10 =0	0
	65	15	10	N		
	65	15 ↔	15	Y	15-15 =0	0

7.15

For supra-aural headphones, it would be necessary to mask whenever the dB level of the presented speech stimuli in the test ear exceeds any of the pure-tone BC thresholds (from 250 to 4000 Hz) in the non-test ear by 40 dB or more. For insert earphones, it would be necessary to mask whenever the presented level of the speech stimuli exceeds any of the pure-tone BC thresholds in the non-test ear by 55 dB or more.

7.16

Whenever masking is needed for the SRT, masking would also be needed when determining the WRS. However, it may be necessary to mask for the WRS even if masking was not needed in determination of the SRT. Similar to SRT masking, it is necessary to mask for WRS, when the presentation level of the speech stimuli minus the IA value of the transducer (40 dB HL for headphones and 55 dB HL for inserts) is greater than any of the BC thresholds in the non-test ear (from 250 to 4000 Hz).

7.17

The speech noise masker contains a band of frequencies above 1000 Hz at an attenuation rate of 12 dB per octave to be similar to the overall spectrum of speech.

7.18

Case A.

SRT: Minimum masking = 25 dB HL; maximum masking = 85 dB HL. The minimum level of speech noise needed in the NTE can be calculated by subtracting the IA value from the SRT presentation level (PL) and then adding 5 dB to guard against overmasking. For this patient, this would be 60 − 40 + 5 = 25 dB. The maximum amount of masking is 50 dB (best BC in the TE) + 40 − 5 dB (to avoid overmasking) = 85 dB HL.

WRS: The minimum level of speech noise needed in the NTE for a PL of 80 dB HL would be 80 − 40 + 5 = 45 dB HL. For a PL of 95 dB HL, the minimum amount of masking would increase to 60 dB HL (95 − 40 + 5). The maximum amount of masking, without overmasking = 85 dB HL, the same as for the SRT.

Case B.

SRT: Minimum masking = 30 dB HL; maximum masking = 100 dB HL. The minimum masking level for this patient would be 80 − 55 + 5 = 30 dB. The maximum amount of masking is 50 (best BC in the TE) + 55 − 5 dB (to avoid overmasking) = 100 dB HL.

WRS: The minimum level of speech noise needed in NTE for a PL of 95 dB HL would be 95 − 55 + 5 = 45 dB HL. For a PL of 105 dB HL, the minimum amount of masking would increase to 55 dB HL (105 − 55 + 5). The maximum amount of masking, without overmasking = 100 dB HL, the same as for the SRT.

Case C.

SRT: Minimum masking = 20 dB HL; maximum masking = 75 dB HL. The minimum masking level for this patient would be 55 − 40 + 5 = 20 dB. The maximum amount of masking would be 40 (best BC in the TE) + 40 − 5 = 75 dB HL.

WRS: The minimum level of speech noise needed in NTE for a PL of 70 dB HL would be 70 dB − 40 dB + 5 = 35 dB HL. For a PL of 85 dB HL, the minimum amount of masking would increase to 50 dB HL (85 − 40 + 5). The maximum amount of masking, without overmasking = 75 dB HL, the same as for the SRT.

7.19

Output limits based on Table 5–2 from Chapter 5.

A.

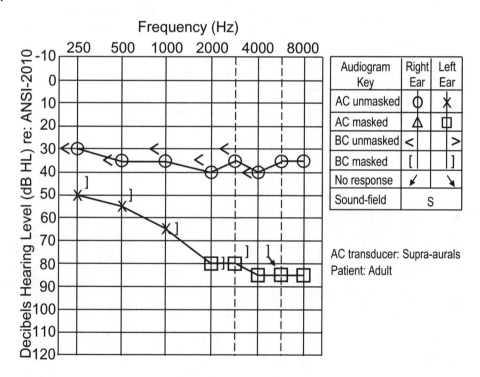

B.

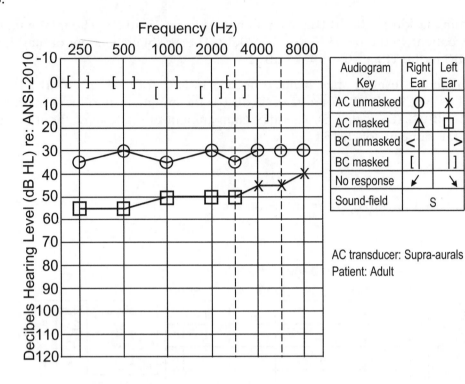

AC transducer: Supra-aurals
Patient: Adult

C.

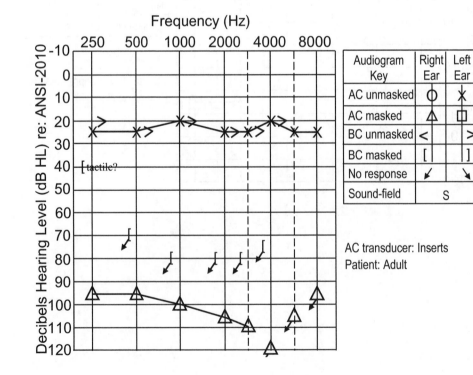

AC transducer: Inserts
Patient: Adult

8 Answers for Immittance

8.1

A. The probe-tone generator/speaker produces a pure tone (usually 226 Hz at 85 dB SPL) that is delivered through the probe assembly to the ear canal. The changes in the level of this probe tone are used to estimate how the admittance of the outer and middle is affected during tympanometry and acoustic reflex testing. In some applications, higher frequency probe tones or probe tones that are swept across a range of frequencies are used instead of only using 226 Hz.

B. The microphone is used to measure/monitor the dB SPL of the probe tone in the ear canal.

C. The automatic gain control (AGC) automatically adjusts the level of the probe tone as it is being measured by the microphone in the ear canal in order to maintain the probe tone at 85 dB SPL. The changes in the AGC are used as estimates of the changes in admittance, i.e., if the AGC increases the dB SPL of the probe tone to maintain 85 dB SPL, this implies that there is an increase in admittance (more of the probe tone energy is admitted by the ear).

D. The air-pressure pump (manometer) is used to apply air pressure during tympanometry. The applied pressure is usually swept from +200 daPa to −400 daPa relative to atmospheric pressure (indicated by 0 daPa on the tympanogram).

E. The reflex-eliciting tones (typically 500, 1000, and 2000 Hz) are individually delivered to either of the ears at varying levels in order to try to determine the level that activates the bilateral acoustic reflex. Activation of the stapedius muscle results in a decrease in admittance as monitored by a change in the dB SPL of the probe tone (see above). When the reflex-eliciting tone is delivered to the same ear as the probe tone, it is referred to as the ipsilateral reflex; when the reflex-eliciting tone is delivered to the ear without the probe tone, it is referred to as the contralateral reflex.

8.2

A. The acoustic equivalent volume of the ear canal (V_{ea}) is related to the admittance, in units of mmho or mL, that is measured by the immittance instrument at +200 daPa, which, therefore, provides an assessment of the admittance associated only with the ear canal (as the tympanic membrane is rendered nonfunctional by the applied air pressure). The measured V_{ea} is based on the admittance of calibrated cavity sizes, and compared to the expected range of normal ear canals for different ages. The V_{ea} can provide information about the status of the tympanic membrane. For example, a larger than normal V_{ea} suggests a perforation or the presence of a patent pressure equalization tube; a smaller than normal V_{ea} suggests an obstructed ear canal (e.g., impacted cerumen). Normal ranges for V_{ea} can be found in Table 8–1 for different age ranges.

B. The admittance at the tympanic membrane (Y_{tm}) is the amount of admittance, in units of mmho or mL, that is associated only with the middle ear, i.e., after the admittance of the ear canal is subtracted out. The Y_{tm} is the height of the tympanogram along the y-axis from the point measured at +200 to the peak of the tympanogram. Normal ranges for Y_{tm} can be found in Table 8–1 for different age ranges.

C. The tympanometric peak pressure (TPP) is the point along the x-axis of the tympanogram, in units of daPa, that corresponds to the maximum admittance, i.e., the pressure associated with the peak admittance of the tympanogram. If a peak admittance is not present (e.g., the line is flat), the TPP is usually designated as "No Peak" (NP). Normal ranges for TPP can be found in Table 8–1 for different age ranges.

D. The tympanometric width (TW) is a calculation, in daPa, that characterizes the width of the tympanogram at half of its height. It is obtained by finding the absolute value of the difference, in daPa, associated with the intersections of the half-height values for the negative and positive intersections drawn downward to the x-axis pressure scale. Normal ranges for TW can be found in Table 8–1 for different age ranges.

8.3

A non-compensated (baseline-off) tympanogram is an option available in many immittance instruments in which the tester can choose to plot/graph the admittance value that includes both the V_{ea} and the Y_{tm}. A compensated (baseline-on) tympanogram is an option selected by the tester to plot the tympanogram "normalized," in which the instrument automatically subtracts out the admittance of V_{ea} and only plots the Y_{tm}. In a compensated tympanogram, the value of the V_{ea} is displayed as a number alongside the tympanogram. The compensated method of plotting tympanograms is typically used clinically when measuring with a 226 Hz probe tone; however, the non-compensated method is used when using higher frequency probe tones.

8.4

A. This tracing shows a flat tympanogram (compensated), as characterized by low admittance with no change in admittance across the pressure range, known as a

Type B. Disorders associated with a flat tympanogram include otitis media with effusion, a perforation or patient pressure equalization tube, or impacted cerumen. In many cases, the associated disorder for a flat tympanogram can be differentiated by the accompanying V_{ea} (see 8.2.A)

B. This tracing shows a normal tympanogram (compensated), characterized by a peaked shape with normal Y_{tm} and TPP around 0 daPa, known as a Type A. Type A suggests normal middle ear function; however, sometimes otosclerosis or ossicular chain disarticulation can appear within the range of a normal tympanogram.

C. This tracing shows a high admittance tympanogram (compensated), characterized by a very high-peaked tracing above the normal range but with the TPP around 0 daPa, known as a Type A_d. A high admittance tympanogram is usually associated with an ossicular chain disarticulation/discontinuity.

D. This tracing shows a negative pressure tympanogram (compensated), characterized by a peaked shape with either normal or reduced Y_{tm} but with a TPP in the negative pressure range (more negative than the normal range of TPP), known as a Type C. A negative pressure tympanogram suggests a temporary dysfunction of the eustachian tube or resolving stage of otitis media with effusion.

E. This tracing shows a reduced admittance tympanogram (compensated), characterized by a peaked shape that has a lower than normal Y_{tm} range but with the TPP around 0 daPa, known as a Type A_s. A reduced admittance tympanogram is typically associated with otosclerosis or in some cases of otitis media.

8.5

The TW is approximately 200 daPa (/−270 to −70/). Based on data shown in Table 8–1 this tympanogram is wider than the expected normal range.

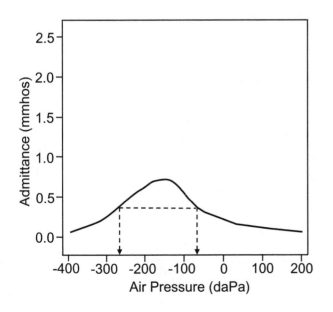

8.6

These two examples are non-compensated tympanograms; V_{ea} and Y_{tm} can be obtained from the tympanogram.

A. V_{ea} = 1.5 mmho
   Y_{tm} = 0.5 mmho
   TPP = −160 daPa
   TW = 200 daPa

B. V_{ea} = 0.5 mmho
   Y_{tm} = 1.0 mmho
   TPP = 0 daPa
   TW = 70 daPa

8.7

These two examples are compensated tympanograms; V_{ea} is not directly available from the tympanogram but would be printed out as a number. For these examples, the V_{ea} was obtained from Table 8–1.

A. V_{ea} (assume a perforation) = 3.5 mmho
   Y_{tm} = No peak (NP)
   TPP = No peak (NP)
   TW = Could not be calculated (NP)

B. V_{ea} = 0.7 mmho (or any value in the normal range)
   Y_{tm} = 1.3 mmho
   TPP = −290 daPa
   TW = 70 daPa

8.8

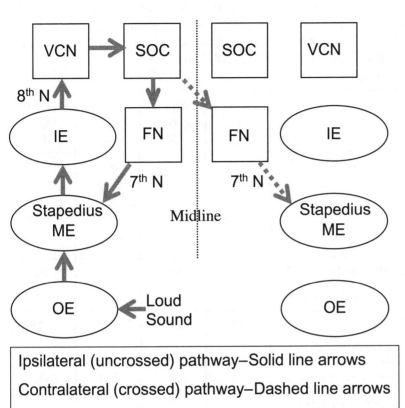

8.9

The middle ear acoustic reflex threshold (ART) is either determined by the tester or automatically determined by some instruments. A typical strategy is to select the lowest dB HL of a reflex-eliciting tone that produces an admittance change of at least 0.02 mmho. The ART should also be verified by:

1. Ruling out any artifact by testing at a low level, i.e., there should not be any response.
2. Showing that the response is repeatable (at least once) at the value to be selected as the ART.
3. Showing that there is a larger (growth) deflection when tested at a level 5 dB higher than the value considered to be the ART.

8.10

The answers shown here are the expected ranges for expected ARTs based on Gelfand et al., (1990). Clinically, one would have a single value that occurs within these expected ranges. Note: NR = no response (absent) at upper test limit. Upper limit of instrument assumed to be 115 dB HL; if upper limit is 110 dB HL, results could vary slightly.

		R Ipsi	Stim L Probe R	L Ipsi	Stim R Probe L
1	RE: Normal hearing and function LE: 45 dB conductive loss	≤95	NR	NR	NR
2	RE: 60 dB cochlear loss LE: 40 dB cochlear loss	≤110	≤95	≤95	≤110
3	RE: Impacted cerumen; 15 dB air–bone gap LE: 7th N problem distal to stapedial branch	NR	NR	≤95	100–115
4	RE: 70 dB cochlear loss LE: Normal hearing and function	≤115	≤95	≤95	≤115
5	RE: 8th N tumor; mild sensorineural loss LE: Normal hearing with small perforation	NR	≤95	NR	NR
6	RE: 40 dB cochlear loss LE: 40 dB conductive loss	≤95	NR	NR	NR
7	RE: 50 dB cochlear loss LE: 70 dB mixed loss (with 40 dB ABG)	≤100	NR	NR	NR
8	RE: 7th N proximal to stapedial branch LE: Normal hearing and function	NR	NR	≤95	≤95
9	RE: 25 dB conductive loss LE: 25 dB conductive loss	NR	NR	NR	NR
10	RE: 35 dB cochlear loss LE: normal hearing with patent PE tube	≤95	≤95	NR	NR
11	RE: Normal hearing and function LE: 8th nerve tumor with 50 dB loss	≤95	NR	NR	≤95
12	RE: 35 dB cochlear loss LE: 45 dB cochlear loss	≤95	≤95	≤95	≤95

		R Ipsi	Stim L Probe R	L Ipsi	Stim R Probe L
13	RE: 40 dB mixed loss (15 dB ABG) LE: 40 dB cochlear loss	100–115	NR	≤95	100–115
14	RE: 25 dB conductive loss; perforation LE: Normal hearing and function	NR	NR	≤95	100–115
15	Both ears normal hearing, but with intra-axial brainstem tumor	≤95	NR	≤95	NR

8.11

Acoustic reflex decay is typically measured using a contralateral recording setup (because it has a higher output range) with the stimulus being presented to the suspect ear. The reflex-eliciting tone (500 or 1000 Hz) is presented at a level that is 10 dB higher than the patient's acoustic reflex threshold (ART), and the stimulus is presented continuously for 10 s. Abnormal acoustic reflex decay would show a relatively large acoustic reflex deflection at the onset of stimulation, followed by a return toward baseline (decay) of at least 50% of its deflection height/amount within 5 seconds of stimulation. Abnormal acoustic reflex decay is a reflection of abnormal neural adaptation that suggests an 8th cranial nerve tumor. Acoustic reflex decay testing can only be done if an ART was obtained and one can increase the stimulus 10 dB over the ART.

9 Answers for Otoacoustic Emissions (OAEs) and Auditory Brainstem Responses (ABRs)

9.1

Signal averaging is a computer-based software program (part of the recording instrument) in which the physiologic activity that is being recorded is sampled repeatedly over a specified time interval. Any response that is in the same time period during the recording epoch will accumulate/build in magnitude over repeated trials, whereas any physiologic randomly occurring "noise" will be reduced in magnitude during the same trials. For stimulus evoked responses like OAEs and ABRs, which are very low level physiologic responses, the time-locked recorded activity will be enhanced and the background noise will be reduced.

9.2

Otoacoustic emissions (OAEs) are very low level acoustic signals recorded from the ear canal with a sensitive microphone. The source of the OAE is a normal functioning cochlea, specifically the outer hair cells (OHCs). The OHCs produce activity on the basilar membrane resulting in vibrational activity (reverse traveling wave) that travels through the middle ear to create acoustic vibrations in the ear canal. Traditionally, the two main types of evoked OAE are transient (click) evoked otoacoustic emissions (TEOAE) and distortion product otoacoustic emission (DPOAE).

9.3

Distortion products are frequencies that are not part of the signal delivered to the ear, and are generated due to the ear's nonlinearity. For example, if two tones are delivered to the ear, the nonlinearities create combination tones, difference tones, as well as more complex arithmetic interactions of the two tones. The distortion component/product most often used for clinical DPOAE testing is called the cubic difference tone, $2f_1 - f_2$ (i.e., two times the lower frequency tone minus the higher frequency tone). The $2f_1 - f_2$ is typically recorded by stimulating the ear with two tones (called primary tones) that are relatively close together ($f_2/f_1 = 1.22$).

A. If $f_2 = 1000$ Hz, then $f_1 = 819$ Hz. The $2f_1 - f_2$ distortion product would be 638 Hz.

B. If $f_2 = 2000$ Hz, then $f_1 = 1639$ Hz. The $2f_1 - f_2$ distortion product would be 1278 Hz.

C. If $f_2 = 4000$ Hz, then $f_1 = 3278$ Hz. The $2f_1 - f_2$ distortion product would be 2556 Hz.

9.4

Spontaneous otoacoustic emissions (SOAEs) are low level emissions (in many cases lower than evoked OAEs) that occur without any externally applied signal. The SOAEs are recorded in the ear canal during a specified period of time (e.g., 1–2 minutes) and the frequency components (spectrum) are displayed. There are typically 3–4 identifiable frequencies between 1000 and 8000 Hz. The source of these emissions is the normally functioning OHCs, similar to that of evoked OAEs. However, SOAEs are not (yet) used clinically, primarily because not all normal ears have SOAEs large enough to be measured. In addition, less is known about these emissions and how they relate to normal cochlear conditions or abnormal cochlear conditions (more research is needed).

9.5

Signals used to evoke OAEs travel through the middle ear, and the low level OAEs generated in the cochlea must travel back out through the middle ear to be recorded at the entrance to the ear canal. Even in a normal functioning middle ear, the reverse transmission through the middle ear causes considerable loss of energy. When the middle ear function is compromised, the OAE energy is significantly reduced and usually becomes too small to be measured in the ear canal.

9.6

A. TEOAEs are typically considered present (normal) when the emission level is at least 3 dB (ideally 6 dB) above the dB level of the noise (called noise floor), i.e., signal-to-noise ratio (SNR) = 3 or more. This criterion is used for each of the frequency regions being measured to indicate normal or abnormal response.

B. DPOAEs are typically considered present (normal) when the emission level is at least 6 dB above the dB level of the noise, i.e., the SNR = 6 or more. This criterion is used for each of the frequency regions being measured to indicate whether the response is considered to be normal or absent (abnormal). Many instruments also allow recording of the absolute levels of the noise and emissions and then relate the emission levels to a template that represents the expected normal range, questionable range, or not-present range. The template approach is used more often with DPOAEs than with TEOAEs.

9.7

A. If OAEs are found to be normal (appropriate level above the noise floor), it is reasonable to infer that the OHCs are functioning normally, the middle ear is functioning normally, and there are no problems in the outer ear. Normal OAEs only reflect the physiologic function of the ear up to the level of the OHCs and do not provide any information regarding the patient's actual hearing ability, which could be affected by other parts of the auditory system and his/her ability/willingness to respond to sounds.

B. If OAEs are found to be abnormal (no measurable emission above the noise floor), one does not know if the problem is originating in the outer ear, middle ear (conductive loss), and/or OHCs (cochlear loss or mixed loss). Too much noise in the recording could also cause abnormal readings. Additional information about the patient and/or other tests would need to be completed to determine the source of the absent OAEs. Abnormal OAEs only reflect the physiologic function of the ear up to the level of the OHCs and do not provide any information regarding the patient's actual hearing ability, including type and degree of hearing loss. An absent OAE can occur with any degree of hearing loss above 30 dB HL.

9.8

A. Time-domain waveform of the applied signal (click) that is present in the ear canal. Although the stimuli are brief rectangular signals, there is some ringing of the signal in the ear canal. The example in the figure is an acceptable stimulus (indicating good probe placement).

B. Time-domain waveform of the OAE being measured in the ear canal. As it is the response to a click, there is a wide distribution of frequencies in the wave, with the higher frequencies having the shorter latencies (coming from the base of the cochlea) and the lower frequencies having the longer latencies (coming from the apex of the cochlea).

C. Level of the averaged TEOAE in the different recorded frequency bands (1–4 kHz).

D. Level of the averaged noise floor that was present in the patient in the different recorded frequency bands (1–4 kHz). The size of the TEOAE is the difference between D and C.

9.9

A. These TEOAE recordings show normal emissions in both ears from 1 to 4 kHz. These results were based on the presence of signal-to-noise ratios (SNRs) well above 3 dB (see column on the right for each recording) in each of the frequency bands typically recorded for TEOAEs. In addition, the absolute level of the emission in each frequency band was fairly robust. These normal TEOAEs were also apparent in the well-defined and superimposed (repeatable) time-domain waveforms for each ear (top of figure) that demonstrated the presence of components with high frequencies (short latency) to lower frequencies (longer latencies).

B. These TEOAE recordings show no emissions in the frequency bands, except for 2 kHz in the right ear. These results were based on the signal-to-noise ratios (SNRs) that were well below the minimum of 3 dB (see column on the right for each recording), except at 2 kHz in which the SNR was 10.4 dB. Looking at the time-domain waveforms, the superimposed (repeatable) semi-sinusoidal response was seen and was consistent with the presence of a response in the 2 kHz band. For the left ear, the noise levels were fairly high, and no emissions above the noise were found, i.e., SNRs considerably less than 3 dB. The noisy recordings and lack of emissions were also apparent in the time-domain waveform for the left ear.

9.10

A. The DPOAE recording for the right ear shows normal emissions from 1 to 2 kHz and no emissions above 2 kHz (consistent with a high frequency deficit). This is based on the presence of signal-to-noise ratios (SNRs) that are above 6 dB from 1 to 2 kHz and below 6 dB above 2 kHz (see column on the right of each recording). In addition, the absolute levels of the emissions are in the expected normal ranges for 1–2 kHz, but extremely small/not present above 2 kHz. The DPOAE recording for the left ear shows no emissions in any of the frequency bands. This is based on the SNRs that are well below 6 dB.

B. These DPOAE recordings show normal emissions in both ears from 1 to 6 kHz. These results were based on the presence of signal-to-noise ratios (SNRs) well above 6 dB (see column on the right for each recording) in each of the frequency bands typically recorded for DPOAEs. In addition, the absolute level of the emission in each frequency band was fairly robust.

Note: DPOAE recording instruments may also provide a template of the normal expected DPOAE levels as a function of frequency that is displayed on the recording screen. With this method, the patient's recorded DPOAEs can be compared with the normal template to determine if the responses are normal or not.

9.11

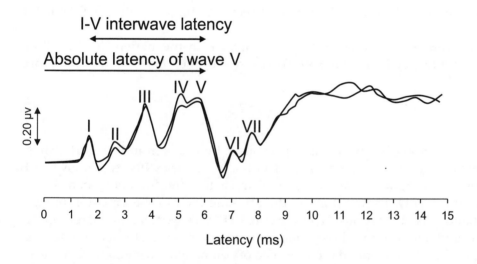

The following is based on animal studies by Møller (1994):

Wave I: Distal part of 8th nerve entering/within the internal auditory canal.

Wave II: Proximal part of 8th nerve within/exiting the internal auditory canal.

Wave III: Ipsilateral cochlear nucleus (pontine region of the brainstem).

Wave IV: Superior olivary complex, primarily contralateral to ear stimulated.

Wave V: Lateral lemniscus and input to the inferior colliculus (midbrain region of the brainstem), primarily contralateral to ear stimulated.

9.12

A. Absolute latency is the time, in milliseconds (ms), from the onset of the presentation of the stimulus as indicated by the beginning of the recording window, to the wave of interest.

B. Interpeak latency (IPL) is the time difference (ms) between any of the waves. The most often used IPLs are I–III, III–V, I–V.

C. Interaural latency difference (ILD) is the time difference between ears for the wave of interest. Wave V is most often used to calculate the ILD.

D. Amplitude is the size, in microvolts (μv), from the positive wave of interest to the negative trough immediately following the positive wave. Amplitude can also be measured (in μv) from the baseline to the positive wave or negative trough, although this is not typically used with ABR recordings.

E. Amplitude ratio is the comparison of the amplitude of one wave to another wave. This is typically done comparing wave V amplitude with that of wave I, i.e., V/I amplitude ratio.

9.13

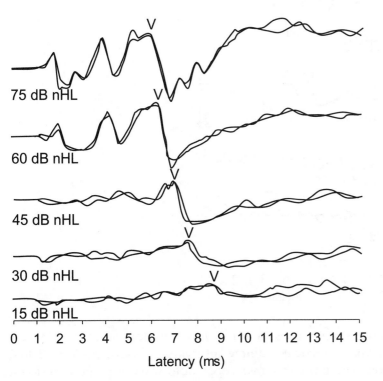

In a normal functioning ear, as intensity decreases, the earlier waves tend to not be identifiable and only wave V is robust enough to be identified. Wave V shows a systematic *increase* in latency as intensity is decreased. For those identifiable waves, the latencies increase by a similar amount, thus the interpeaklatencies (IPLs) remain constant. In addition, the amplitudes of the waves *decrease* as intensity decreases, and typically only wave V can be seen at the lower intensities.

9.14

The click evoked ABR outcomes, recorded at a high intensity, that would be expected in an ear with an acoustic neuroma (vestibular schwannoma) may include any of the following:

- Presence of only wave I.
- Abnormal (more than +2 standard deviations) of IPL for I–III (as well as I–V).
- No identifiable waves even though there is sufficient hearing to expect an ABR.
- Reduced V/I amplitude ratio.

9.15

A.

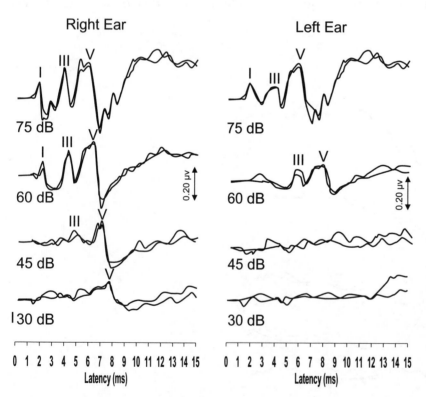

The right ear shows repeatable wave V responses down to levels as low as at least 30 dB nHL with normal latencies and normal interpeak latency intervals for I–III, III–V, and I–V, suggesting normal auditory function. The left ear shows repeatable wave V responses down to 60 dB nHL, but no responses at lower levels. The wave V latency at 75 dB HL was in the normal range (similar to right ear) consistent with a moderate cochlear hearing loss. Neural function was normal, as evident by the normal interpeak latency intervals for I–III, III–V, and I–V (similar to right ear).

B.

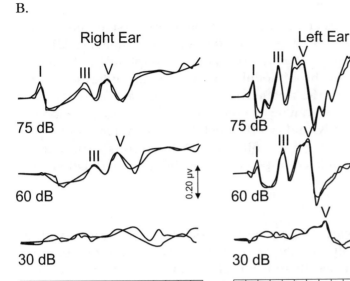

The left ear shows repeatable wave V responses down to levels as low as at least 30 dB nHL with normal latencies and normal interpeak latency intervals for I–III, III–V, and I–V, suggesting normal auditory function. The right ear shows repeatable wave V responses down to 60 dB nHL, but no clear repeatable waves at 30 dB nHL. The interpeak latency intervals for I–III and I–V are prolonged (greater than +2 standard deviations) relative to normal expectations. In addition, the interaural latency differences for waves III and V are significantly prolonged. The results for the right ear are consistent with an acoustic neuroma (vestibular schwannoma).

9.16

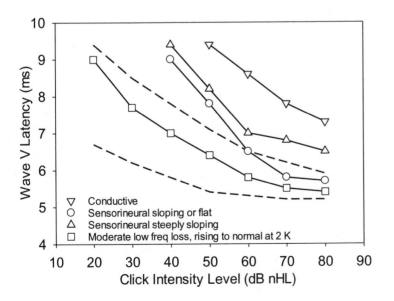

9.17

The auditory steady-state response (ASSR) is an additional technique used to measure evoked electrical responses at the level of the brainstem. It is recorded in a manner similar to ABR, but with stimuli that have carrier frequencies (e.g., 1000 Hz) that are then amplitude or frequency modulated at different rates. Detection of these modulations can be an indication of the patient's ability to respond to the various carrier frequencies. One of the benefits of the ASSR (over ABR) is that multiple carrier frequencies can be combined (e.g., chirps) to get responses from many frequency regions simultaneously, and can be much faster than doing frequency-specific ABRs. Rather than plot the waveform (as in ABR), the ASSR performs a spectral and phase analyses to see if there are stimulus-related responses at the different modulation rates.

9.18

If one found normal OAEs in a patient with a significant sensorineural hearing loss (with no conductive involvement), this would imply that the hearing problem is either due to a loss of only the inner hair cells (very rare) or that there is a problem in the 8th cranial nerve or central auditory system. Another possibility would be pseudohypoacusis.

The presence of normal OAEs and absent ABRs is an indication that there is something abnormal with the 8th nerve. This pattern is typically characteristic of auditory neuropathy spectrum disorder (auditory dyssynchrony), a congenital disorder.

10 Answers for Screening for Hearing Loss

10.1

The primary goal of an EHDI program is to identify permanent and significant hearing loss that can affect and/or delay development of audition and speech-language abilities, which if left untreated would impact educational and psychological factors.

10.2

An effective screening test should be:

- Reasonably safe
- Acceptable to society
- Cost-effective
- Initiated as early as possible

10.3

Validity refers to how well a test measures what it was designed to measure. Reliability refers to the consistency of test results upon repeated administration of the test by one or more people.

10.4

Universal screening is a test that is performed with a relatively large population, such as hearing screening of all newborns. Targeted screening is performed with a subgroup of the larger population, such as newborn infants who are at high risk for hearing loss. Targeted screening is more cost-effective and, as it focuses on a population with a higher prevalence rate of the disorder, will improve the positive predictive value (PPV) of the test.

10.5

(a) Initial screening performed at birth (usually before the infant is discharged from the hospital).

(b) Follow-up screening performed at birth (after initial screening) or within 1 month.

(c) Diagnostic testing of those who fail the screening by three months of age.

(d) Initiation of treatment of those confirmed to have a hearing loss by six months of age.

10.6

(Answers may vary)

* Quick to administer (can be completed in approximately 10 minutes).

* Automated decision analysis eliminates the need for a professional to make a pass/fail interpretation/decision.

* Considered to have good reliability and validity.

* Have acceptable outcomes, including referral rates and false positive rates of approximately 2%.

10.7

1. In the presence of any outer or middle ear involvement, such as vernix/debris in the ear canal or middle ear fluid, the OAE response will be absent due to the conductive component.

2. Infants with auditory dyssynchrony (auditory neuropathy spectrum disorder) will be missed because this disorder is characterized by normal OAEs (good OHCs hair cell function) and abnormal ABRs (poor neural synchrony).

10.8

According to the ASHA (2017) and/or AAA (2011) guidelines for hearing screening, school-aged children should be screened at 1000, 2000, and 4000 Hz, at a presentation level of 20 dB HL. Adults should be screened at the same frequencies, using a presentation level of 25 dB HL.

10.9

(Answers may vary)

* Audiologists
* Speech-language pathologists
* Supervised graduate students
* Trained nurses
* Individuals holding an audiometrist certificate (this can vary by state)
* Supervised speech-language pathology aides and assistants
* Supervised audiology aides and assistants

10.10

If a child does not give an appropriate response at 20 dB HL for any of the three test frequencies (1000, 2000, or 4000 Hz) for either ear, the child would be considered to have "failed" the hearing screening and should be referred for a full audiologic evaluation.

10.11

A child should be referred for a medical evaluation if the hearing screening reveals any of the following:

- Structural abnormality of the ear
- Drainage in the ear canal
- Foreign object in the ear canal
- Impacted cerumen
- Suspected ear infection
- Tympanic membrane abnormal appearance
- Tympanic membrane perforation (not due to the presence of a pressure equalization tube)

10.12

The addition of 500 Hz for pure-tone screening is recommended if tympanometry is not included in the screening program. This is only appropriate if the test environment has acceptable background noise levels, as high levels of background noise or intermittent distracting sounds could make 500 Hz difficult to detect and lead to a false positive outcome.

10.13

1. True positive (TP) (a.k.a. a hit): This would occur when the test correctly identifies the presence of hearing loss.
2. True negative (TN): This would occur when the test correctly identifies the absence of hearing loss.
3. False positive (FP): This would occur when the test incorrectly identifies the presence of hearing loss (i.e., identifies the individual as having a hearing loss when he or she actually does not have a hearing loss).
4. False negative (FN) (a.k.a. a miss): This would occur when the test incorrectly identifies the absence of hearing loss (i.e., identifies the individual as not having a hearing loss when he or she actually does have a hearing loss).

10.14

1. Sensitivity defines how well a test correctly identifies the targeted disorder. It indicates the proportion of TPs to all individuals whose test result indicates the disorder is present, i.e., TP / (TP + FN).
2. Specificity defines how well a test correctly identifies individuals without the targeted disorder. It indicates the proportion of TNs to all individuals whose test result indicates the disorder is absent, i.e., TN / (TN + FP).

3. Positive predictive value indicates the percentage of people who actually have the disease among all who test positive, i.e., TP / (TP + FP).

4. Negative predictive value indicates the percentage of people who actually do not have the disease among all who test negative, i.e., TN / (FN + TN).

10.15

Using 10 dB HL for screening would cause more individuals to fail the hearing screening than if 50 dB HL is used. Using 10 dB HL would greatly increase the test's sensitivity (the test would correctly identify more individuals who actually have a hearing loss); however, the test's specificity would decrease, with a corresponding increase in the number of false positives (the test would fail more individuals who have normal hearing). Using 50 dB HL for screening would cause more individuals to pass the screening than if 10 dB HL had been chosen. Using 50 dB HL would greatly increase the test's specificity (the test would correctly identify more individuals who have normal hearing); however, the test's sensitivity would decrease, with a corresponding increase in the number of false negatives (misses) (the test would pass more individuals who have a hearing loss. This example demonstrates that sensitivity and specificity are inversely related, i.e., as sensitivity increases, specificity decreases, and vice versa.

10.16

A. Sensitivity = TP / (TP + FN) = 15/18 = 83%

Specificity = TN / (TN + FP) = 422/445 = 95%

PPV = TP / (TP + FP) = 15/38 = 39%

NPV = TN / (TN + FN) = 422/425 = 99%

B. The sensitivity of this screening test was quite good, reflecting the fact that the test correctly identified hearing loss in 83% of the population tested, with a false negative (FN) rate of 17% (100%–83%). The specificity of this test indicates that the test correctly identified those without a hearing loss 95% of the time, with a very low false positive (FP) rate of 5% (100%–95%).

The positive predictive value (PPV) of this test suggests that of all individuals with a positive test result (TP + FP), only 39% will actually have a hearing loss. On the other hand, the negative predictive value (NPV) suggests that of all individuals who have a negative test result (TN + FN), 99% will not have a hearing loss.

10.17

A. Sensitivity = TP / (TP + FN) = 25/35 = 71%

Specificity = TN / (TN + FP) = 120/145 = 83%

PPV = TP/ (TP + FP) = 25/50 = 50%

NPV = TN / (TN + FN) = 120/130 = 92%

B. Sensitivity = TP / (TP + FN) = 50/70 = 71%

   Specificity = TN / (TN + FP) = 91/110 = 83%

   PPV = TP/ (TP + FP) = 50/69 = 72%

   NPV = TN / (TN + FN) = 91/111 = 82%

C. The sensitivity and specificity for the two populations tested are identical because both of these indices are measures of the specific test being given, regardless of the population being tested. The prevalence of the disease has no bearing on these measures.

D. When comparing PPV and NPV across the two populations (using the same test), it is evident that as disease prevalence increases, there is a corresponding increase in the PPV and a corresponding decrease in the NPV. With increased incidence of disease, the more probable it is that a positive test result will indicate the presence of the disease, and the less probable it is that a negative test result will indicate the absence of the disease.

11 Answers for Disorders of the Auditory System

11.1

A. outer ear; none

B. cochlea; sensorineural

C. middle ear; conductive or none

D. middle ear; conductive

E. outer ear; conductive

F. cochlea; sensorineural

G. cochlea, 8th nerve, and/or central; sensorineural

H. outer ear; none

I. 8th nerve; sensorineural

J. cochlea; sensorineural

K. cochlea; sensorineural

L. outer ear; none

M. middle ear; conductive

N. cochlea; sensorineural

O. cochlea (could also have ruptured tympanic membrane); sensorineural

P. middle ear (could also invade cochlea); conductive, sensorineural (or mixed) if cochlea affected

Q. outer ear; none

R. outer ear; conductive

S. 8th nerve or central; sensorineural

T. middle ear; conductive

U. cochlea; sensorineural

V. middle ear; none or slight conductive

W. outer ear; none or conductive if also has atresia

X. middle ear; conductive

Y. outer ear; none

11.2

A genetic hearing loss is a disorder that occurs due to abnormal gene expression, usually passed on through a hereditary/familial pathway, and is also called hereditary or familiar hearing loss; however, a genetic mutation can also occur spontaneously without a hereditary link. A genetic hearing loss can manifest itself at birth or with a later onset. Examples: connexin-26 gene mutation; hereditary syndromes like Down, Treacher-Collins, Goldenhar, Paget, Apert, Usher, Klippel-Feil, Waardenburg, Crouzon, Hunter, Mobius, etc.

A congenital hearing loss is one that is present at birth and can be due to hereditary factors, genetic mutations, infections, and other prenatal or perinatal trauma. Example: cytomegalovirus, high-risk factors, anoxia, CHARGE, and genetic losses (see above).

An acquired hearing loss is one that is not of hereditary or congenital origin but occurs any time after birth. Acquired hearing losses are usually caused by disease, infections, trauma, drugs, and/or aging, but can also be of unknown (idiopathic) origin.

11.3

An acute disorder/condition is one that is usually in its initial phase, comes on suddenly, and lasts a relatively short time. A chronic disorder/condition is one that persists over a period of time.

11.4

A. (otitis externa) Bacterial or fungal infection that causes an acute reaction to the skin lining of the external ear.

B. (exostoses) Repeated exposures to cycles of warm and cold water resulting in bony growths in the external auditory canal (a.k.a. surfer's ear).

C. (atresia) Congenital, developmental abnormality causing the absence of the external auditory canal in one or both ears.

D. (otitis media) Poor eustachian tube function, causing an accumulation of fluid in the middle ear that may become infected with bacteria, typically during an upper respiratory infection.

E. (cholesteatoma) Retraction pocket or congenital condition of the tympanic membrane in the affected ear that creates a benign cyst that grows due to dead skin that sluffs off and is trapped in the pocket, which can invade the middle ear.

F. (disarticulation) Trauma to the middle ear that results in a break in the ossicular chain of the affected ear.

G. (otosclerosis) Idiopathic or late-onset genetic cause that arises from an abnormal growth of bone around the stapes at the oval window, leading to fixation of the stapes or depositing of toxins into the cochlea in one or both ears.

H. (glomus tumor) Idiopathic (possibly hereditary), benign, slow-growing, highly vascularized tumor/mass in the middle ear arising from neural tissues either from the jugular bulb or other nerves around the promontory of the affected ear.

I. (Meniere's disease) Unknown cause/event (possibly viral, genetic predisposition, idiopathic) associated with an abnormal buildup of endolymph in the inner ear of one or both ears.

J. (presbycusis) Decline of hearing associated with aging due to damage of the hair cells, stria vascularis, and/or neural pathways, typically in both ears.

K. (autoimmune inner ear disease) Idiopathic condition whereby the body's cells begin to attack normal cells in one or both ears.

L. (acoustic trauma/noise-induced hearing loss) Excessive exposure to loud sounds causing damage to hair cells in both ears, and/or rupture of tympanic membrane in the affected ear.

M. (ototoxicity) Exposure to drugs and substances that systemically poison the auditory system, especially the hair cells in both ears.

N. (acoustic neuroma) Idiopathic/spontaneous benign tumor arising from the vestibular branch of the 8th cranial nerve, leading to an impingement/compression on the cochlear branch of the 8th cranial nerve in the affected ear.

O. (auditory dyssynchrony/neuropathy) Congenital abnormality of the 8th cranial nerve that disrupts the synchrony of the neural discharges, typically in both ears.

11.5

(Answers may vary; not all symptoms and treatments apply in each case)

A. (otitis externa)

Symptoms: Itchy/painful feeling in the ear canal, redness, fever in the affected ear(s).

Treatments: Topical antibiotics.

B. (exostoses)

Symptoms: None, unless debris/cerumen becomes trapped, causing an uncomfortable feeling in one or both ear canals.

Treatments: Surgical removal of the bony growths and/or cleaning out the ear canal(s).

C. (atresia)

Symptoms: Hearing loss in the affected ear(s)

Treatments: Bone conduction hearing aid, surgical reconstruction of the ear canal.

D. (otitis media)

Symptoms: Ear pain, fever, discharge, hearing loss.

Treatments: Wait and watch/follow-up monitoring, antibiotics, PE tubes.

E. (cholesteatoma)

Symptoms: Smelly discharge in the ear canal, possible hearing loss in the affected ear.

Treatments: Surgical removal of the cyst from the middle ear, antibiotics if needed.

F. (disarticulation)

Symptoms: Hearing loss in the affected ear.

Treatment: Ossicular chain reconstruction or bone conduction hearing aid.

G. (otosclerosis)

Symptoms: Hearing loss in the affected ear(s).

Treatments: Stapedectomy to replace the stapes with a prosthesis in the affected ear(s).

H. (glomus tumor)

Symptoms: Aural fullness, audible pulse/whooshing sound in the ear, ear pain (otalgia), hearing loss if it affects the middle ear structures of the pathological ear.

Treatments: Surgical removal of the tumor, reconstruction of the ossicles, a hearing aid if appropriate.

I. (Meniere's disease)

Symptoms: Vertigo, aural fullness, hearing loss, low-pitch tinnitus.

Treatments: Dietary reduction of salt/caffeine, diuretics, endolymphatic shunt, vestibular nerve section.

J. (presbycusis)

Symptoms: Hearing loss in both ears, difficulty understanding speech, possibility of high-pitched tinnitus.

Treatments: Hearing aids, counseling, speechreading.

K. (autoimmune inner ear disease)

Symptoms: Progressive hearing loss with relative sudden onset.

Treatments: Corticosteroids (hearing may improve with early treatment), hearing aid(s) if appropriate.

L. (acoustic trauma/noise-induced hearing loss)

Symptoms: High-pitched tinnitus, hearing loss of varying degrees, typically in both ears, possible perforation in the affected ear if exposed to loud impulse noise, speech perception difficulty (especially in noise).

Treatments: Hearing protection around noise, hearing aids if appropriate.

M. (ototoxicity)

Symptoms: Hearing loss, especially in the extended high frequencies in both ears, high-pitched tinnitus.

Treatment: Regular monitoring of hearing thresholds during drug administration, hearing aids if appropriate.

N. (acoustic neuroma)

Symptoms: High-pitched, unilateral tinnitus, asymmetric hearing loss, difficulty understanding speech, especially in the affected ear, e.g., when trying to use the telephone, possible balance problems.

Treatments: Surgical removal of the tumor, hearing aid if needed following surgery.

O. (auditory dyssynchrony/neuropathy)

Symptoms: Failed newborn auditory brainstem hearing screening, normal otoacoustic emissions. Hearing loss, poor speech-language development.

Treatments: Speech-language therapy, possible cochlear implant.

11.6

1. aminoglycosides
2. chemotherapeutic (neoplastic) agents
3. loop diuretics (hearing loss often reversible when treatment ended)
4. salicylates (hearing loss often reversible when treatment ended)

11.7

A longitudinal fracture is a temporal bone fracture from a closed head injury that occurs parallel to but not involving the petrous part of the temporal bone. A transverse fracture is a fracture that is perpendicular/transverse to the petrous part of the temporal bone that causes damage to the otic capsule. A large number of fractures are combinations of the above and are often called oblique fractures. An alternate classification scheme is to refer to the fracture as either involving the petrous part/otic capsule (inner ear), or not involving the petrous part/otic capsule. Longitudinal (non-otic capsule) fractures generally have conductive hearing losses due to fluid or other damage in the middle ear; transverse (otic capsule fractures) are more severe and result in sensorineural or mixed hearing losses.

11.8

Common reasons that a person might feign a hearing loss include:

- Financial gain
- Attention
- Excuse for some behavior or to get out of an activity
- Underlying psychological problem

11.9

The Stenger phenomenon is a psychoacoustic perception whereby a listener who is presented with a tone (typically 1000 Hz) or a word in both ears simultaneously will only perceive the louder of the two stimuli. For a patient suspected of feigning a hearing loss in the right ear (left ear thresholds normal) a tone or word is presented simultaneously at 10 dB below (softer) the patient's "threshold" in the right ear and 10 dB above (louder) the threshold in the left ear. If the patient is feigning a hearing loss in her right ear, she will not respond to the stimuli because she only hears the tone in her right ear, and as that is the ear she is pretending has a hearing loss, she does not admit to hearing it. If the patient is not feigning a hearing loss, she should respond because she only hears the tone in the left ear.

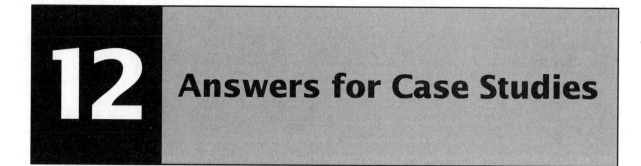

12 Answers for Case Studies

The answers provided for each of the cases are examples: Your data and descriptions can vary somewhat but should be consistent across tests and history, and your write-up should be based on your data.

Case Study 1

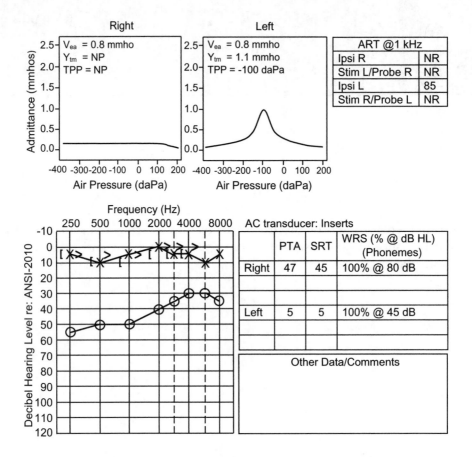

Results: Right ear showed a conductive loss, moderate through 2000 Hz and rising to mild in the higher frequencies. Left ear has normal hearing. Immittance testing revealed a flat tympanogram in the right ear and a normal tympanogram in the left ear; both ears had a normal acoustic equivalent volume (V_{ea}). Acoustic reflexes were absent for all conditions except left ipsilateral, consistent with a moderate conductive loss in the right ear and normal hearing in the left ear. Speech recognition thresholds were consistent with the pure-tone averages, and word recognition scores were excellent in both ears.

Impression/Diagnosis: Moderate conductive loss in right ear. Normal V_{ea} rules out impacted cerumen and perforation. Consistent with OTITIS MEDIA in right ear.

Recommendations: Medical referral for middle ear involvement and a repeat audiogram following treatment to ensure that the conductive component has resolved. Preferential seating at school should be considered until hearing improves.

Case Study 2

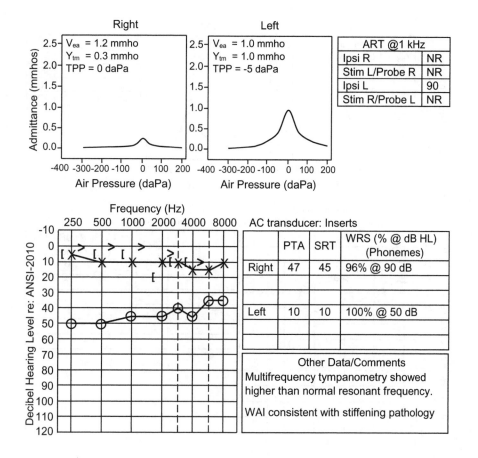

Results: Right ear showed a conductive loss, moderate through 4000 Hz and rising to mild in the higher frequencies. A dip (notch) in the BC threshold occurred at 2000 Hz for the right ear. Left ear showed normal hearing. Immittance testing revealed a reduced admittance tympanogram (Type A$_s$) in the right ear and a normal (Type A) tympanogram in the left ear; both ears had a normal acoustic equivalent volume (V$_{ea}$). Acoustic reflexes were absent for all conditions except left ipsilateral, consistent with a moderate conductive loss in the right ear and normal hearing in the left ear. Multifrequency tympanometry and wideband acoustic immittance were consistent with a stiffening pathology. Speech recognition thresholds were consistent with the pure-tone averages, and word recognition scores were excellent in both ears.

Impression/Diagnosis: Moderate conductive loss in right ear of gradual onset. Notch in BC at 2000 Hz (Carhart's notch), reduced admittance tympanogram, stiffening pathology on advanced immittance measures, and family history are consistent with OTOSCLEROSIS in right ear.

Recommendations: Medical referral for middle ear involvement and a repeat audiogram following treatment to ensure that the conductive component has resolved. A trial period with a hearing aid, with medical clearance, may be appropriate should medical intervention not be an option.

Case Study 3

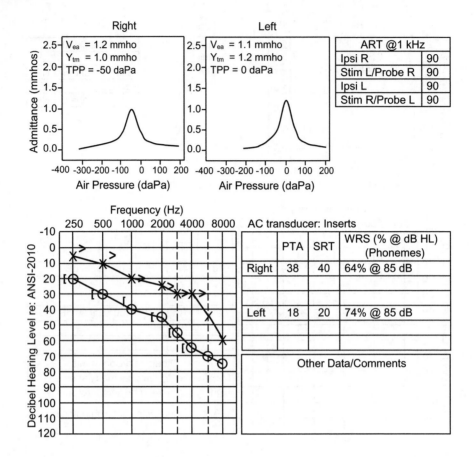

Results: Left ear showed hearing within the normal range through 2000 Hz, sloping to a moderately severe sensorineural loss in the higher frequencies. Right ear was about 20–30 dB poorer than the left ear, with hearing within the normal range at 250 Hz, sloping to severe in the higher frequencies. Immittance testing revealed normal tympanograms, and acoustic reflex thresholds (tested only at 1000 Hz) were present at normal levels, consistent with the degree of cochlear hearing loss at 1000 Hz based on data from Gelfand et al. (1990). Speech recognition thresholds were consistent with the pure-tone averages. Word recognition scores (WRSs) were fair. Although the right WRS was 10% poorer than the left WRS, these were not significantly different from each other based on critical difference values of the binomial distribution.

Impression/Diagnosis: Asymmetric sensorineural hearing loss, right ear poorer than left ear. Degree of hearing loss and speech results are consistent with her reported hearing and communication difficulties, which are most likely due to PRESBYCUSIS.

Recommendations: Trial period with binaural hearing aids, and aural rehabilitation as needed.

Case Study 4

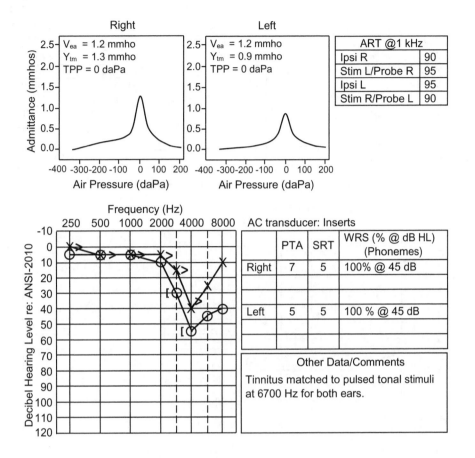

Results: Normal hearing except for a characteristic notched sensorineural hearing loss, bilaterally, with right ear about 15 dB poorer than left ear. Immittance testing revealed normal tympanograms and acoustic reflex thresholds (tested at 1000 Hz), consistent with normal puretone thresholds. Speech recognition thresholds were consistent with the pure-tone averages, and WRS was excellent, bilaterally.

Impression/Diagnosis: Bilateral, asymmetric, NOISE-INDUCED HEARING LOSS, most likely related to her reported use of firearms, police radio, and recreational vehicles. The slightly worse threshold at 4000 Hz for the right ear compared with the left ear may be due to her use of the police radio on her right shoulder (often without ear protection).

Recommendations: Consistent use of hearing protection devices when exposed to high levels of sound/noise. Periodic hearing evaluations to monitor any change in hearing loss. She was given information today about tinnitus; however, should she continue to be concerned about the tinnitus, she should consider being seen for a more complete tinnitus evaluation and discussion of treatment options.

Case Study 5

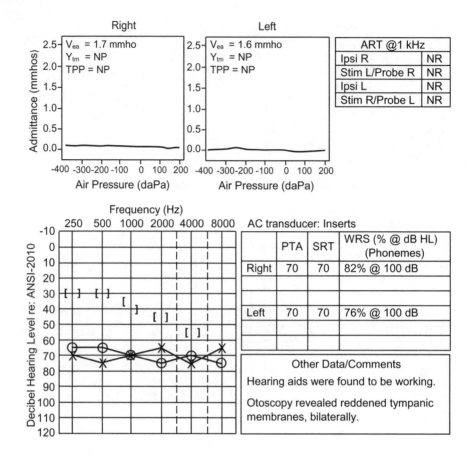

Results: Moderately severe to severe, relatively flat, mixed hearing loss, bilaterally. Air–bone gaps ranged from about 35 dB in the lower frequencies to about 15 dB in the higher frequencies. Immittance testing revealed flat tympanograms and normal acoustic equivalent volume (V_{ea}), bilaterally, and absent reflexes for all testing conditions, consistent with the conductive component in both ears. Otoscopy revealed reddened tympanic membranes. Speech recognition thresholds were 70 dB HL in each ear, and consistent with the pure-tone averages. Word recognition scores (at 100 dB HL) were 82% in the right ear and 76% in the left ear, which are not significantly different from each other based on critical differences of the binomial distribution.

Impression/Diagnosis: Mixed hearing loss, bilaterally, due to a recent episode of OTITIS MEDIA adding a conductive component to his long-standing sensorineural hearing loss. His hearing aids were found to be working appropriately, and from his mother's report he has been doing quite well with them prior to his recent drop in hearing.

Recommendations: Medical referral for middle ear involvement and a repeat audiogram following treatment to ensure that the conductive component has resolved. May benefit from preferential seating at school, at least until his conductive component to his hearing loss resolves. It is also recommended that he have hearing evaluations annually, or sooner if a change in hearing is noticed.

Case Study 6

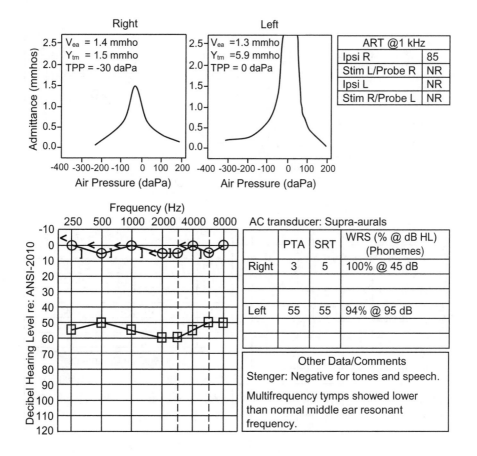

Right

V_{ea} = 1.4 mmho		
Y_{tm} = 1.5 mmho		
TPP = -30 daPa		

Air Pressure (daPa)

Left

V_{ea} =1.3 mmho		
Y_{tm} =5.9 mmho		
TPP = 0 daPa		

Air Pressure (daPa)

ART @1 kHz	
Ipsi R	85
Stim L/Probe R	NR
Ipsi L	NR
Stim R/Probe L	NR

Frequency (Hz)

AC transducer: Supra-aurals

	PTA	SRT	WRS (% @ dB HL) (Phonemes)
Right	3	5	100% @ 45 dB
Left	55	55	94% @ 95 dB

Other Data/Comments
Stenger: Negative for tones and speech.
Multifrequency tymps showed lower than normal middle ear resonant frequency.

Results: Right ear showed normal hearing. Left ear showed a moderate conductive loss. The tympanogram for the left ear had a normal shape, but with a very high admittance (Type A_d). Multifrequency tympanometry revealed a lower than normal resonant frequency. Acoustic reflexes were absent in all conditions except right ipsilateral, consistent with a left ear conductive hearing loss. Speech recognition thresholds were 5 dB HL for the right ear and 55 dB HL for the left ear, and were consistent with pure-tone averages. Word recognition scores were excellent in both ears. The negative results of the Stenger test validated the conductive hearing loss in the left ear.

Impression/Diagnosis: Left ear has a moderate conductive loss following a blow to the head by a baseball. The high admittance tympanogram and lower resonant frequency support a DISARTICULATION of the ossicles. There was no evidence of a functional hearing loss.

Recommendations: Medical referral for left ear middle ear involvement and a repeat audiogram following treatment to determine if conductive component has resolved. If conductive loss continues, a hearing aid for the left ear may be of benefit.

Case Study 7

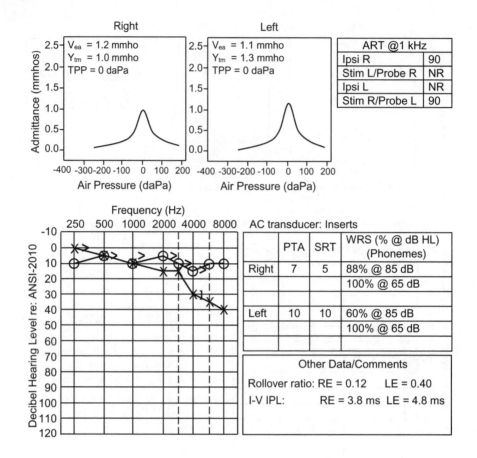

Results: Left ear shows normal hearing through 3000 Hz with a mild sloping high frequency sensorineural loss in the higher frequencies. Right ear has normal hearing throughout the frequency range. Tympanograms were normal for both ears. Acoustic reflex thresholds were absent for conditions in which stimulation occurred in the left ear. Speech recognition thresholds were within normal range and consistent with the pure-tone averages. Maximum word recognition scores were significantly different between the ears based on the critical difference scores from the binomial distribution. Word recognition scores were measured at two presentation levels in each ear in order to determine if there was any rollover. The rollover ratio was within the normal range for the right ear and were in the abnormal range (0.40) for the left ear. Results from the auditory brainstem response (ABR) test revealed abnormally delayed I-V interpeak latency interval for the left ear.

Impression/Diagnosis: Asymmetric (left ear), high frequency sensorineural loss, with high-pitched ringing in the left ear, along with absent reflexes for left ear stimulation, abnormal rollover, and abnormal ABR results, are suggestive of an ACOUSTIC NEUROMA in the left ear. Hearing loss most likely was not due to the fall from the scaffold; the fall may have occurred due to dizziness/unsteadiness.

Recommendations: Medical referral to rule out 8th nerve involvement in the left ear.

Case Study 8

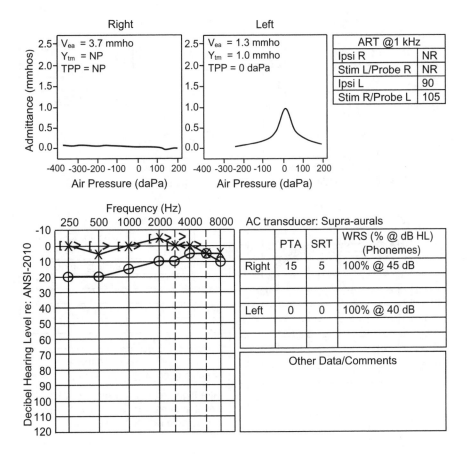

ART @1 kHz	
Ipsi R	NR
Stim L/Probe R	NR
Ipsi L	90
Stim R/Probe L	105

AC transducer: Supra-aurals

	PTA	SRT	WRS (% @ dB HL) (Phonemes)
Right	15	5	100% @ 45 dB
Left	0	0	100% @ 40 dB

Other Data/Comments

Results: Right ear showed normal hearing through 1000 Hz; however, there was a 15–20 dB air–bone gap through 2000 Hz consistent with a conductive component. Left ear showed normal hearing with no other abnormalities. The tympanogram for the right ear was flat (Type B) with a larger than normal acoustic equivalent volume (V_{ea}), and the tympanogram for the left ear was normal. Acoustic reflex thresholds were absent when the probe was in the right ear, and elevated for contralateral recording with right ear stimulation. Speech recognition thresholds were within the normal range and consistent with the pure-tone averages. Word recognition scores were excellent.

Impression/Diagnosis: Right ear has normal hearing, but has slightly worse thresholds than the left ear due to the small conductive component, as evident by the air–bone gap, flat tympanogram, and acoustic reflex pattern. The large V_{ea} in the right ear is consistent with a PERFORATION—most likely resulting from the incident with the cotton swab—that has resulted in the small decline in hearing thresholds.

Recommendations: Medical referral for the possible right ear perforation and a repeat audiogram following treatment to determine if conductive component has resolved. Avoidance of cotton swabs for cleaning the ears was also recommended.

Case Study 9

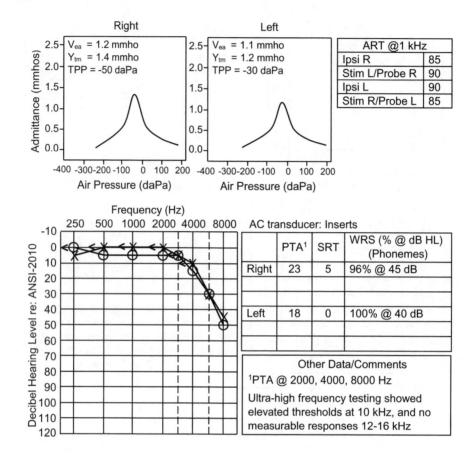

Results: Normal hearing through 4000 Hz, sloping to a moderate sensorineural hearing loss at 8000 Hz, bilaterally. Extended-high-frequency audiometry revealed elevated threshold at 10,000 Hz and no measurable responses from 12,000 to 16,000 Hz, bilaterally. Tympanograms and acoustic reflex thresholds were normal. Speech recognition thresholds were normal and consistent with the conventional PTA (500, 1000, 2000 Hz). The high frequency PTAs (2000, 4000, 8000 Hz) were reflective of the sloping high frequency hearing loss in both ears. Word recognition scores were excellent, bilaterally.

Impression/Diagnosis: Symmetric high (and extended-high) frequency hearing loss. Given the recent treatment for a urinary tract (gram negative bacilli) infection, most likely with aminoglycosides, results are consistent with hearing loss due to OTOTOXICITY. Delayed effects of ototoxic medications may continue to affect hearing, even after discontinuation.

Recommendations: Report/send findings of the audiologic evaluation to the physician who treated the infection. Regular monitoring of hearing is recommended until hearing stabilizes. Should hearing affect communication in the future, the possibility of hearing aids should be considered.

Case Study 10

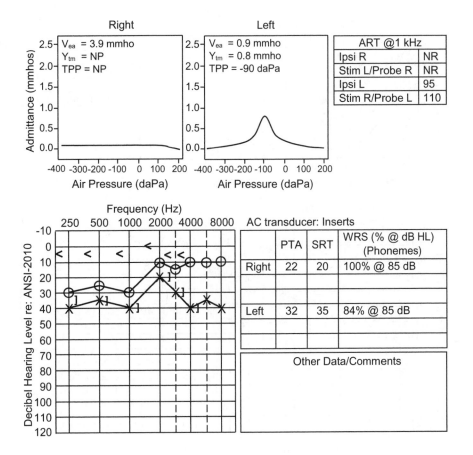

Results: Right ear showed a mild conductive loss through 1000 Hz. Left ear showed a mild sensorineural hearing loss, relatively flat except for normal threshold at 2000 Hz. Right ear tympanogram was flat (Type B) with a large V_{ea}. Left ear tympanogram was normal (Type A). Acoustic reflexes were absent when probe was in the right ear, and elevated in the contralateral condition when stimulating the right ear. Left ear ipsilateral reflex was in the normal range, consistent with the degree of cochlear hearing loss based on data from Gelfand et al. (1990). Speech recognition thresholds were 20 and 35 dB HL for the right and left ears, respectively, and were in agreement with the pure-tone averages. Word recognition score was excellent (100%) for the right ear and good (84%) for the left ear.

Impression/Diagnosis: Based on the patient's complaints/symptoms, along with the sensorineural hearing loss, the left ear appears to have MENIERE'S DISEASE. The right ear's conductive loss, flat tympanogram, large V_{ea}, and pattern of acoustic reflex thresholds are consistent with a PERFORATION.

Recommendations: Return to ENT for continued medical treatment of dizziness and perforation. Treatment options for the Meniere's disease can range from diet (reduce salt/caffeine), diuretics, and endolymphatic shunt to control endolymph buildup to vestibular nerve surgery should dizziness become a debilitating problem. Repeat audiologic evaluation as needed.

Case Study 11

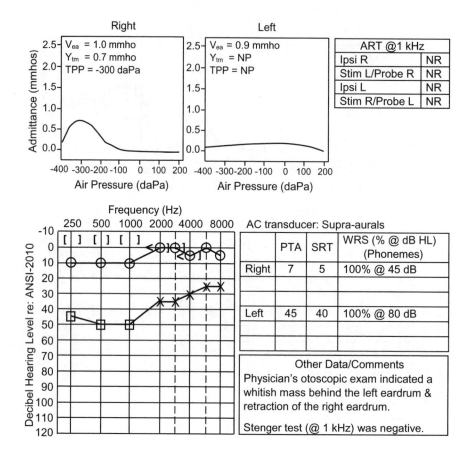

Results: Left ear showed a moderate conductive loss through 1000 Hz, rising to a slight conductive hearing loss in the higher frequencies. Right ear showed normal hearing; however, there was a conductive component (15 dB air–bone gap) from 250 to 1000 Hz. Tympanograms were relatively flat (Type B) with normal V_{ea} for the left ear and negative pressure (Type C) for the right ear. Acoustic reflex thresholds were absent for all conditions, consistent with the bilateral conductive component. Speech recognition thresholds were 40 dB HL and 5 dB HL for the left and right ears, respectively, and were consistent with the pure-tone averages. Word recognition scores were excellent in both ears. The negative results of the Stenger test validated the conductive hearing loss in the left ear.

Impression/Diagnosis: The left ear conductive loss and flat tympanogram, along with otoscopic observation of a white mass behind the tympanic membrane, are consistent with a CHOLESTEATOMA. The right ear's tympanogram and small air–bone gap, along with the otoscopic appearance of a retracted tympanic membrane, are consistent with NEGATIVE MIDDLE EAR PRESSURE.

Recommendations: Return to ENT for medical treatment of the conductive loss in the left ear, which would require surgical removal of the cholesteatoma. Repeat audiologic evaluation following medical treatment, or as needed to monitor hearing, especially if the right ear hearing worsens.

Case Study 12

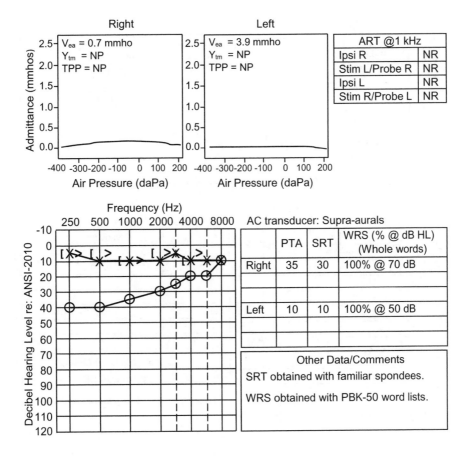

Results: Right ear showed a mild conductive loss through 2000 Hz, rising to a slight conductive loss. Left ear showed normal hearing. The tympanogram for the right ear was flat (Type B) with normal V_{ea}. The tympanogram for the left ear was flat (Type B) with large V_{ea}. Acoustic reflexes were absent for all conditions, consistent with the conductive loss in the right ear and the tube in the left ear. Speech recognition thresholds were 35 dB HL for the right ear and 10 dB HL for the left, and consistent with the pure-tone averages. Word recognition scores (PBK-50) were excellent in both ears.

Impression/Diagnosis: The right ear conductive loss, along with the normal V_{ea} indicates OTITIS MEDIA WITH EFFUSION AND A NON-PATENT (blocked) PE TUBE, which may be clogged by the fluid and/or debris. His left ear has normal hearing and he PE tube appears to be patent (open), as evident by the large V_{ea}.

Recommendations: Return to ENT for treatment of the right ear conductive loss and non-patent tube. Repeat audiologic evaluation following medical treatment, or as needed to monitor hearing, especially if hearing worsens.

Case Study 13

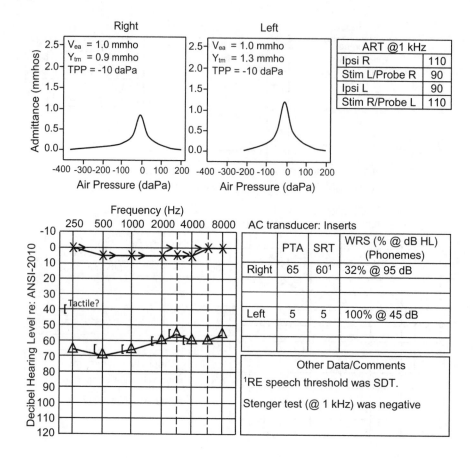

Results: Right ear showed a moderately severe, relatively flat, sensorineural hearing loss. Left ear had normal hearing. Tympanograms were normal, bilaterally. Acoustic reflex thresholds were in the normal range for left ear stimulation and were elevated (110 dB HL) for stimulation of the right ear, consistent with the degree of cochlear hearing loss based on data from Gelfand et al. (1990). Speech detection threshold for the right ear was 60 dB HL, which was appropriate based on the pure-tone thresholds. The word recognition score was poor (32%) in the right ear and excellent (100%) in the left ear, and the difference in scores was considered significantly different between the ears based on the critical difference scores from the binomial distribution. The negative results of the Stenger test validated the presence of the hearing loss in the right ear.

Impression/Diagnosis: Right ear has a SUDDEN SENSORINEURAL HEARING LOSS. The potential causes could be autoimmune inner ear disease, viral attack, or idiopathic. Given the lack of any dizziness, it is not likely that this is due to a perilymph fistula. Left ear is normal.

Recommendations: Return to ENT for medical treatment; timely treatment may improve or stabilize the hearing loss. Regular monitoring of hearing is recommended until hearing stabilizes. Hearing aid for the right ear should also be considered, with medical clearance, should the hearing loss continue and/or worsen; however, this may not be of much benefit unless speech understanding improves.

Case Study 14

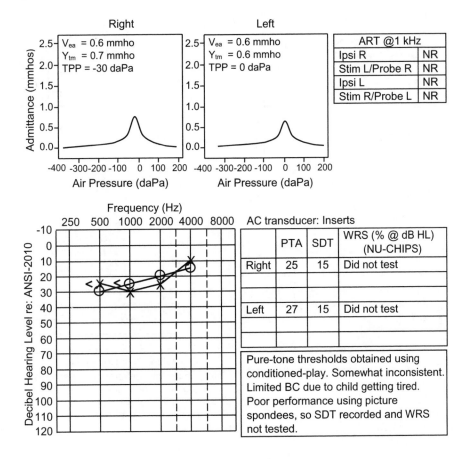

Results: Although testing was somewhat inconsistent, pure-tone thresholds suggested bilateral slight to mild sensorineural hearing loss. Tympanograms were normal, bilaterally; however, acoustic reflex thresholds were absent, which was not consistent with her degree of hearing loss. Speech recognition thresholds were attempted with picture spondees, but she had difficulty correctly identifying the words (less than 30%); therefore, speech detection thresholds were assessed, and were consistent with the pure-tone results. Word recognition testing was not done due to poor performance with the picture spondees.

Impression/Diagnosis: The absent acoustic reflexes and poor word recognition scores, in light of the relatively good pure-tone results, are consistent with AUDITORY NEUROPATHY SPECTRUM DISORDER (ANSD). It is likely that the newborn hearing screening was done with otoacoustic emissions, in which a "pass" would be expected with ANSD. Automated auditory brainstem response screening at birth may have picked up on the ANSD.

Recommendations: Follow-up testing with auditory brainstem responses and otoacoustic emissions, along with continued pure-tone behavioral testing, are recommended. It is also recommended that the family be seen for a speech-language evaluation, as well as referral to social work and/or psychology for appropriate counseling and appropriate follow-up.

Case Study 15

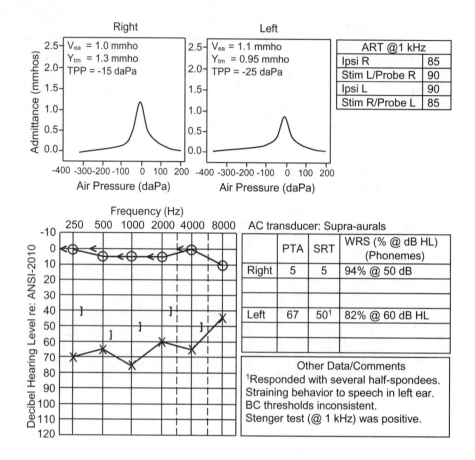

ART @1 kHz	
Ipsi R	85
Stim L/Probe R	90
Ipsi L	90
Stim R/Probe L	85

Right: V_{ea} = 1.0 mmho, Y_{tm} = 1.3 mmho, TPP = -15 daPa

Left: V_{ea} = 1.1 mmho, Y_{tm} = 0.95 mmho, TPP = -25 daPa

AC transducer: Supra-aurals

	PTA	SRT	WRS (% @ dB HL) (Phonemes)
Right	5	5	94% @ 50 dB
Left	67	50[1]	82% @ 60 dB HL

Other Data/Comments
[1]Responded with several half-spondees.
Straining behavior to speech in left ear.
BC thresholds inconsistent.
Stenger test (@ 1 kHz) was positive.

Results: Right ear showed normal hearing. Left ear showed a moderately severe hearing loss, with some air–bone gaps, which is not consistent with the immittance results. In addition, air conduction thresholds in the left ear were obtained without masking and the volunteered thresholds were higher than those that would be expected to cross over to the right ear. Tympanograms were normal, bilaterally. Acoustic reflex thresholds were in the normal range for all conditions, and for conditions with left ear stimulation, were not consistent with the degree of cochlear hearing loss. Speech recognition threshold testing for the left ear had several "half-spondee" responses, and was 17 dB better than the pure-tone average. Word recognition score for the left ear was good (82%), even though the presentation level was lower than his pure-tone average. Patient also exhibited some "straining" behavior while listening to speech in the left ear. Stenger test was positive for a non-organic basis for the hearing loss in the left ear.

Impression/Diagnosis: The inconsistency of the left ear pure-tone thresholds with the immittance results and the speech results, along with the positive Stenger, suggests that the results obtained today may not be an accurate indication of his hearing ability (i.e., FUNCTIONAL HEARING LOSS) for the left ear. It is unlikely that the noisy event at work contributed to the results obtained today.

Recommendations: None at this time. Should a need arise for more validation of the hearing ability, it is recommended that otoacoustic emissions and/or auditory brainstem response testing be performed.

13 Answers for Vestibular Anatomy, Physiology, Disorders, and Assessment

13.1

Three primary purposes of the vestibular system are to: (1) maintain the body's orientation in space relative to gravity (e.g., maintain an upright position), (2) provide information about changes in head movement (linear and rotational accelerations/decelerations) to perform coordinated movements, and (3) maintain a visual target while moving.

13.2

Peripheral Vestibular Component	Sensory Organ	Acceleration/Deceleration
Horizontal semicircular canal	Crista	Rotational/angular (e.g., head turn left-right)
Superior semicircular canal	Crista	Rotational/angular (e.g., head pitch forward-backward)
Posterior semicircular canal	Crista	Rotational/angular (e.g., head tilt/yaw left-right)
Utricle	Macula	Linear in horizontal planes (e.g., left-right, forward-backward)
Saccule	Macula	Linear in vertical plane (e.g., up-down)

13.3
Answers for labels in figure.

a. superior semicircular canal
b. posterior semicircular canal
c. horizontal semicircular canal
d. ampullae
e. vestibule
f. oval window
g. cochlea
h. cochlear branch of 8th cranial nerve
i. inferior vestibular branch of 8th cranial nerve
j. superior vestibular branch of 8th cranial nerve

13.4
Answers for labels in figure.

a. membranous labyrinth of superior semicircular canal
b. membranous labyrinth of horizontal semicircular canal
c. membranous labyrinth of posterior semicircular canal
d. utricle
e. ductus reuniens
f. saccule
g. cochlea
h. cochlear aqueduct
i. endolymphatic duct
j. endolymph

13.5
Answers for labels in figure.

a. cristae of the semicircular canals
b. endolymphatic sac
c. macula of the utricle
d. macula of the saccule
e. scala media of the cochlea (or organ of Corti)
f. endolymph

13.6
Answers for labels in figure.

a. hair cells within the crista of a semicircular canal
b. cupula of a crista of a semicircular canal
c. ampulla of a semicircular canal
d. afferent neurons of a crista
e. otoconia crystals of a macula
f. otolithic (gelatinous) membrane of a macula
g. hair cell of a macula
h. kinocilium of a hair cell of a macula

13.7

The superior vestibular branch of the 8th cranial nerve is associated with neurons from the cristae of the superior and horizontal canals, the macula of the utricle, and part of the macula of the saccule. The inferior vestibular branch is associated with neurons from the crista of the posterior canal and a large part of the macula of the saccule.

13.8

The three functional pairs of semicircular canals (SCC) in a normal vestibular system are:

1. The horizontal SCC on the left side works with the horizontal SCC on the right side.
2. The superior SCC on the left side works with the posterior SCC on the right side.
3. The posterior SCC on the left side works with the superior SCC on the right side.

13.9

When the head accelerates or decelerates, there is a centrifugal force that occurs in the cristae of the appropriate pair of semicircular canals in that plane of motion. This centrifugal force results in the fluid lagging behind the motion of the head and exerting a force on the cupula of the crista. The displacement of the cupula results in deflecting the stereocilia of the hair cells one way or the other, causing excitation or inhibition.

13.10

A. The neural discharge patterns for head rotation to the left on a horizontal plane of reference for a normal peripheral vestibular system would show an increase in the neural discharge rate from the left horizontal SCC and a decrease in the neural discharge rate from the right horizontal SCC.

B. For a pathology in the right peripheral vestibular organ, even without rotating the head, there would be an absence (or reduction) of neural discharges from the right horizontal SCC and a normal neural discharge rate from the left horizontal SCC, giving a sensation of head movement to the left (and sensation of the room spinning).

13.11

The utricles from each side of the head work together as a functional pair to signal changes in linear horizontal head movement. The hair cells within each macula are separated into two groups characterized by the position of their kinocilia. The dividing line between these two groups of hair cells is called the striola, which is near the middle of the macula. In the utricle, the kinocilia of both groups of hair cells are situated toward the striola (in the saccule both groups are oriented away from the striola). During forward or backward directed accelerations of the head, the utricular hair cells in one group increase their neural discharge rate (deflection of stereocilia is toward the kinocilia) and the hair cells in the other group decrease their neural discharge rate (deflection of stereocilia is away from the kinocilia). Once the head movement reaches a steady velocity, the discharge rates are back in balance.

13.12

The vestibular system works together with inputs from the visual, auditory, somatosensory, and proprioceptive systems to maintain good balance and position in space, and is well integrated with the cerebellum and the cortex.

13.13

The central vestibular nuclei for the VOR are located in the pontine-medullary region of the brainstem (as are those for the VSR). The VOR has direct connections from parts of the vestibular nuclei to the oculomotor nuclei through the medial longitudinal fasciculus (MLF), and indirect connections through the reticular formation. During head rotation, the VOR is responsible for maintaining a steady gaze/focus on an object.

13.14

The central vestibular nuclei for the VSR are located in the pontine-medullary region of the brainstem (as are those for the VOR). The VSR has direct connections from portions of the vestibular nuclei to motor neurons in the spinal cord (vestibulospinal tracts), and indirect connections through the reticular formation (reticulospinal tracts).

13.15

The corneoretinal potential (CRP) is a resting voltage between the front and back of the eye that is generated within the retina. Electro-oculography (EOG) is a method of recording electrical potentials from surface-electrodes placed near the eyes. These electrodes register voltage changes of the corneoretinal potential as the eyes move.

13.16

Nystagmus is the repetitive back and forth movement (beating) of the eyes, typically involuntarily, resulting from induced stimulation of the vestibular system during portions of the vestibular exam, or spontaneously occurring in some vestibular disorders. Each beat of the eye is called a saccade, which is composed of a slow phase and a fast phase (looks like a saw tooth). For example, for a head turn to the right, the vestibular connection to the eyes causes them to rotate to the left (slow phase); as the eyes can only move so far in their orbits, there is an additional connection from the reticular formation that quickly brings the eyes back to the center (fast phase). For spontaneous or pathological nystagmus, the eyes appear to beat without any stimulation. The nystagmus is named by the direction of the fast phase (e.g., right-beating nystagmus), and quantified by the velocity (distance/time) of the slow phase.

Right beating   Slow   Fast

Left beating   Fast   Slow

13.17

Consuming too much alcohol alters the specific gravity of the cupula of the semicircular canals, i.e., makes it lighter than the surrounding endolymph, which causes it to become more sensitive to rotational acceleration or may even produce a sensation of spinning while standing or lying still. In addition, too much alcohol may result in vomiting that could result in vertigo as a symptom of dehydration.

13.18

Motion sickness is caused by getting mixed signals from different sensory systems. It occurs when your vestibular system senses the movements, but the other sensory systems do not have the same sensation or are not able to counteract the sensation of movement. This can happen when your body is moving, but your eyes cannot adjust to the movement. It can also happen if your eyes see movement (video game) and your body does not sense movement. Vertigo is also a relatively big problem for astronauts because they have to adapt to changes in gravitational forces that are monitored by the vestibular system and may give an incorrect spatial orientation.

13.19

A. Benign paroxysmal positional vertigo (BPPV) occurs when some of the calcium carbonate crystals of the otoconia within the macula of a utricle become dislodged and fall into one or more of the semicircular canals (usually the superior canal). The inappropriate accumulation of the crystals alters the normal movement of the fluid within the semicircular canals, resulting in incorrect neural information being sent to the central vestibular system, giving rise to vertigo, especially when the head is moved into a certain position.

B. Bilateral vestibular hypofunction is a loss/reduction of vestibular function on both sides as a secondary effect to a known disorder (e.g., ototoxicity, vestibular neuritis) or from an unknown cause (idiopathic). The loss of vestibular function reduces the ability to make coordinated movements and results in a generalized feeling of being off-balance (as opposed to vertigo attacks) or difficulty walking, especially when other sensory input is not able to be effectively used, such as in the dark or on irregular surfaces.

C. Endolymphatic hydrops/Meniere's disease is a condition resulting from excessive buildup of endolymph within the inner ear (due to unknown causes). The increased pressure from the buildup of endolymph produces a sensation of aural fullness and may eventually rupture the inner ear membrane (thought to occur in Reissner's membrane). When the membrane ruptures, there is a mixing of perilymph with endolymph that has a temporary (at least initially) toxic effect on the hair cells. The membrane can repair itself, returning the fluids to a more normal balance, and the hair cells may regain normal function. The patient experiences repetitive episodes of vertigo, usually accompanied by hearing loss and tinnitus (typically lower pitch/buzzing).

D. <u>Enlarged vestibular aqueduct (EVA).</u> The vestibular aqueduct is the very narrow bony canal in which the membranous endolymphatic duct is located. An enlarged vestibular aqueduct is a developmental malformation. The hearing loss can be syndromic or non-syndromic, can be present at birth or a later onset, and may progress over time. Hearing loss, typically sensorineural, and balance symptoms may be related to the enlarged endolymphatic duct and sac within the aqueduct.

E. <u>Labyrinthitis/vestibular neuritis</u> is an infection (commonly viral) of the inner ear labyrinth and/or vestibular nerve that causes temporary disruption of vestibular function, producing dizziness, balance problems, nausea, and/or hearing and vision problems.

F. <u>Perilymph fistula (PLF)</u> is a rupture or defect in the oval window or round window membranes (most often from head trauma) that causes some of the perilymphatic fluid of the inner ear to leak into the middle ear and may result in a feeling of unsteadiness, vertigo, and/or nausea, especially during changes in middle ear pressure or when in certain positions.

G. <u>Persistent postural-perceptual dizziness (PPPD)</u> is usually a chronic sequela lasting at least three months following an acute vertigo or balance problem (e.g., Meniere's disease, BPPV), without any obvious ongoing abnormalities. The main symptom of PPPD is a persistent (every day or two) sensation of unsteadiness, described as rocking or swaying, without vertigo.

H. <u>Superior canal dehiscence (SCD)</u> is a small opening in the bony labyrinth of the superior semicircular canal. This opening acts like a third window of the inner ear (the other two are the oval window and the round window) and allows the membranous portion of the superior semicircular canal to be displaced during sound or increased pressure. Symptoms include vertigo and oscillopsia (apparent motion of stationary objects) that can be caused by loud noises and/or by pressure changes of the middle ear or intracranial pressures from coughing, sneezing, or straining. Many patients experience a low-frequency conductive hearing loss that occurs because some of the energy of the vibrations entering the middle ear are "diverted" to the third window and less energy is routed through the normal pathway to the cochlea.

I. <u>Vestibular schwannoma</u>, also known as an acoustic neuroma, is a benign, non-hereditary, slow-growing tumor that arises from an overproduction of Schwann cells of the 8th nerve fibers (usually from the vestibular branch). As the acoustic neuroma grows, it compresses the 8th nerve, causing a unilateral hearing loss, tinnitus (high pitched), aural fullness, and/or balance problems. There is a genetic version of this disorder, called neurofibromatosis (NF2), in which vestibular schwannoma (acoustic neuroma) occurs bilaterally, and can lead to deafness if the tumors are not removed.

J. <u>Vestibulotoxicity (ototoxicity)</u> refers to "poisoning" of the vestibular organs and/or vestibular nerve from drugs or chemicals. The amount of damage depends on the drug/chemical involved, and can be temporary or permanent. Symptoms will vary but typically cause dizziness, balance problems, and, when there is also damage to the auditory system, hearing loss and tinnitus.

13.20

Electronystagmography (ENG) and videonystagmography (VNG) are methods to monitor eye movements and record nystagmus during a vestibular evaluation. The ENG has traditionally been used, whereas VNG is a newer method that has become increasingly popular. The ENG measures changes in the corneoretinal potential of the eye through surface electrodes taped at the outer canthi of the eyes for horizontal eye movements and above and below one or both eyes to record vertical eye movements. The VNG is a video-recording method using special goggles that can track the horizontal and vertical movements of the pupil, and does not require electrodes. Many of the vestibular tests are done with and without vision, which would be done with eyes open and closed for ENG, or with a visor up or down on the VNG goggles.

13.21

A. The <u>caloric</u> (bithermal, bilateral) test is used to induce peripheral vestibular nystagmus from each ear and make comparisons of the resulting nystagmus between the two sides. The caloric irrigation system delivers warm and cold (bithermal) water or pressurized air to the ear canals that is sufficient to stimulate the horizontal semicircular canals and induce nystagmus. The different temperatures, indirectly, alter the density of the endolymph in a part of the horizontal canal and causes the endolymph to flow, thus causing stimulation of the crista within the canal. Warm water or air reduces endolymph density and causes endolymph to flow toward the ampulla (ampullopetal), resulting in an excitatory neural response in that ear: Cold water or air increases endolymph density and causes the endolymph to flow away from the ampulla (ampullofugal), resulting in an inhibitory neural response in that ear. Normal results would be no unilateral weakness or directional preponderance (see Question/Answer 13.22).

B. The <u>gaze</u> test assesses the patient's ability to maintain visual fixation, without moving the head, on a spot or finger positioned alternately in the center position (same as testing for spontaneous nystagmus), and then at 30 degrees left or right (horizontal plane) and 30 degrees up or down (vertical plane). Normal results would be no nystagmus at the different gaze points.

C. The <u>optokinetic</u> test induces nystagmus by having the patient look at bars of light that are projected onto a curved surface (or black and white stripes on a revolving drum) as they move right-to-left or left-to-right across his/her field of vision at a slow and fast velocity (20–60 degrees/second). A normal response should show the presence of nystagmus with the fast phase directed away from the direction of the stimulus movement and the velocity is comparable to the velocity of the stimulus and relatively symmetric for both directions.

D. The <u>paroxysmal nystagmus</u> (a.k.a. positioning test) is used to evaluate benign paroxysmal positional vertigo (BPPV). In patients with BPPV, the displaced otoconia alters the fluid movement, giving rise to vertigo and rotary nystagmus (eyes rotate about the visual axis). The test involves rapidly moving the patient's head from a sitting position backward and with the head rotating to the right or the left and hanging off the table (supported by the tester) in order to stimulate the posterior semicircular canal (called the Dix-Hallpike maneuver or modified Hallpike maneuver). Normal results would not show the classic pattern of BPPV. The classic pattern of BPPV is a slightly delayed burst of strong rotary nystagmus after the movement is completed with the involved ear underneath, then a period of buildup in intensity of the nystagmus, and then slow dissipation of the nystagmus over 10–15 seconds.

E. The <u>positional</u> test looks for nystagmus in different *stationary* positions of the head/body, i.e., monitoring effects of linear gravitational forces on the otolith organs (saccule and utricle). Positional testing should be done after the Dix-Hallpike or head-roll positioning tests. Positional testing is done without vision (20 seconds) and with vision (20 seconds). The normal result would not show nystagmus, with or without vision.

F. The <u>saccade/ocular dysmetria</u> test should always be done before any of the other tests in order to calibrate the recording instrument and to be sure the patient has the ability to perform saccades. Saccades are quick movements of the eye that occur when trying to refixate on a target that is quickly moved from one point to another. A light bar or video projection is used to intermittently present visual spots/flashing lights at 10–30 degrees in the horizontal and vertical planes, and the patient is instructed to follow/find the target as quickly as possible without moving the head (and can also be used to calibrate the system to have 20 mm = 20 degrees of eye movement). Too much undershooting or overshooting of the target is called ocular dysmetria. Normal results would not show significant dysmetria.

G. The <u>spontaneous nystagmus</u> test looks for nystagmus that is not induced by normal vestibular stimulation or induced vestibular stimulation. The nystagmus can be observed on the printout with eyes closed during an ENG exam, or with eyes open using Frenzel lenses, with which the tester can see the eyes (magnified), but the patient cannot see out. With VNG, the spontaneous nystagmus would be recorded with the goggle visor pulled down.

13.22

A. Unilateral weakness (UW): Compare right ear responses to left ear responses.

$$\frac{(RW + RC) - (LC + LW)}{RW + RC + LC + LW} \times 100 = \% \text{ UW}$$

$$\frac{(10 + 13) - (34 + 30)}{10 + 13 + 34 + 30} = \frac{-41}{87} \times 100 = -47\% \text{ (UW on the right; significantly abnormal)}$$

Note: A negative total value in the calculation of UW indicates right weakness. (A positive number would have indicated left weakness.) If the absolute value of the UW is greater than about 20%–30% it is usually considered an abnormal peripheral sign on the side of the weakness.

B. Directional preponderance (DP): Compare right beating responses to left beating responses.

$$\frac{(RW + LC) - (RC + LW)}{RW + LC + RC + LW} \times 100 = \% \, DP$$

$$\frac{(10 + 34) - (13 + 30)}{10 + 34 + 13 + 30} = \frac{1}{87} \times 100 = 1\% \, (\text{DP to the right; within normal range})$$

Note: DP is according to the direction of the stronger response. A positive total value indicates a DP to the right. (A negative value would have indicated a DP to the left.) If the absolute value of the DP is greater than about 30% it is usually considered abnormal involvement of either the peripheral or central system.

13.23

VEMPs are short-latency myogenic (muscle) potentials that can be elicited by relatively high intensity air-conduction or bone-conduction auditory stimuli. VEMP recordings are done using surface-mounted electrodes and signal averaging (similar to auditory brainstem response measures). The VEMP responses occur around 10–15 ms, and are characterized by a negative polarity peak (N1) followed by a positive polarity peak (P1).

A. The cVEMP is recorded from the surface of the sternocleidomastoid (cervical) muscle on the neck, and assesses vestibular function through the vestibulocollic reflex (VCR). It is thought to reflect activity of the <u>ipsilateral saccule</u>.

B. The oVEMP is recorded from the eye muscles, and assesses vestibular function through the vestibulo-ocular reflex (VOR). It is thought to reflect activity of the <u>contralateral utricle</u>.

References

American Academy of Audiology (AAA). (2011). *Childhood hearing screening guidelines.* Retrieved from http://audiology-web.s3.amazonaws.com/migrated/ChildhoodScreening Guidelines.pdf_5399751c9ec216.42663963.pdf

American National Standards Institute (ANSI). (2004). *Methods for manual pure-tone threshold audiometry*, ANSI S3.21-2004. New York, NY: Author.

American National Standards Institute (ANSI). (2010). *Specifications for audiometers.* New York, NY: Author.

American Speech-Language-Hearing Association (ASHA). (2005). *Guidelines for manual pure-tone threshold audiometry.* Retrieved from http://www.asha.org/policy

American Speech-Language-Hearing Association (ASHA). (2017). *Childhood hearing screening: Overview.* Retrieved from http://www.asha.org/Practice-Portal/Professional-Issues/Childhood-Hearing-Screening/

Baloh, R. W., & Honrubia, V. H. (2001). *Clinical neurophysiology of the vestibular system.* New York, NY: Oxford University Press.

Barber, H. O., & Stockwell, C. W. (1976). *Manual of electronystagmography.* St. Louis, MO: Mosby.

Bloom, W., & Fawcett, D. W. (1962). *A textbook of histology* (8th ed.). Philadelphia, PA: W. B. Saunders.

Boothroyd, A., & Cawkwell, S. (1970). Vibrotactile thresholds in pure-tone audiometry. *Acta Otolaryngologica, 69*, 381–387.

Dubno, J. R., Lee, F. S., Klein, A. J., Matthews, L. J., & Lam, C. F. (1995). Confidence limits for maximum word-recognition scores. *Journal of Speech and Hearing Research, 38*(2), 490–502.

Fletcher, H. (1940). Auditory patterns. *Review of Modern Physics, 12*, 47–65.

Furman, J. M., & Cass, S. P. (1996). *Balance disorders: A case-study approach.* Philadelphia, PA: F. A. Davis.

Gelfand, S. A., Schwander, T., & Silman, S. (1990). Acoustic reflex thresholds in normal and cochlear-impaired ears: Effects of no-response rates on 90th percentiles in a large sample. *Journal of Speech and Hearing Disorders, 55*(2), 198–205.

Guthrie, L., & Mackersie, C. (2009). A comparison of presentation levels to maximize word recognition scores. *Journal of the American Academy of Audiology, 20*(6), 381–390.

Humes, L. E. (1991). Understanding the speech-understanding problems of the hearing impaired. *Journal of the American Academy of Audiology, 2*(2), 59–69.

Hunter, L. L. (2013). 20Q: Acoustic immittance—What still works & what's new. *Audiology Online* (September 9, 2013). Retrieved from http://www.audiologyonline.com/articles/20q-acoustic-immittance-what-still-works-what-s-new-12131

Killion, M. C., & Mueller, H. G. (2010). Twenty years later: A new count-the-dots method. *Hearing Journal, 63*, 10–17.

Margolis, R. H., & Hunter, L. L. (2000). Acoustic immittance measurements, In R. J. Roeser, M. Valente, & H. Hosford-Dunn (Eds.), *Audiology diagnosis* (pp. 381–423). New York, NY: Thieme.

Møller, A. R. (1994). Neural generators of auditory evoked potentials. In J. T. Jacobson (Ed.), *Principles and applications in auditory evoked potentials*. Boston, MA: Allyn & Bacon.

Møller, A. R. (2013). *Hearing: Anatomy, physiology, and disorders of the auditory system*. San Diego, CA: Plural.

Nober, E. H. (1970). Cutile air and bone conduction thresholds of the deaf. *Exceptional Children, 36*(8), 571–579.

Roush, J., Bryant, K., Mundy, M., Zeisel, S., & Roberts, J. (1995). Developmental changes in static admittance and tympanometric width in infants and toddlers. *Journal of the American Academy of Audiology, 6*(4), 334–338.

Sanders, J. W., & Rintleman, W. F. (1964). Masking in audiometry. *Archives of Otolaryngology, 80*, 541–556.

Seidel, H. M., Ball, J. W., Dains, J. E., & Benedict, G. W. (2003). *Mosby's guide to physical examination*. St. Louis, MO: Mosby.

Sklare, D. A., & Denenberg, L. J. (1987). Interaural attenuation for tubephone insert earphones. *Ear and Hearing, 8*(5), 298–300.

Tonndorf, J. (1972). Bone conduction. In J. V. Tobias (Ed.), *Foundations of modern auditory theory* (pp. 84–99). New York, NY: Academic Press.

Yacullo, W. S. (1996). *Clinical masking procedures*. Boston, MA: Allyn & Bacon.